PRAISE FOR *THE INCLU*

CW01511863

'Inclusion is not just a moral imperative but a strategic one. *The Inclusion Journey* offers a masterclass in transforming inclusion from an abstract ideal into actionable, quantifiable progress. It's essential reading for leaders who are serious about making real change.'
Dan Södergren, keynote speaker on the future of work, technology and AI

'I hoped this would be a game-changing book to help us on our diversity and inclusion journeys. It exceeded my expectations. It is a brilliantly conceived, evidence-based, challenging, practical and an expertly written guide. It inspires action. Inclusion is not enough – everyone belonging is the aim. It's a must-read for every leader and leadership group. The business benefits from taking the actions described are proven and well worth the challenges and costs.'
Tony Robinson OBE, Director of the Organisation for Responsible Businesses

'Gives an invaluable clear approach as to what you should be looking at and the impact the analysis shows – and, vitally, how you can act. Expectations have changed in our workforce; the skill is to listen and act to protect the longevity of the business and, quite frankly, it's the right thing to do for society.'
Hanna Smith, Chief People Officer

'To be included and to feel we belong is one of our most basic human needs. This book outlines in detail a map of how we can offer this to all employees from all backgrounds. A must for anyone who believes this subject is important but needs help building momentum. I love how practical and easy to read this book is.'
Matt Phelan, Co-Founder, The Happiness Index

'There are so many informative and educational moments in the text that do not preach, but allow space for exploration and reflection, empowering you to take a beat and to challenge yourself to improve a little more. Even when

you feel you might have cracked it, this book reminds you that the journey is not complete. The desire is to reach the destination, but the journey is always more important.'
Paul Mortimer, workplace inclusion practitioner, ex-footballer, broadcaster, coach and motivational speaker

'The authors create a vital road map for change with clarity and rigour. This highly engaging and brilliantly written book will prepare you for the journey towards real transformation, guiding you along the way with comprehensive data, actionable steps and proven strategies for overcoming the inevitable obstacles and setbacks. Quite simply, this is an essential book to bring about the change that we need for a fairer society.'
Sheela Banerjee, award-winning author, academic and journalist

'The authors have done an incredible job breaking down the steps into practical actions to help any organization implement an inclusive culture. Their writing style is easy to read, and you feel like they are advising you directly. It's a must-read for leaders who care about their colleagues and those who are ready to be intentional and take effective action so they can create a space where everyone can thrive.'
Advita Patel, internal comms and workplace culture strategist, and co-author of *Building a Culture of Inclusivity*

'Highlights how everyone, from leadership to frontline employees, plays a crucial role in creating a culture where every individual feels valued and empowered to thrive. The authors' comprehensive advice will equip anyone committed to make real change with actionable strategies to ensure that inclusion is not just a policy, but a deeply ingrained practice that enhances workplace culture and drives overall success.'
Andi Fletcher, Director of People and Culture, The Athenaeum Hotel

'As a disabled disrupter, the journey from exclusion to inclusion has been long. This book makes me bounce. It sets out the same route map for business, provides the why and delivers on how it can be done and at speed.'
Mike Adams, CEO, We Are Purple

'This is a brilliant book for anyone wanting to create a culture of inclusivity in their organization. It's jam packed with practical tools and advice to help managers communicate and implement inclusivity strategies. It should be required reading for every human who works with other humans.'
Nadia Finer, Founder of Shy and Mighty and author

'An essential guide for leaders who want to embed inclusion in their workplaces. The book takes you through the steps to follow in a clear and concise way. The actions you need to take are detailed, as well as the things to watch out for along the way. I recommend this to all leaders who want to drive change.'
Dr Sam Collins, CEO, Aspire for Equality

'EDI must be taken seriously, by people, policy and processes. This is about showing up and speaking out, and knowing, as they say, that diversity is not a black-or-white issue but impacts us all. I would recommend that companies take a read and reference their actions – let's create the change together.'
Sonya Barlow, diversity coach and author of *Unprepared to Entrepreneur*

The Inclusion Journey

Creating a strategy that improves employee engagement and company results

Allegra Chapman
Mousumi Kanjilal Williams

KoganPage

First published in Great Britain and the United States in 2024 by Kogan Page Limited

2nd Floor, 45 Gee Street
London
EC1V 3RS
United Kingdom

8 W 38th Street, Suite 902
New York, NY 10018
USA

www.koganpage.com

Kogan Page books are printed on paper from sustainable forests.

ISBNs
Hardback   978 1 3986 1674 5
Paperback   978 1 3986 1672 1
Ebook   978 1 3986 1673 8

British Library Cataloguing-in-Publication Data
A CIP record for this book is available from the British Library.

Library of Congress Cataloging-in-Publication Data
Names: Chapman, Allegra, author. | Williams, Mousumi Kanjilal, author.
Title: The inclusion journey : creating a strategy that improves employee
   engagement and company results / Allegra Chapman, Mousumi Kanjilal
   Williams.
Description: London, United Kingdom ; New York, NY : Kogan Page, 2024. |
   Includes bibliographical references and index.
Identifiers: LCCN 2024021000 (print) | LCCN 2024021001 (ebook) | ISBN
   9781398616721 (paperback) | ISBN 9781398616745 (hardback) | ISBN
   9781398616738 (ebook)
Subjects: LCSH: Diversity in the workplace. | Social integration. | BISAC:
   BUSINESS & ECONOMICS / Human Resources & Personnel Management | BUSINESS
   & ECONOMICS / Diversity & Inclusion
Classification: LCC HF5549.5.M5 C4774 2024 (print) | LCC HF5549.5.M5
   (ebook) | DDC 658.3008–dc23/eng/20240508
LC record available at https://lccn.loc.gov/2024021000
LC ebook record available at https://lccn.loc.gov/2024021001

Typeset by Integra Software Services, Pondicherry
Print production managed by Jellyfish
Printed and bound by CPI Group (UK) Ltd, Croydon CR0 4YY

For Chloe and Noah, in the hopes that you will inherit a fairer world, where you will shine as your fullest selves – Allegra

For all the people who have ever felt excluded for being different, this is how we change the world so there's space for everyone – Mousumi

CONTENTS

ACKNOWLEDGEMENTS

When we first founded Watch This Sp_ce, we talked about our ultimate goals for the business. Very near the top of the list was to write a book. As two people with a passion for writing, this is a real dream come true, and we're so grateful to everyone who has helped to make it happen.

Huge thanks to Lucy Carter, for inviting us to embark on this project, and for encouraging us along the way. Thank you also to Joe Ferner-Reeves and all the team at Kogan Page for helping us to turn our vision for this book into a reality and for being so supportive of what we wanted to create.

We are so lucky to work with such an incredible team at Watch This Sp_ce, and we are deeply grateful to Kaia Allen-Bevan, Megan Wellman, and everyone else who has been part of the journey so far. We have a lot of exciting plans for the future, so watch th– no, let's not do that.

Thanks also to the experts and big thinkers who contributed their thoughts and experiences to this book: Danielle Alsey, Marc Caulfield, Helen Curr, Paul Deemer, Karen Dobres, Alex Farbon, Nadia Finer, Liva Jones, Dina Knight, Dee Mathieson, Natalie Rathner, Sitara Rivers, Julian Roberts, Diane Tapner-Evans and Bonamy Waddell.

We are glad to be part of a wonderful community of business people – many of whom are also writers as well. Thanks for all the support, encouragement and 'oh my goodness can we really do this? Yes we can' chats with Areej AbuAli (author and founder of Crawlina and Women in Tech SEO), Sheela Banerjee (author, journalist and academic), Dr Sam Collins (author and founder of Aspire) and Sarah Lewis (author, epic writer person and founder of Writers' HQ), as well as to those who have supported us and our business along the way: Fiona Anderson, Liz Cadman, Samantha Harland, Vicky King, Holly Mapstone, Emma Mills-Sheffield, Stephanie Prior, Joanne Simmons, Mark Vaesen, Amy White, Nisanka Wickramarachchi, Sarah Wilson and many, many more!

We have both dreamt of writing a book since we were little girls, and we are so grateful for the continued belief our parents always held that one day we would make that dream a reality.

Last, but not least, we have to thank our husbands, Peter Chapman and Stuart Williams, who have been unwavering in their support and encouragement of the book, the business and us as humans from the very beginning.

Introduction

If you want to go fast, go alone. If you want to go far, go together.
AFRICAN PROVERB, ORIGINS UNKNOWN

Back in the depths of the 2020 pandemic lockdown, employers were frantically rewriting the rules of work overnight. Those who had previously said it was impossible for their staff to work flexibly from home, suddenly found ways to make it happen. Parents had to find creative ways to work and manage childcare with everyone at home. People had to find spaces to work in their already full living environments. What we saw around us was a radical re-thinking of work within only a few weeks. It magnified what had long been apparent: that work was not working for everyone. The pandemic shone a light on existing inequalities and the compelling case for change. This is largely what prompted us to start Watch This Sp_ce, and to help organizations to find better ways to work together.

As people were forced to change how, where and when they worked, they started to find new approaches that worked for them. We saw people moving out from cities, we saw hiring processes change and we saw different types of leadership styles emerging. The work paradigms we had previously been living with were created for different lives, and different people. Before 2020, the workplace had not seen disruptive change for a long time. Our structures, processes and cultures have long been due for an overhaul, so that businesses become places where everyone can thrive.

Before the pandemic, there was already widespread dissatisfaction. A poll in 2017 showed that, globally, only 15 per cent of people[1] were engaged in their roles. Add in an international health crisis, disruptive change and global economic uncertainty, and it's no wonder this increased. A more recent survey by Indeed showed that one in three[2] people are now actively *un*happy at work. When you consider that we spend an average of 3,515 days[3] at work in our lifetimes, that's a lot of time to be unhappy.

The disruption of 2020 has not necessarily led to permanent change, though. It has not taken long for flexible working practices to be removed,[4] for adapted interview styles to be reversed and for people to feel they are being forced back into old ways again. After all, for those in dominant groups, things were fine as they were. Employers have buildings to fill, commercial landlords have rents to be paid and leaders have their favourites already lined up for promotion. For those of us on the frontlines of the drive for inclusion, it's clear that it's not going to be plain sailing ahead.

Time for change

When we founded Watch This Sp_ce in 2020, during those uncertain times, we had no idea where it would take us. What we did know was that this was the time to explore the ideas we had to make work better for everyone. After experiencing the inequalities of work ourselves and facing personal struggles, and through our volunteering and community work, we knew the why behind the drive for change. People had shared their stories with us long before the pandemic. We could see that Covid-19 had highlighted and exacerbated the frustrations and inequalities of the workplace, and that there was so much opportunity for improvement. So, we got started on helping employers to begin the journey of change. Since then, we have won multiple awards,[5] and worked with a range of employers in various sectors. We've seen the impact when there is a desire for change, with a clear roadmap and employee engagement. This creates a more positive and productive working environment for everyone, and it also improves results and performance.

From the beginning, we have always wanted to be clear that inclusion is good for business. Creating workplaces that include everyone is the right thing to do, but this isn't a one-way street. When inclusion improves, everyone wins. Diversity and inclusion should be core to any business strategy, because of the impact on business performance and the imperative to create working environments fit for the future.

The changes and new paths that emerged in the wake of the pandemic were not completely new ideas. There were many who could see for a long time that the world of work needed to change. There were research papers and studies which showed the value of diversity, inclusion and inclusive work practices. Many of the research papers were government-funded, with targets set to increase diversity on boards and across organizations in some countries. Despite this wealth of research and evidence showing the benefits, little actual progress has been made. We will go into greater detail later in this book, but for now just know that:

- Female CEOs run less than 5% of the world's largest businesses.[6]
- Only 11% of top roles in the UK's top companies are held by people of colour.[7]
- Just 7% of business leaders identify as disabled, despite 15% of people worldwide having disabilities.[8]
- Nordic countries lead on social mobility, but most countries are very far behind.[9]
- Up to 75% of C-suite roles are held by extroverts.[10]

You get the picture? Most working environments are dominated by those from dominant groups. There is little space created for different types of people to be involved, particularly in leadership roles. So we are missing the valuable contributions of so many people, and creating and deepening inequalities.

It doesn't make business sense either.

If we want to solve the world's problems, then we need different types of people on the case to bring different perspectives. Our businesses are all creating products, services and solutions to tackle the varied challenges of our fellow humans, and we can't do a good job of that by only considering the perspectives of dominant groups. Otherwise, we're creating environments where phones are designed that are too big for women's hands[11] or the best ideas are never heard in meetings dominated by extroverts.[12] What will move us forward are the voices that say "How about this though?" or "I have a different idea." And for those people to feel confident to speak up and say what they think, and for them to be heard, there is work to do to create cultures that make that possible.

There is overwhelming evidence for the power of diverse teams, which we will look at in detail in Chapter 1. There is more innovation, more creativity, higher productivity, better problem-solving and improved decision-making when teams include different types of people. It doesn't just happen, though. It takes work, dedication and engagement to create inclusive teams where people feel they can belong.

As the evidence mounts, it's getting harder to ignore. When people are faced with statistics about how their productivity will increase, how innovation thrives and that people deliver better results in inclusive teams, they sit up and listen. If they don't, employees are increasingly voting with their feet. In a working environment where people have a variety of potential employers to choose from, and where there is a scarcity of candidates, creating inclusive environments becomes ever more important.

With any work like this, it takes buy-in from stakeholders and needs to feel like it's been worth it to keep things moving. But we know data alone is not going to be the driver for most people to change things. They need to feel a pain point. They need to feel the discomfort, feel lost and confused before they will be willing to look at a map and consider a new direction. When you're stuck in the mud, the benefits of diversity and inclusion offer a rope to pull you out. People are often convinced by evidence that they will directly benefit themselves from a change. These tangible rewards are more convincing than targets, legislation and metrics. And that's what we need to focus on to create movement, direction and pace to create the inclusive teams of the future.

It's the journey

Creating work cultures and environments where people feel genuinely included is a journey, not a finite destination. There is no single box to tick, form to fill in or one action to take which means the work is done and can be checked off a list. Employers need to think about how to engage and inspire people and set out with a clear roadmap. People need to see why the journey is needed, how to get on board, the route you are taking and the vision ahead for destinations you will reach. And that there is not one endpoint. Every employer takes a different journey and reaches different stops and rest points along the way. As you progress along different stages of the journey, there are sights and summits to savour, there can be challenges to face and changes in direction to navigate, and there will be celebrations as you reach each milestone.

So we need to focus, plot a roadmap, create frameworks and talk about bold new ideas for the future of work. We need to embrace different types of people, different styles of work and different workplace practices. This process is not a static one; it evolves as we progress. This is about creating the workplaces of the future, which can adapt with the times, and take people along the way so we're ready when the next disruption comes along.

Through our work in diversity and inclusion since founding Watch This Sp_ce, we have learnt a lot about what it takes for an organization to make an inclusion journey. We have seen what works, and what doesn't, and we have built frameworks to help people understand how to engage employees on the way. Here, we want to share our insights with you.

- In Part One of this book, you will learn about what progress has been made on a global scale, and how you can get things moving for your organization.

- Part Two shows you how to draw a map of where you are now and where you want to go, as well as how to keep moving and track your progress as you go.

- Part Three will look at the potential problems you might encounter along the way, and help you with maintaining enthusiasm, handling bumps in the road and course corrections you might need to make.

- In Part Four we look at how to celebrate your achievements, and how to maintain momentum for ongoing progress.

So come with us on this journey. We will look at how you can prepare to set out, and how to create a map for change with actionable steps. We will take an honest look at the challenges and problems you might face and help you to celebrate the progress you will make. We have worked with a lot of different types of organizations since we started our business, and we have spoken to many others along the way. We will share stories of struggles and success to pave a smoother route for your organization.

We hope this book can form a travel guide for your inclusion journey, with the recommendations, practical information and inside knowledge you need, that we've gained from walking this path many times before. We aim to make your progress more straightforward and enjoyable for having this guidance to turn to.

Good luck on your travels. Do send us a postcard.

Notes

1 J Clifton. The world's broken workplace, Gallup, 13 June 2017, https://news.gallup.com/opinion/chairman/212045/world-broken-workplace.aspx?g_source=position1&g_medium=related&g_campaign=tiles (archived at https://perma.cc/956V-DZ2U)

2   Indeed. Indeed Work Wellbeing Score: Discover work wellbeing, https://uk. indeed.com/employers/work-happiness (archived at https://perma.cc/PGH3-QZ7E)

3   C Marton. How much time do we spend at work?, Understanding ModernGov, 5 December 2019, https://blog.moderngov.com/2019/02/how-much-time-do-we-spend-at-work (archived at https://perma.cc/6XDF-3EDJ)

4   A Christian. The companies backtracking on flexible work, BBC, 7 February 2023, www.bbc.com/worklife/article/20230206-the-companies-backtracking-on-flexible-work (archived at https://perma.cc/L8FA-X4S8)

5   C Smith. Diversity and inclusion consultancy wins our £25K Business Boost grant, Simply Business, 22 October 2021, www.simplybusiness.co.uk/knowledge/articles/2021/10/inclusion-consultancy-wins-business-boost-grant/ (archived at https://perma.cc/ZTW2-CMAL)

6   Fortune 500 – female CEO, 2023, https://fortune.com/ranking/global500/2023/search/?ceowoman=true (archived at https://perma.cc/X8QG-Q3KU)

7   C Powell. Only 11 top roles across FTSE 100 held by ethnic minority leaders, research finds, People Management, 13 August 2021, www.peoplemanagement.co.uk/article/1743111/only-11-top-roles-ftse-100-held-ethnic-minority-leaders-research-finds (archived at https://perma.cc/WN2Q-GD9S)

8   Valuable 500. Disability absent from leadership strategy in majority of global businesses, Press Release, 14 January 2019, www.thevaluable500.com/press-release/disability-absent-from-leadership-strategy-in-majority-of-global-businesses (archived at https://perma.cc/A8SK-ART2)

9   World Economic Forum. Global Social Mobility Index 2020: why economies benefit from fixing inequality, 19 January 2020, www.weforum.org/reports/global-social-mobility-index-2020-why-economies-benefit-from-fixing-inequality/ (archived at https://perma.cc/2AAM-K8KZ)

10   ZynQ360. Introverts and extroverts in business, www.zynq360.com/blog/team-blog-posts/introverts-and-extroverts-in-business/ (archived at https://perma.cc/SCF6-KKX6)

11   C Criado Perez (2019) *Invisible Women: Exposing data bias in a world designed for men*, Chatto & Windus

12   N Finer (2022) *Shy and Mighty: Your shyness is a superpower*, DK Children

PART ONE

Preparing for the journey

1

Why do we have to go anywhere?

You've probably heard a lot of talk about why you need to be working on your organizational approach to diversity and inclusion, but you'd be forgiven for wondering exactly why you need to bother. Is diversity and inclusion *really* something that businesses need to worry about? Or is it just a fluffy ideal that's nice in theory but not all that important in the context of the many urgent priorities that you currently have on your plate? This chapter will demonstrate that diversity and inclusion is an imperative for all organizations and will show you how it is a vital ingredient for the success of all those other priorities you're grappling with.

What's this all about?

There's a general feeling that seems to pervade business and media circles that diversity and inclusion are simply part of a left-wing 'woke' agenda, designed to make us all be overly nice to each other for the sake of it. But that view is born largely from fear of change and a desire from some to maintain a status quo that they believe benefits them. That's not unreasonable – why would you want to rock a boat that's keeping you nicely afloat? Except that the status quo *isn't* really benefiting you as much as you might think. You're currently sitting comfortably in a rowboat where you could be stretching out on the deck of a cruise liner.

The business case for inclusion is incredibly powerful. A wealth of research demonstrates that inclusion drives productivity, innovation, results and profits. But before we dive into that, let's start at the beginning – what do we mean by diversity and inclusion in a workplace context?

Diversity: The variety that exists amongst the human population with regards to background and identity, including gender identity, ethnicity, physical ability, cognitive function, religion, sexuality, culture, socio-economic background and so on.

Inclusion: Ensuring that diverse individuals of all backgrounds and identities are able to access, participate in, progress within or benefit from, and influence spaces, structures and systems.

Inclusion, however, should be just the beginning. We need to move on to driving a sense of belonging, where individuals from under-represented groups aren't just accepted alongside their colleagues from dominant groups, but where they are just as much a part of the fabric of the organization, and *everyone* feels deeply connected to that organization.

Belonging: A sense of being at home in an organization, fully aligned with its mission and values, welcomed and valued as your full self, able and eager to contribute your full potential, and integral to its future success.

When we drive inclusion, and belonging, in our workplaces, we don't just benefit people as individuals – our organizations and wider economy reap vast rewards. We will look at these rewards in more detail in this chapter.

The inclusion imperative

Study after study and book after book have set out the benefits of inclusion and how they support organizational growth. We're not going to replicate them in detail here, because the information is already out there, and we've got a lot more ground we want to cover. But here are the highlights of what you can expect to gain from a more inclusive culture, and why.

Innovation

Diverse organizations have a 19 per cent higher output of innovation[1] than their competitors. Why should this be the case? Well, a diverse team of people bring with them a diverse range of experiences, perspectives, opinions and ideas. In Figure 1.1 we can see a Venn diagram of the knowledge of different members of a team. When looking at a particular topic, a homogeneous group will have largely overlapping knowledge.

FIGURE 1.1 Overlap of knowledge of a topic within a homogeneous group

Topic

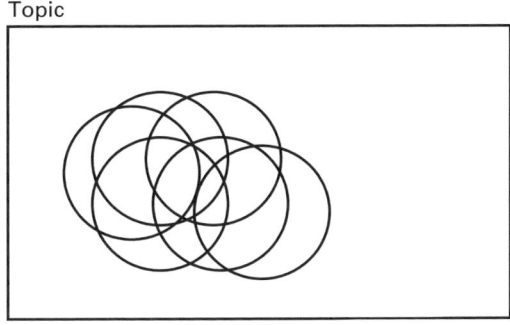

A more diverse group, however, will have different perspectives, experiences and ranges of knowledge. So together their understanding will cover a broader area of the topic (see Figure 1.2).

FIGURE 1.2 Overlap of knowledge of a topic within a diverse group

Topic

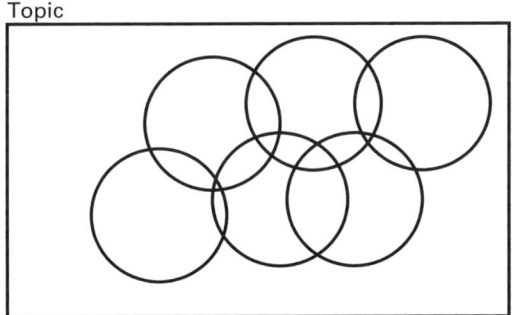

Between them, diverse individuals cover a broader knowledge space, and can bring in different ideas, or challenge one another on their ideas to make them even better. They're also more likely to spot potential holes in new ideas so that they can be fixed before they hit the market. In *Invisible Women*, Caroline Criado Perez offers numerous examples of organizations releasing products that were unsuitable for half the population, including the Apple iPhone that was too large for women's hands despite the majority of their customers being female.[2] Having a little more gender diversity on the team would have saved them huge amounts of time and money.

It's not only the simple ability of a diverse team to be more innovative that makes the difference, though. Having a diverse team is often an indication of an inclusive culture. If you have attracted and retained diverse talent, it's likely that your working environment allows everyone to contribute and progress, and to feel that they will be heard, respected and valued. This environment of psychological safety is what makes staff feel able to bring up those potentially ground-breaking ideas and challenge potentially problematic issues. It's this culture of open discussion and collaboration that enables you to benefit from the diverse perspectives in your team and drives impactful innovation.

Decision-making

Who will deliver a better decision, an individual or a group? The group seems like the obvious choice, surely? Two heads are better than one, and multiple heads should be even better able to figure out the best solution. Except research shows that's not the case. As with the knowledge space problem we saw above, a homogeneous group will have a limited view of the issue at hand. In decision-making environments, this has a powerful effect, as groups have a tendency towards shared information bias – focusing on information that is shared by the whole group at the expense of potentially vital information held only by a minority. But that's not the only problem with group decisions.

We're hardwired to be part of a group. That caveperson brain that's still doing so much of the driving remembers a time when being expelled from the group would mean starving to death alone or not having protection from predators. Fostering good relations with the people around us still feels like a matter of life and death. So, in group discussions, we're highly sensitive to peer pressure and following the line thrown out by the most vocal members of our team. But it goes deeper than that – research shows that, even when we would have had an entirely different opinion independently, in a group situation we will convince ourselves that we genuinely agree with the opinion of the group.[3] So we don't even realize that we're suppressing our real thoughts and ideas, which makes the effect even more dangerous.

As a species, we're also very sensitive to hierarchy,[4] and we don't want to go against the group leader, particularly if we think our job (and therefore our means of survival) might depend on it. So, groups will often line up, consciously or not, behind the opinion of the most senior person in the room.

All of this means that groups can make misjudgements in decision-making, and often ones that are more risky and less balanced than they would have been if made by any of the involved individuals alone.[5] Yet a group does still have a wider knowledge base than an individual, so they can supply a greater volume of useful inputs; a group can generate more ideas, and therefore more solutions, than an individual; and a group has the potential to identify more potential problems or counter-arguments that can be used to refine the solution.

So why aren't groups routinely outperforming individuals?

Given what you've read so far, it will probably come as no surprise that the answer lies with inclusion. Groups will amplify any biases its members might hold, leading to a polarization effect, so a group that makes active attempts to recognize and challenge their own biases – conscious and unconscious – will be less likely to drift towards faulty assumptions. An inclusive environment that promotes psychological safety encourages group members to challenge decisions and to try to think about matters from different angles. These are also environments in which leaders invite their teams to try to find holes in their decisions or build on their ideas. Although, in a group discussion that you are hoping to get the best from, you'd be wise to ensure the leader speaks last to make space for everyone else to voice their true opinions without influence from the top. Inclusive groups will benefit from the broad knowledge base that diverse individuals can bring, and that's why inclusive teams make better decisions 87 per cent of the time.[6]

Not only that, but inclusive teams make decisions twice as fast, with half the number of meetings.[7] Perhaps counter-intuitively, the likelihood that diverse groups will disagree and think differently actually accelerates the process. Rather than moving forward with an easy consensus, then finding blockers and having to rethink without a full understanding of where they're going wrong, inclusive teams can thrash out a wider view of the problem straight away. And when there are clear processes in place to support healthy disagreement and encourage diversity of thought, teams are clear on how they can reach the best solution. So they get the job done.

Crisis management

As we have seen, diverse groups have a greater ability to identify potential issues, and an inclusive environment allows them to voice their concerns, which means the problem can be addressed. But inclusive teams are also more likely to be aware of possible crises before they ever occur, and are therefore proactively preparing for them.[8] When a crisis does hit, diverse and inclusive teams are able to understand the problem more quickly, and come up with a wider variety of solutions. Partly because of this head start, and partly because of a wider skillset and more collaborative culture, they respond more quickly to the problem and are more likely to have the variety of skills needed to address the problem effectively. We have already seen that they are more innovative, and so will their solutions to a crisis be.

Inclusive teams are also more resilient.[9] They are more likely to be able to get through whatever problems are thrown at them together. An inclusive culture, and especially a culture of true belonging, also means that staff genuinely *want* to solve the problem – they care enough about the organization and their colleagues to throw their all into overcoming these challenges, and are less likely to simply desert a leaky ship. After the storm has blown over and the dust has settled, inclusive teams are more able to reflect effectively on what happened and take useful learnings forward into the future. They also do so in a psychologically safe environment, free from blame attribution, where staff can share honestly and openly what could be improved.

This is why, in times of crisis, inclusive teams significantly outperform the competition. For example, while the stock market was declining by 35 per cent between 2007 and 2009, inclusive organizations saw a 14 per cent *increase* in stock performance.[10] When the Covid-19 pandemic struck, organizations that had already embraced inclusive methods, such as remote and flexible working, had a head start on everyone else and were better placed to adapt. Make no mistake, future crises will come for us, and an inclusive culture is a strong predictor of our ability to survive.

Productivity

Inclusion leads to an uplift in productivity of around 20 per cent.[11] This is partly owing to the increased innovation and more effective decision-making that we've already discussed, but it also has a lot to do with employee engagement. Only 23 per cent of the world's employees are currently actively engaged at work,[12] which is something that should worry all of us. A lot of staff have basically mentally checked out and don't feel motivated to give their best. That's obviously bad news for businesses, but the good news is that there is a fix. Millennials – those born between 1981 and 1996, and so a considerable portion of the workforce – are 83 per cent more likely[13] to feel engaged in an inclusive organization.

Organizations that prioritize inclusion are also more likely to create environments that facilitate productivity. Different people work effectively in different ways – some people like quiet, some like noise and activity; some people like discussion, some prefer reflection; some people have different needs that require different support or different working approaches; the ways in which people vary are, as we will see in the next chapter, almost infinite. When you try to force everyone to work in the same way, you will only get the best from staff that suit that approach. If you strive for inclusion, however, and allow adaptations and varied approaches to benefit everyone, you enable everyone to give their best. Which further encourages them to *want* to give their best.

Furthermore, happy and engaged staff take less time off. Mental health issues are costing employers £56 billion each year in the UK,[14] and around $48 billion annually in the US,[15] because of sick days and resignations; and, when you are under stress or unhappy, you are also more likely to suffer *physical* ill-health. A sense of belonging at work, on the other hand, leads to a 75 per cent reduction in sick days.[16] And staff tend to work considerably more productively when they're not unwell.

Recruitment and retention

The so-called Great Resignation, an ongoing trend for staff to leave jobs where they don't feel valued to either move elsewhere, become self-employed or leave the workforce entirely, means that there is currently a talent shortage. Globally, 77 per cent of businesses are struggling to recruit,[17] so it is more important than ever for organizations to make themselves attractive to prospective candidates. Since 76 per cent of people say that diversity and inclusion are important factors when choosing where they want to work,[18] it's vital that inclusion is high on the agenda.

Candidates are pretty savvy when it comes to sizing up organizations, as well. They will look closely at the leadership team, the people shown on your company's website and social media, the way you talk about your culture and working conditions, the words you use to describe the role and the wider organization, the wider reputation of the business, and the values you put forward (and whether or not you seem to live up to them). Some 39 per cent of job seekers[19] won't even apply for a role if they don't believe that the organization is inclusive – think how much talent you could be missing out on.

Hiring talent is only half the battle though – you then have to keep them in the face of this trend for quitting. Thirty-nine per cent of staff say they would leave their current employer for a more inclusive one, and 23 per cent have already done so.[20] Inclusive organizations, on the other hand, have 5.4 times higher rates of retention.[21] Employees who feel that their workplace is inclusive are three times happier than those who do not.[22] And it stands to reason that people who are happy in their jobs tend to stay put. These same employees also feel more satisfied with their pay and more positive about their progression prospects – whether that's because inclusive organizations are also more likely to ensure these elements are fair and work for all staff, or because staff simply have a more positive perception of an inclusive organization across the board, is hard to say, but it's clear that inclusion is a powerful reason for talented people to join, and stay at, your organization.

Results

Given that we already know that inclusive teams are more productive and make better decisions, and that inclusive organizations have a stronger chance of recruiting and retaining the best talent, it follows inevitably that inclusive organizations will achieve better results. Employee performance is 12 per cent higher in diverse organizations,[23] but the value of going beyond simple diversity and creating a culture of inclusion is clear when we consider that inclusive teams perform up to 30 per cent better in high-diversity environments.[24]

So much rests on the culture of the organization, and the leadership is a key part of that, setting the tone for what is expected of the team. In fact, inclusive leaders increase team performance by 17 per cent.[25] This is likely owing to all the factors we have already discussed: the breadth of ideas and perspectives, the psychological safety to feel able to share them, the desire to give your all for the organization and an environment that empowers you to do so. Inclusive teams are also better enabled and encouraged to work together – teams in inclusive organizations have a 36 per cent higher rate of collaboration[26] – which cannot fail to bring them better results.

As we've said before, though, belonging is the ultimate goal. A culture of belonging leads to a 56 per cent increase in job performance,[27] and surely that's what all organizations want to strive for?

Growth

If your organization is looking to sell something (and, ultimately, every organization is selling something, whether it's a necessity, like food you need for survival, a support service, like accounting, that will help your business run more effectively, a luxury, like a holiday, or a sense of being part of something, like contributing to the fight against cancer), then inclusion will help you do it more effectively. When it comes to reaching new customers, you should know that 59 per cent of customers prefer to buy from brands that stand for diversity and inclusion.[28] Sixty-one per cent of women and 67 per cent of people from minority ethnic backgrounds are more trusting of brands that represent them in their advertising[29] – when you consider that 54 per cent of customers currently don't feel represented in advertising, there's a potentially easy win for you in growing your customer base right there. Just representing different people in your ad campaigns could steal consumers from your competitors without much effort. When you come to build relationships with clients, having diverse team members enables you to connect more effectively. A team member who shares a client's ethnicity, for example, is 152 per cent more likely to understand that client.[30] All of this goes a long way to explaining why diverse and inclusive organizations are 45 per cent more likely to report increased market share.[31]

If you're hoping to expand your business, different perspectives, understanding of different backgrounds, cultures and needs, and diverse approaches to challenges all play a pivotal role, which is why inclusive organizations are 70 per cent more likely to capture new markets.[32]

Profits

Ultimately, and probably unsurprisingly, these factors add up to a significant increase in organizational profits. Gender-diverse teams are 25 per cent more likely to generate higher profits,[33] and ethnically diverse teams have 33 per cent higher profits.[34] Statistics like this are helping previously unenthusiastic leaders to wake up to the value of inclusion, and 78 per cent of people now say that diversity and inclusion give a competitive advantage.[35] When research demonstrates that inclusive practices generate 30 per cent higher revenue per employee[36] and 25 per cent higher revenue growth,[37] it's hard to see how you could argue otherwise. Diverse organizations are also a better bet for investors, generating 53 per cent higher returns on equity and 66 per cent higher returns on invested capital.[38]

Overall, businesses that prioritise diversity and inclusion are 35 per cent more likely to achieve above-average returns, with business performance increased by 31 per cent.[39] Everything we have discussed so far shows how much better organizations work when they are not only diverse, but when they operate inclusively and strive for belonging. The bottom line is that inclusion will make you more money, so it's a very shrewd investment.

Time to get moving

Hopefully this chapter has convinced you that working on diversity and inclusion isn't just the right thing to do – although it is the right thing to do. We should all want a world that is fairer, more equitable and offers opportunities for everyone. We need to think about the kind of world we want to live in, that we want our children to grow up in and that we want to leave able to face the challenges of the future. But luckily, we don't have to choose between what is right for the world and what benefits us. Inclusion will make your organization more successful and will put more money in your pocket. So it's a win-win. That's the good news. The bad news is, now the real work begins.

Notes

1   R Lorenzo, N Voigt, M Tsusaka, M Krentz and K Abouzahr. How diverse leadership teams boost innovation, BCG, 23 January 2018, www.bcg.com/publications/2018/how-diverse-leadership-teams-boost-innovation (archived at https://perma.cc/D2P9-89MM)
2   C Criado Perez. Sexist smartphone designs may be hurting women's health, according to a new book, Bustle, 8 March 2019, www.bustle.com/p/in-invisible-women-caroline-criado-perez-argues-that-one-size-fits-all-usually-means-one-size-fits-men-16822238 (archived at https://perma.cc/YF7T-2G78)
3   *Principles of Social Psychology*, 1st International H5P edn. Chapter 10. Working Groups: Performance and Decision Making: 10.3 Group Decision Making, https://opentextbc.ca/socialpsychology/chapter/group-decision-making/ (archived at https://perma.cc/B75Z-94PG)
4   J Koski, H Xie and I R Olson. Understanding social hierarchies: The neural and psychological foundations of status perception, *Social Neuroscience*, 2015, 10 (5), 527–50, www.ncbi.nlm.nih.gov/pmc/articles/PMC5494206/ (archived at https://perma.cc/5LJM-MUDY)
5   CFA Society. Group polarisation and risky decisions, 6 September 2019, www.cfauk.org/pi-listing/group-polarisation-and-risky-decisions#gsc.tab=0 (archived at https://perma.cc/46UF-B7PL)
6   H Obaidy. How a diverse team drives better decision-making, emtrain, August 16, 2019, https://emtrain.com/blog/diversity/better-decision-making/ (archived at https://perma.cc/4Q23-4RLL)

7 Cloverpop. Learn how inclusion + diversity = better decision making at work, www.cloverpop.com/hacking-diversity-with-inclusive-decision-making-white-paper (archived at https://perma.cc/CCL7-TFYP)

8 A Reynolds and D Lewis. Teams solve problems faster when they're more cognitively diverse, Harvard Business Review, 30 March 2017, https://hbr.org/2017/03/teams-solve-problems-faster-when-theyre-more-cognitively-diverse (archived at https://perma.cc/8DVZ-2AZT)

9 S Duchek, S Raetze and I Scheuch. The role of diversity in organizational resilience: A theoretical framework, Business Research, 2020, 13, 387–423, https://link.springer.com/article/10.1007/s40685-019-0084-8 (archived at https://perma.cc/Z4FH-HRG6)

10 M Swaminathan. Opinion: During crises, diversity and inclusion should lead the way, devex, 29 October 2020, www.devex.com/news/opinion-during-crises-diversity-and-inclusion-should-lead-the-way-98408 (archived at https://perma.cc/Y4H9-QE26)

11 C Wood. 7 ways diversity and inclusion help teams perform better, CIO, 24 October 2023, www.cio.com/article/189194/5-ways-diversity-and-inclusion-help-teams-perform-better.html (archived at https://perma.cc/Y4H9-https://perma.cc/PL6Y-DF9N)

12 *State of the Global Workplace: 2023 Report*. Gallup, www.gallup.com/workplace/349484/state-of-the-global-workplace-2022-report.aspx (archived at https://perma.cc/HJ8L-CHA7)

13 Hive. 7 research-backed benefits of diversity in the workplace, www.hive.hr/blog/benefits-of-diversity-in-the-workplace/ (archived at https://perma.cc/Y2NJ-3QGD)

14 Deloitte. Poor mental health costs UK employers up to £56 billion a year, Press Release, 1 April 2022, www2.deloitte.com/uk/en/pages/press-releases/articles/poor-mental-health-costs-uk-employers-up-to-pound-56-billion-a-year.html (archived at https://perma.cc/L3S8-5JAM)

15 D Witters and S Agrawal. The economic cost of poor employee mental health, Gallup, 3 November 2022, www.gallup.com/workplace/404174/economic-cost-poor-employee-mental-health.aspx (archived at https://perma.cc/3FM4-KFU7)

16 rewardian. Diversity and inclusion can boost employee engagement, 9 September 2020, https://blog.rewardian.com/diversity-inclusion#:~:text=Research%20shows%20that%20companies%20with,to%2087%25%20of%20the%20time (archived at https://perma.cc/BX2Q-YJ89)

17 ManpowerGroup. 2024 Global talent shortage, https://go.manpowergroup.com/talent-shortage (archived at https://perma.cc/237T-6Z4E)

18 Glassdoor. What job seekers really think about your diversity and inclusion stats, 12 July 2021, www.glassdoor.com/employers/blog/diversity/ (archived at https://perma.cc/AC32-WMWE)

19 McKinsey & Company. Not inclusive? You're losing 39 percent of job applicants, 29 June 2020, www.mckinsey.com/featured-insights/sustainable-inclusive-growth/chart-of-the-day/not-inclusive-youre-losing-39-percent-of-job-applicants (archived at https://perma.cc/SNS5-ZNC8)

20 Deloitte. Unleashing the power of inclusion: Attracting and engaging the evolving workforce, www2.deloitte.com/content/dam/Deloitte/us/Documents/about-deloitte/us-about-deloitte-unleashing-power-of-inclusion.pdf (archived at https://perma.cc/Z7P4-BZ9B)

21 M Bush. Why is diversity and inclusion in the workplace important?, Insights, 25 August 2023, www.greatplacetowork.com/resources/blog/why-is-diversity-inclusion-in-the-workplace-important (archived at https://perma.cc/WJ5E-ZEP3)

22 M Krentz, A Dartnell, D Khanna and S Locklair. Inclusive cultures have healthier and happier workers, BCG, 14 September 2021, www.bcg.com/publications/2021/building-an-inclusive-culture-leads-to-happier-healthier-workers (archived at https://perma.cc/H7Y5-K8ZS)

23 C Wood. 7 ways diversity and inclusion help teams perform better, CIO, 24 October 2023, www.cio.com/article/189194/5-ways-diversity-and-inclusion-help-teams-perform-better.html (archived at https://perma.cc/4G3Q-29XG)

24 Gartner. How HCM technologies can scale inclusion in the workplace, 22 January 2020, www.gartner.com/en/documents/3979855 (archived at https://perma.cc/58K7-9AGA)

25 J Bourke and A Titus. Why inclusive leaders are good for organizations, and how to become one, Harvard Business Review, 29 March 2019, https://hbr.org/2019/03/why-inclusive-leaders-are-good-for-organizations-and-how-to-become-one (archived at https://perma.cc/6GYH-VG4Q)

26 Qlearsite. How Diversity and Inclusion is linked to productivity and profitability [blog], 21 October 2020, www.qlearsite.com/blog/how-diversity-and-inclusion-is-linked-to-productivity-and-profitability/#:~:text=Recent%20research%20shows%20that%20companies,be%20able%20to%20recruit%20millennials (archived at https://perma.cc/RT7D-T69B)

27 rewardian. Diversity and inclusion can boost employee engagement, 9 September 2020, https://blog.rewardian.com/diversity-inclusion#:~:text=Research%20shows%20that%20companies%20with,to%2087%25%20of%20the%20time (archived at https://perma.cc/GE89-VHTC)

28 K McCormick. 76 perspective-broadening stats about diversity & inclusion in marketing for 2024, WordStream, 25 January 2024, www.wordstream.com/blog/ws/2023/02/27/diversity-inclusion-marketing-statistics#:~:text=Some%2059%25%20of%20consumers%20polled ,in %20online%20advertising%20(Facebook) (archived at https://perma.cc/5M29-Y42U)

29 R Sukhraj. 36 eye-opening inclusive marketing statistics that prove its power for 2022, Impact, 6 October 2021, www.impactplus.com/blog/diverse-inclusive-marketing-statistics (archived at https://perma.cc/4SE3-Q9GE)

30 S A Hewlett, M Marshall, and L Sherbin. How diversity can drive innovation, Harvard Business Review, December 2019, https://hbr.org/2013/12/how-diversity-can-drive-innovation (archived at https://perma.cc/U2EH-EZGE)

31 S A Hewlett, M Marshall, and L Sherbin. How diversity can drive innovation, Harvard Business Review, December 2019, https://hbr.org/2013/12/how-diversity-can-drive-innovation (archived at https://perma.cc/Q5PJ-7WB8)

32 L Sands. What is inclusive leadership & how can it help you grow your business?, breathe, 13 July 2022, www.breathehr.com/en-gb/blog/topic/equality-and-diversity/what-is-inclusive-leadership-how-can-it-help-you-grow-your-business#:~:text=In%20fact%2C%20research%20indicates%20that, we%20do%20things%20round%20here' (archived at https://perma.cc/ACE3-FPFT)

33 A Watts. 17 Statistics Highlighting the Importance of Workplace Diversity and Inclusion, eduMe, www.edume.com/blog/workplace-diversity-statistics (archived at https://perma.cc/D9FA-H3KE)

34 Dame V Hunt, L Yee, S Prince, and S Dixon-Fyle. Delivering through diversity, McKinsey, 18 January, www.mckinsey.com/business-functions/people-and-organizational-performance/our-insights/delivering-through-diversity (archived at https://perma.cc/5WLA-DFJB)

35 J Bourke, S Garr and 王大威. Diversity and inclusion: The reality gap, Deloitte, 2017, www2.deloitte.com/us/en/insights/focus/human-capital-trends/2017/diversity-and-inclusion-at-the-workplace.html (archived at https://perma.cc/D588-VPQ3)

36 H Dickinson. Why inclusion is fundamental to success, Abstract, www.abstractuk.co.uk/why-inclusion-is-fundamental-to-success (archived at https://perma.cc/3PGT-TCM9)

37 C Hastwell. Racially diverse workplaces have largest revenue growth [blog], Insights, 5 January 2020, www.greatplacetowork.com/resources/blog/racially-diverse-workplaces-have-largest-revenue-growth (archived at https://perma.cc/W6MC-6BEC)

38 RICS. Why Diversity and Inclusion is crucial in the built environment sector, 1 April 2020, https://www.rics.org/news-insights/why-diversity-and-inclusion-is-crucial-in-the-built-environment-sector (archived at https://perma.cc/C7X6-G8P4)

39 Qlearsite. How Diversity and Inclusion is linked to productivity and profitability [blog], 21 October 2020, www.qlearsite.com/blog/how-diversity-and-inclusion-is-linked-to-productivity-and-profitability/#:~:text=Recent%20research%20 shows%20that%20companies,be%20able%20to%20recruit%20millennials (archived at https://perma.cc/HR47-JGHU)

2

Are we nearly there yet?

There are many who say we've already achieved equality, or perhaps we're nearly there, so why worry about it? People think we live in multicultural societies where anyone can achieve the things they want to. Many believe we live in a world of meritocracy, where people get ahead through hard work alone. There are those who talk about not seeing skin colour, about judging people purely on their merits, and how it doesn't matter where someone grew up and what their education was. Is that true though? If that is the case, why does the data show us something different? In this chapter we will look at what the reality is, and why there is still work to do and progress to make. We are moving forward, but we are definitely not there yet.

It's true that our world *is* full of diversity. We encounter rich variety every day of our lives. A lack of diversity isn't the issue. But before we get to that, let's look at the environment around us.

The diversity landscape

We already live in a fantastically diverse society. Take the UK, where we live, as an example. According to the 2021 census, a quarter of the population of England and Wales are from varied ethnic backgrounds distinct from the dominant white British group.[1] Ethnicity is not recorded in the same way in every country,[2] and as many as 20 of the 38 OECD countries prohibit the collection of race and ethnicity data, which makes it difficult to be precise on a global scale; but it is estimated that people of colour make up around 85 per cent[3] of the world's population. Increasingly we see the term 'global majority' being used, instead of referring to people of colour as minorities. Women, often talked about as if they were a minority group, actually make up slightly more than half of the population of most countries.[4]

Back in the UK, 11 per cent of people have sexualities other than hetero-sexual,[5] up to 20 per cent of the population is neurodivergent,[6] and 18 per cent of people in England and Wales live with a disability.[7] While the major-ity of adults speak English as a first language, almost one in 10 do not.[8] We could go on, but you get the picture. We live within a wonderfully varied environment, rich with a wide range of perspectives, experiences, opinions, ideas and imaginings.

Of course, who you encounter and work with depends on your personal world. Cities, for example, tend to have a wider range of people, and those who work in international companies are even more likely to come into contact with a wide variety of people. But no matter where you go, you don't have to look too hard to find a breadth of human identities and experi-ences. In many ways, 'diversity' in business is an outdated concept. The real issue is whether a wide range of people are able to access, influence and progress within businesses.

Diversity is widely available to us, yet we are being denied the benefits of all of those unique inputs. There is no lack of women in the UK, yet more CEOs of UK FTSE 100 companies are named Peter than are female.[9] Some 15 per cent have entirely male executive committees. No country has yet achieved full gender parity.[10] Meanwhile, more of these UK CEOs are named Steve than are from minority ethnic backgrounds.[11] More than half of FTSE 100 companies have exclusively white board members. Out of the 8 million people who are not white to choose from, it cannot be the case that only 10 of them were suitable for FTSE 100 leadership roles – yet only 10 have been appointed.[12]

We live on this wonderfully diverse planet, surrounded by human beings who are not only fantastically varied from one another but also have a rich spectrum of experience contained within each individual. How have we so spectacularly failed to harness all of the benefits of these different views, experiences and ideas? Why isn't belonging our default state? This is how our societies limit opportunities for many individuals:

- Around 2.4 billion women of working age do not have equal economic opportunities.[13]

- 54,000 women[14] lose their jobs in the UK every year because of maternity discrimination.

- The employment rate of people with disabilities globally is 27 per cent lower than for people without disability.[15]

- UK job seekers from ethnic backgrounds need to send out an average of 60 per cent more applications[16] to get the same number of interviews as candidates from majority groups. When fictitious CVs were sent out with identical skills and experience, 24 per cent of those from white backgrounds were invited to interview compared to 15 per cent from minority backgrounds.

- People with 'non-English' sounding names have to send 60 per cent more job applications to get a response in the UK than equally qualified peers with more anglicized names.[17]

- Black pupils are routinely marked down by their teachers – when their work is marked externally by people unaware of their ethnic background, they receive higher grades.[18] White children from neighbourhoods with high poverty rates also tend to be under-assessed compared to their more advantaged peers.

- 42 per cent of LGBTQIA+ people[19] have experienced non-inclusive behaviour at work owing to their sexual orientation.

- One in three employers say they would be 'less likely' to hire a trans person.[20]

Unfortunately, there are many, many more examples we could list of ways people are excluded from opportunities. The result of pushing these people out of key positions and limiting their contributions is that we have been left with a blinkered view of the world that centres white maleness as the default and the optimal way to be human. We have excluded other points of view, and our organizations, our communities, our society has suffered as a result.

The full scale of the problem isn't known, either, because data isn't gathered on any except the largest organizations that are required to release it, and no data at all is being gathered on the representation of people with disabilities, trans and non-binary people, neurodiversity, socioeconomics and so on.

An organization might lack diversity, but that's not an accident of location or available candidates – it's down to how people are employed and developed. The population it exists within is rich with diversity that it could benefit from if it had the right structures and processes in place. If we are going to build a way of working that will succeed into the evolving future, we need to move the focus away from diversity.

The issue is inclusion.

Diversity is not just a black and white issue

When the word 'diversity' is mentioned, most people immediately think of race. Over the last few years, the media have focused their discussion of the topic on issues of racial discrimination, and the Black Lives Matter movement brought more attention to the need to challenge racism and increase opportunities for people of colour. It is incredibly important and right that this has become such a key issue and about time that organizations have been forced to consider it more closely. But it is not the only issue.

Other people might think predominantly of gender and tackling the huge inequalities in pay and progression that exist between men and women. Or maybe you think about disability and making the world more accessible. Often, it's the issue closest to your life that determines your focus. All of these are incredibly important issues, and there's no doubt that most of us will be judged initially and most powerfully by the most visible characteristics that differentiate us from others. When you first enter a room, you cannot escape the fact that you will be judged on people's immediate perceptions, which will be hugely fuelled by the way that you look and the identity that you present.

Many organizations, too, get hung up on characteristics protected by law. In the UK, the key legislation is the Equality Act 2010,[21] which protects age, disability, sex, gender reassignment, marriage and civil partnership, pregnancy and maternity, race, religion or belief, and sexual orientation. Other countries have similar legislation around similar characteristics,[22] although in many countries there is a long way to go for some of the laws needed for equality.

Some countries have introduced further regulations to track workplace equality. The UK has mandatory gender pay gap reporting for businesses with more than 250 employees, and there is talk of ethnicity pay gap reporting becoming a requirement soon, too. UN Women monitor the number of women in leadership roles, and factors such as socioeconomic mobility are tracked by world organizations.

Legislation and regulations are where your legal obligations lie, certainly; and if you're motivated entirely by risk mitigation, then that is where to focus. But it's a narrow and limiting view to take.

There are a number of diversity issues that aren't visible, aren't obvious and don't come with legal obligations. Some might not be causing direct prejudices, but can still be unfairly limiting a person's potential. The world is designed for a very specific type of person, and people who don't fit that mould can find themselves disadvantaged and held back for no good reason. Other areas of diversity people may choose to keep hidden, if they can, because they fear being sidelined or dismissed if they are open about who they are. Yet creating cultures where we feel afraid to be open is hurting our organizations. It's only by feeling able to be our full selves that we are able to contribute our best, and only in environments where we feel psychologically safe to think, act and be in different ways that we can move forward with innovation, collaboration and effective decision-making. So creating spaces that are considerate of, and inclusive to, a wide range of differences is vital.

Here are a few examples of areas of diversity that you might not have considered.

Socioeconomics

We have to acknowledge that there is an 'old boys' network' which is still a considerable force in the world of business in most countries. Fewer than a third of UN member states have ever had a woman as their leader [23] and that will also be the case for many companies. In the UK, 20 out of 55 UK prime ministers have been to Eton.[24] Does Eton just generate a particularly superior breed of political mind? Very unlikely. No one school, however brilliant, can be responsible for generating 36 per cent of the country's top talent. But the people at the top are automatically more likely to pass opportunities down to people they are connected to or share history with, or who remind them of themselves and come from similar backgrounds.

People from more privileged backgrounds are more likely to have access to professional networks, mentors and connections that help them to progress in their careers. The media and pervasive stereotypes have trained us all to make certain assumptions based on someone's accent or style of clothing. Certain industries expect new entrants to spend a long time working for free as an intern before they can achieve a paid job, and that makes those roles simply inaccessible to many people. How many times have you seen that someone has been given an amazing role somewhere based on an introduction from a friend or family member?

A university education in most countries costs money. (Although there are some countries, many in the European Union, which do offer free or minimal cost higher education.[25]) In the UK, a university education costs most domestic students £9,000 per year, and the average student will graduate with £40,000 worth of debt. Worldwide, most people without large reserves of family financial support will have to think long and hard about whether higher education is a burden they want to take on. When a job advert says that a degree is a requirement, is that because someone really needs a degree to do that job? Or are you needlessly stripping a vast amount of talented and motivated people from your potential talent pool?

Caring responsibilities

Five million people in the UK are juggling caring responsibilities with work,[26] and there are a further 13 million working parents who are trying to balance employment and childcare.[27] That means 55 per cent of the working population have some kind of additional caring to do on top of their day job. Globally, 84 per cent of carers are women and girls.[28] This is having a dramatically negative effect on people, where 48 per cent of carers worldwide are worried about their own health.

If we focus on UK data, 72 per cent of carers have struggled with their mental health, and 61 per cent have seen an impact on their physical health,[29] which is probably why 600 people give up work every day to look after an older or disabled relative.[30] In 2021/22, the number of women leaving the workforce to look after young children rose by 12.6 per cent,[31] with one in four women having to reduce their hours because of caregiving, and one in five unable to work longer hours even though they would like to do so.[32] And this is largely a gender issue – because of existing structural inequalities, societal expectations and wage gaps, women are more than twice as likely than men[33] to be pushed out of the workforce to take on caring responsibilities. What we see when we look globally is that it's a gender issue worldwide.

It isn't only women affected, though. Many fathers would like to take on their share of parenting duties but are often faced with the response of 'can't your wife do that?' when they ask for flexible hours or time away from the office to enable them to be more involved in key moments of their children's lives. This has an impact on their mental health and morale. Men who do take advantage of shared parental leave or flexible working options often face sexism and mockery in the workplace. And work social events that take place only late on a Friday night can exclude parents who want to see their children for a few fleeting moments before they go to sleep. A number of parents are made unhappy and disengaged by a long commute and inflexible work hours that mean they get little quality time with their families.

Why should you care? Well, the UK economy is missing out on an estimated £1 billion just from the mothers who have been excluded from the workplace.[34] We're losing skills and knowledge, as well as varied perspectives.

And your organization is losing experienced employees who have built up significant insights into the way you work, having to spend money recruiting and training new people, and missing out on talent that could take you to the next level. The more women that leave you, or avoid you in the first place, because of motherhood, the more women in general will avoid you, because they don't see your organization as a place where they can have a long-term career. With growing numbers of jobseekers prioritizing inclusion as a criterion for choosing an employer, that will lead to you missing out on a much wider pool of top talent. The ripple effect is significant. On top of all this, if you are draining the energy of working parents physically and mentally and creating a conflict between their work life and home life, how much do you expect them to have to give to their job? How much will they *want* to give? Do you want coming to work to be an exciting opportunity to channel their insights and creativity, or an exhausting source of guilt, frustration and resentment? Which do you think will lead to the best results for your business?

Neurodiversity

As we have seen, humans are infinitely varied, and that includes the ways our brains work. Neurodiversity refers to the range of differences in the way that human beings experience and interpret the world around them. Now, you could make an argument that we are all neurodiverse, as no two brains work in the same way. Every individual person's brain interacts slightly differently with their environment, which means that everyone experiences the world in a slightly different way. When you really start to examine it, there is actually no such thing as an objective reality and we're all actually living in distinct, co-existing realities shaped by our own thoughts, experiences, feelings and perceptions. But now we're straying into the realms of philosophy, which is slightly off-remit for this book.

While we are all different, it's important to recognize that there are people who are considered 'neurotypical', whose brain processes and functions are within the range expected by society, and people who are described as 'neurodivergent', whose brain processes and functions in some way fall outside the expected range. This could include autism, ADHD, dyslexia, dyspraxia, dyscalculia, OCD, depression, anxiety, seasonal affective disorder and much more. The world is very much designed for neurotypical people, and those people will therefore find the world much easier to navigate. For people who are in some way neurodivergent, unnecessary barriers have been created that might limit their potential or their contributions. You might be missing out on a huge array of talent, inputs and ideas by inadvertently limiting the types of people who can contribute to, and thrive in, your organization.

This isn't limited to people who identify as neurodivergent, either. Since everyone's brain operates differently, everyone has different strengths and weaknesses, different approaches and different personalities. These all result in different ways of working and communicating. Every human being you interact with will interpret and process the information you give them in different ways. People give and receive feedback differently, they need instructions and guidance in different forms, they will approach tasks in different ways, they communicate more effectively through different methods, and they may need different kinds of support to be enabled to contribute and participate in full. Considering the varied ways in which people work, communicate and collaborate can unlock a vast amount of potential. Would you rather find someone's particular skills and passions and help them use those to their fullest, or would you prefer to try to force a square peg into a round hole which causes frustration for everyone?

These are just three examples of types of diversity. We could also discuss culture, politics, nationality, language… and go on forever. The point, though, is that we are all different in more ways than we can realistically quantify. All of the various ways in which we differ from each other affect the way that we see and experience the world, and therefore influence our perspectives and our ideas. These varied viewpoints coming together is what drives innovation and problem-solving and success. They're all important elements to be considered and affect the dynamics of any group we bring together.

We should also be careful not to neglect the importance of intersectionality – the ways in which those different identities co-exist within one person. The experience of misogyny, for example, is different for a white woman and a Black woman. Being proud of your LGBTQIA+ identity might also be a very different challenge depending on your cultural background or which country you live in. Human beings aren't just diverse as a species, we are diverse within ourselves.

One person is never just one thing, and we should be wary of ever seeing them that way.

The inclusion gap

In Chapter 1, we saw the need to move from diversity to inclusion to belonging. But, as a society, we have consistently skipped that step in the middle.

We haven't been including everyone. In fact, based on a combination of self-interest, unconscious bias and downright prejudice, society has actively excluded a number of people. We've already looked at the myriad benefits that we've denied ourselves by maintaining such a narrow group at the top, and that's a shame, but rather than losing ourselves in hand-wringing and defensiveness and recriminations, let's focus on the positive – now that we understand the problem, we can fix it.

The key to fixing it, however, will not lie in head counts and box ticking. That is only measuring diversity, which, as we've seen, is only one part of the process. A diverse range of staff, as measured by demographic criteria, might be an indication as to how inclusive your organization is, but it is not a solution in itself. We shouldn't lose sight of these measurements as useful key performance indicators, but we cannot think that our job is done when we've managed to add a few different people into the room. Rather than counting heads, we want to make space for all that rich diversity to flourish so that we can benefit from it.

If we want to make meaningful change in our organizations, and in the broader world of work in which we operate, we need to move our focus to creating spaces where everyone can thrive. We need to work on creating cultures of inclusion and, ultimately, of true belonging.

Notes

1 Census 2021. Population and household estimates, England and Wales: Census 2021, unrounded data, 2 November 2022, www.ons.gov.uk/ peoplepopulationandcommunity/populationandmigration/populationestimates/ bulletins/populationandhouseholdestimatesenglandandwales/census2021 unroundeddata (archived at https://perma.cc/7SN9-AGSA)

2 World Economic Forum. Why better reporting on racial and ethnic equity can improve diversity and inclusion outcomes, 23 January 2023, www.weforum.org/ agenda/2023/01/davos23-reporting-racial-ethnic-equity-improve-diversity/ (archived at https://perma.cc/Z4R9-ZB8R)

3 Statista. Distribution of the global population 2023, by continent, 5 January 2024, www.statista.com/statistics/237584/distribution-of-the-world-population- by-continent/ (archived at https://perma.cc/Q4W5-ABNU)

4 Statista. Distribution of the global population 2023, by continent, 5 January 2024, www.statista.com/statistics/237584/distribution-of-the-world-population- by-continent/ (archived at https://perma.cc/N7ZW-WCL2)

5   Census 2021. Sexual orientation, England and Wales: Census 2021, 6 January 2023, www.ons.gov.uk/peoplepopulationandcommunity/culturalidentity/sexuality/bulletins/sexualorientationenglandandwales/census2021 (archived at https://perma.cc/HZR8-4XLN)

6   ICAEW Insights. Neurodiversity: the power of thinking differently, 22 March 2023, www.icaew.com/insights/viewpoints-on-the-news/2023/mar-2023/neurodiversity-the-power-of-thinking-differently (archived at https://perma.cc/TPW8-V547)

7   Census 2021. Disability, England and Wales: Census 2021, 19 January 2023, www.ons.gov.uk/peoplepopulationandcommunity/healthandsocialcare/healthandwellbeing/bulletins/disabilityenglandandwales/census2021#:~:text=In%20England%2C%20the%20census%20data,are%20disabled%20within%20the%20household (archived at https://perma.cc/7MED-D5R7)

8   Census 2021. Language, www.ons.gov.uk/peoplepopulationandcommunity/culturalidentity/language (archived at https://perma.cc/X8CN-PZM9)

9   A Cohen. What is a 'Peter problem'? Jaw-dropping study of U.K. CEOs reveals more named Peter than women, Fast Company, 29 July 2020, www.fastcompany.com/90534066/what-is-a-peter-problem-jaw-dropping-study-of-u-k-ceos-reveals-more-named-peter-than-women (archived at https://perma.cc/43X4-JHQR)

10 World Economic Forum, Global Gender Gap Report 2023, June 2023, www3.weforum.org/docs/WEF_GGGR_2023.pdf? (archived at https://perma.cc/FW8R-7CSQ)

11 B Chapman. FTSE 100 has more CEOs called Steve than from ethnic minorities, research finds, *Independent*, 8 February 2019, www.independent.co.uk/news/business/news/ftse-100-ceos-called-steve-ethnic-minorities-diversity-a8769006.html (archived at https://perma.cc/X643-DN9T)

12 BBC. 'People of colour seem to be superglued to the floor', 4 December 2019, www.bbc.co.uk/news/business-50656176 (archived at https://perma.cc/QDN2-9S7K)

13 The World Bank. Nearly 2.4 billion women globally don't have same economic rights as men, Press Release, 1 March 2022, www.worldbank.org/en/news/press-release/2022/03/01/nearly-2-4-billion-women-globally-don-t-have-same-economic-rights-as-men (archived at https://perma.cc/H4DF-QTEJ)

14 A Topping, Maternity leave discrimination means 54,000 women lose their jobs each year, *Guardian*, 24 July 2015, www.theguardian.com/money/2015/jul/24/maternity-leave-discrimination-54000-women-lose-jobs-each-year-ehrc-report (archived at https://perma.cc/DW26-74EK)

15 OECD. Disability, Work and Inclusion: Mainstreaming in All Policies and Practices, 11 October 2022, www.oecd.org/employment/disability-work-and-inclusion-1eaa5e9c-en.htm (archived at https://perma.cc/PYL8-SRN4)

16 H Siddique. Minority ethnic Britons face 'shocking' job discrimination, *Guardian*, 17 January 2019, www.theguardian.com/world/2019/jan/17/minority-ethnic-britons-face-shocking-job-discrimination (archived at https://perma.cc/6UHY-2KLV)

17 I Amrani. Is your name holding you back?, Raconteur, 21 October 2019, www.raconteur.net/talent-culture/ethnic-name-bias (archived at https://perma.cc/S6BA-C7RC)

18 A Asthana, T Helm and T McVeigh. Black pupils 'are routinely marked down by teachers', Guardian, 4 April 2010, www.theguardian.com/education/2010/apr/04/sats-marking-race-stereotypes (archived at https://perma.cc/P68M-6NQF)

19 Deloitte. Deloitte Global 2023 LGBT+ Inclusion @ Work, www.deloitte.com/global/en/issues/work/content/lgbt-at-work.html (archived at https://perma.cc/ZVV2-J79M)

20 Crossland. Transphobia rife among UK employers as 1 in 3 won't hire a transgender person, 18 June 2018, www.crosslandsolicitors.com/site/hr-hub/transgender-discrimination-in-UK-workplaces (archived at https://perma.cc/KV6Q-CVJX)

21 Equality Act 2010, www.legislation.gov.uk/ukpga/2010/15/contents (archived at https://perma.cc/2ZX2-AAYR)

22 Global Campaign for Equal Nationality Rights. Global overview, https://equalnationalityrights.org/countries/global-overview (archived at https://perma.cc/2ZX2-zzzz)

23 L Clancy and S Austin. Fewer than a third of UN member states have ever had a woman leader, Pew Research Center, 28 March 2023, www.pewresearch.org/short-reads/2023/03/28/women-leaders-around-the-world/ (archived at https://perma.cc/B4D2-NB5N)

24 J Self. The school that rules Britain, BBC, 14 April 2021, www.bbc.com/culture/article/20210413-the-school-that-rules-britain (archived at https://perma.cc/BX23-J5Z8)

25 World Population Review. Countries with Free College 2024, https://worldpopulationreview.com/country-rankings/countries-with-free-college (archived at https://perma.cc/6LVA-UKNV)

26 Carers UK. Key facts and figures about caring, www.carersuk.org/news-and-campaigns/press-releases/facts-and-figures (archived at https://perma.cc/E9G2-C8G5)

27 Working Families. Concern about future from UK working parents linked to final restrictions lifting, 17 June 2021, https://workingfamilies.org.uk/news/flextheuk2021/ (archived at https://perma.cc/8HFY-4TNJ)

28 Carers Worldwide. Whoever we are, we will all one day be a carer or be cared for ourselves, https://carersworldwide.org/our-work/carers-issue (archived at https://perma.cc/6N2M-CBRZ)

29   Carers UK. Health, www.carersuk.org/policy-and-research/our-areas-of-policy-work/health/ (archived at https://perma.cc/3UB9-6H57)

30   Carers UK. Key facts and figures about caring, www.carersuk.org/news-and-campaigns/press-releases/facts-and-figures (archived at https://perma.cc/P4PY-KBDC)

31   Pregnant Then Screwed. The number of women leaving the workforce to look after family has increased for the first time in decades, https://pregnantthenscrewed.com/the-number-of-women-leaving-the-workforce-to-look-after-family-has-increased-for-the-first-time-in-decades/ (archived at https://perma.cc/6YVH-X27L)

32   A Topping. Almost half of working-age women in UK do 45 hours of unpaid care a week – study, *Guardian*, 31 March 2022, www.theguardian.com/world/2022/mar/31/almost-half-of-working-age-women-in-uk-do-45-hours-of-unpaid-care-a-week-study (archived at https://perma.cc/TA4X-C7RJ)

33   M Oppemheim. Women more than twice as likely to 'quit job due to caring responsibilities', Independent, 9 March 2021, www.independent.co.uk/news/uk/home-news/women-childcare-job-quit-gender-inequality-b1814526.html (archived at https://perma.cc/QJA2-HCZB)

34   J Farrugia. Why supporting mothers' return to work improves prospects, profitability, and economic prosperity, LinkedIn, 11 October 2021, www.linkedin.com/pulse/why-supporting-mothers-return-work-improves-prospects-john-farrugia (archived at https://perma.cc/9SVE-7PVJ)

3

What's taking so long?

So now we know that diversity and inclusion offer huge benefits for organizational success, but that many businesses are still lacklustre to say the least in the way they approach this area. So why the hesitation? Given that we know this is a path to increased innovation, productivity, performance and profits, surely leaders everywhere should be all over it? Some 87 per cent of global businesses say that diversity and inclusion should be a priority[1]… so why aren't they making it one? In this chapter we'll take a look at why there is still resistance to driving inclusion, and what we might be able to do to overcome it.

Inclusion inertia

In the last chapter, we looked at how the scale of the problem hasn't changed much in recent years, and in our work with organizations we've seen the unwillingness to deal with the issues in action. Many of the senior leaders we speak to are aware that inclusion is something that 'should' be looked at. However, we still see inertia. Even when we show them the vast benefits that it could unlock for their business and how effectively it can support their biggest objectives and help solve the challenges, they still hesitate to act. This seems counterintuitive, but we've come to realize that this inertia is largely rooted in fear.

Scarcity mentality

Imagine the world is a pie. Hopefully, you're not reading this when you're hungry or this metaphor could be quite distracting. If dominant groups already have 90 per cent of the pie, and everyone else is left with 10 per cent, we can see objectively that that's not fair. But persuading individual people from those dominant groups to give up some of their portion of the pie also doesn't seem fair. Why should I have some taken away from me to be given to someone else?

That's the way we tend to look at work and power and wealth. As if there is a finite amount, and more for one group means less for another.

But that's not the case. There is not a finite amount; there is infinite scope to develop new jobs, new positions of status and more money. All we need is the will to do it. Life is not a pie, and we don't have to fight over the crumbs. We need to let go of this scarcity mentality that drives us all to hoard and selfishly guard what we have and treat everyone else as competitors to fight with.

'But only one person can be CEO', we hear you cry. Yes, maybe only one person can be CEO of *your* organization (although we write this as two co-CEOs, so it's not a given that there can only be one). But given that 1,843 companies are founded every day in the UK alone[2] – that's more than one every *minute* – there will always be plenty of other opportunities out there. No one is suggesting that you fire all your white male staff immediately and replace them with people from less dominant groups, and no one is about to remove you from your position. But as people move on to take up one of those myriad other roles out there, or as your company expands and more new jobs are created, the chance to bring in new ideas and perspectives presents itself.

'If I'm hiring more diverse candidates, though,' you continue, 'then there is a reduction in opportunities for people from dominant groups.' I'm sure your organization is a great place to work, and it's wonderful that you see it as the best choice for any candidate, but there are other great places out there too. The candidates you don't choose will be fine elsewhere. You can't hire everyone who applies, anyway.

Let's be totally clear – any form of discrimination is illegal. So-called 'positive discrimination', where candidates from dominant groups are rejected on the basis of their demographic characteristics in favour of candidates from non-dominant groups, is just as prohibited by the Equality Act 2010 in the UK, and by similar legislation around the world, as discrimination the other way around. What we're discussing here is positive *action* – taking steps to create a more level playing field, so that all candidates have the same opportunities to succeed. (As a side note, if you are choosing between two equally qualified candidates for a role with nothing much to separate them, it is perfectly legal, under UK law as a positive action step, to choose the one with a protected characteristic if you have identified that you have a disproportionate lack of people from that group in your business.)

'I don't see colour,' you tell us (or gender, or disability, and so on). We know it's probably starting to seem like we just keep arguing with you, but, frankly, you *should* see these things. They are key elements of people's identities, and if you don't see them then you don't see the people clearly. It's also important that we recognize what a privilege it is to not have to think about these elements of identity – if you don't have to be aware of them, it means there are no barriers in your way because of them. For many people, though, that is not the case. You need to see these elements in order to recognize where barriers are being created and your role in keeping them there – how else can we take them down?

Ultimately, we get it, you don't want to be focusing on someone's demographics, you just want to hire the best person for the job. But if certain people are being excluded or blocked by these unnecessary barriers, then you're not going to be able to do that because your pool of talent is being artificially limited. In order to find the best talent, you need to maximize the amount of talent you are reaching, attracting and engaging, and then give each of those people the best possible chance to show you what they're capable of.

The idea that there is one best person for the job, though, is nonsense. There isn't just one person that can do a particular job. And you'd better hope there's not – what if they quit or went to a competitor? You'd be in serious trouble if they were genuinely irreplaceable. But, of course, multiple people exist with the skills you're looking for. When someone tells us that they don't want to hire with diversity in mind because they want the best person for the job, that does rather imply that they are assuming the best person for the job will be a white man. Why else would hiring diverse people cause a conflict with hiring the best people? So first there's some work to do in overcoming the unconscious bias that tells us that the character of a 'serious business person' looks a certain way. Then it's time to consider that the best person for the job is actually the person you don't have already – it's the person who can bring new ideas, new perspectives, challenge the way you do things to find better possibilities and open up new opportunities. If that means rejecting a white man because he is similar in background and experience to everyone else on your team and can't contribute anything new, then don't worry about him – since research shows that white candidates are 60 per cent more likely to be called to interview for a job,[3] and men are 30 per cent more likely to receive an interview than women,[4] he'll probably be fine.

Status guarding

For someone who's got used to being at the top of the tree, of course it doesn't seem attractive to level the ground. Why would anyone be eager to give up their existing level of status? It's why 55 per cent of white women still voted for Donald Trump in 2020,[5] despite his very clear stance on women's rights – they were keener to protect their privilege as a white person than to risk losing what status they had in order to gamble for new rights as a woman. There's also an immediate desire to justify your position – no one wants to believe that they got where they are because of natural advantages. For many people in leadership roles, accepting the concept that our current system makes it easier for certain types of people to succeed and harder for others equates to admitting that they don't deserve to be in the role they're in or that they've got there unfairly. That's not the case at all.

As with the scarcity pie, levelling the playing field doesn't mean bringing those at the top down, it means lifting everyone else up. It might be a bitter pill to swallow that you won't necessarily receive automatic deference in any room because of who you are, and that you won't necessarily be given a free pass to dominate conversations and decisions, but you may just have to have a spoonful of sugar handy and get it down you. Because when you allow your ideas and views to be challenged, you will find builds and developments to your ideas that will take you even further.

It might be an uncomfortable reality to face, but the fact is that men speak for 75 per cent of meetings[6] and are responsible for 96 per cent of interruptions.[7] Most probably don't realize they're doing it, and there's likely no malice behind it. It's not necessarily down to them that women are quieter in their presence, either – most women have been conditioned, by a system far bigger than any of us, that they are expected to pipe down, and that, if they do speak up, they will be viewed negatively.[8] Accepting that we've benefited from this system can be challenging for any of us. The words 'white privilege' often provoke defensive reactions from white people who have not led anything close to a privileged upbringing and have worked hard to get where they are.

You have worked hard. We all have. You are where you are because of your talent, skill and commitment, and no one is saying anything different. If you can acknowledge, though, that there are other people with equal levels of talent, skill and commitment who simply haven't been permitted by the current structure of our society to progress to the same level you have, then you open yourself up to much wider possibilities. That is what we mean when we talk about privilege in this context – not wealth or comfort, but the basic ability to move through life without having doors slammed in your face because of who you are. It doesn't detract from your achievements to look to make the same opportunities available to a wider range of people. You don't deserve less respect; other people deserve more.

Fear of getting it wrong

Time and time again, leaders in large organizations will whisper to us, 'But what if we get it wrong?' There's a huge panic in our society these days about 'cancel culture' and businesses are terrified of being 'called out' on social media for mistakes. The terminology around inclusion is complex and ever-evolving, and many people feel overwhelmed at the thought of having to get their heads around it, and horrified at the idea they might use a term incorrectly and offend someone. Sometimes the scale of the issue and the number of areas that need to be addressed, and then having to justify why the initial focus has been put in a certain place – or even knowing where to put the initial focus and how to start – is just too much.

The simplest way to avoid being called out for doing the wrong thing is to do the work. Burying your head in the sand is going to seriously inhibit your ability to move forward. Employees and consumers are incredibly aware of these issues now, and they will look beneath the surface. If you have a homogeneous leadership team and are taking no steps to develop future leaders from diverse groups, they will post images of your board on social media with scathing captions. If you're not taking steps to address pay gaps, if your recruitment processes aren't accessible for everyone, if you're not supporting different types of people to progress, if your website can't be used by some people, it will get talked about. If you are putting the work in to drive change, however, and that work is genuine and meaningful, people are far more likely to be sympathetic and supportive. Everyone understands that this challenge is a big one and that change will take a long time – they are willing to forgive a great deal if they know that you are trying to do better. It also provides you with a strong response to any criticism – when you can acknowledge that, yes, you know there is a problem but that here is what you are doing to address it, you will win a lot more supporters and admirers than if you try to ignore it or whitewash over it.

The idea that you'll be cancelled, though, is a myth. No brand or individual has yet been cancelled for a simple slip. If Kevin Spacey can still make a comeback with his acting career, you don't need to worry about inadvertently starting a speech with 'ladies and gentlemen' instead of using inclusive, gender-neutral language like 'everyone'. We promise you, many brands have done far worse than anything you're about to do and lived to tell the tale.

In 2006, Sony sparked outrage by promoting the new white model of its PSP console in the Netherlands using an ad that showed a white person gripping a Black person by the face, while standing over them menacingly. Images of the ad resurface on social media every so often, prompting fresh outrage from people who haven't yet seen it. There's no doubt the ad, which was pulled pretty quickly by the brand, who issued an apology, was grossly misguided at best, yet Sony remains the world's largest gaming brand, with a 45 per cent share of the console market.[9]

In 2020, L'Oréal Paris attracted significant negative attention for posting allegedly hypocritical social media messages in support of the Black Lives Matter movement, after model Munroe Bergdorf claimed she had been fired by the brand in 2017 for discussing racism in the wake of the Charlottesville riots in the US. Although many called for a boycott of the brand, L'Oréal remains the leading beauty manufacturer in the world.[10]

In 2021, Burger King attempted to champion female representation in the restaurant industry, but went about it in a rather controversial way. Their tweet and US newspaper adverts declaring 'women belong in the kitchen' were highly criticized and the company was forced to apologize. The controversy didn't prevent worldwide profits increasing by 24 per cent in that year, though.

Arguably, all these brands had good (or, at least, not evil) intentions, but they made mistakes. Perhaps because of a lack of representation in the decision-making process, no one recognized the drawbacks of the actions they chose. You'll be a lot less likely to make these blunders if you have diverse people in the room, or at least available as sounding boards before you take those actions forward, who can look at your proposals from different perspectives; but the reality is that you are going to mess up at some point.

Everyone makes mistakes. We're all human, and there isn't a business out there that hasn't taken a wrong turn somewhere along the road. The best way to recover from an error in this area is to:

- **Acknowledge the problem** – don't try to cover over it, minimize it or dismiss it; just openly admit that you have made a mistake and show that you recognize the damage done to the people who have been impacted.

- **Apologize** – unequivocally, and straight away; no politician's apology of the 'I'm sorry if you feel this was offensive/I'm sorry if some people were offended' variety, no caveats, no excuses, just a straightforward apology.

- **Listen** – the people telling you that you've got it wrong are a gift; plenty of staff or customers might just desert you without saying a word, and there's no obligation on underrepresented or systemically marginalized people to do the tough emotional work of explaining to you why an action is problematic. So when someone is willing to provide you with that information, listen to them. Take the opportunity to understand where you've gone wrong and what you can do better next time.

- **Learn** – whatever you've taken from the feedback you were given, put those lessons into action. Take steps to change what you're doing or to make sure you do better in future.

- **Communicate** – be clear, to your staff and wider audiences, on what steps you're taking to improve following this incident, and provide mechanisms for further feedback and input to help guide you.

No one likes to hear they've made a mistake, so it's not surprising that it puts us all on edge. But if you accept right now that you are a fallible human who is going to do the wrong thing sometimes, but that doing so offers you huge potential to learn and grow, making you stronger, more effective and more respected in the long-term, then you can move forward and make progress instead of holding back and giving the impression that you simply don't care.

It's worth noting that handling customer complaints effectively has been shown to increase customer loyalty, and that complainants who feel they received a good response from the company go on to spend more money with that business in future.[11] So criticism doesn't need to be all that scary anyway.

Fear of change

The biggest resistance to inclusion is a basic fear of change. Human beings don't like change – we like predictability and familiarity, because the primal side of our brain that governs most of our judgements equates those things with safety. And not getting eaten by a surprise sabre-toothed tiger. In many ways, our brains haven't moved on much from when we first invented fire, and we're still operating with a lot of the same protection mechanisms in place that kept us safe in prehistoric environments.

Society, though, has moved on quite some way, and change is no longer as fraught with danger as our inner caveperson believes. Change offers us new possibilities and innovations. Change is what helps us stay ahead of the game and reach new markets. Change is what keeps us moving forward. But, as we will see in Chapter 4, we need a powerful vision of the future to create a strong enough pull to bring our teams along through the fear of the unknown.

With so many primal fears causing people to hide from the potential successes that diversity and inclusion offer, how can we get this work to actually happen in our organizations?

Overcoming objections

Whilst the root of the hesitancy might be fear, that's rarely the reason anyone gives. As humans, we're very good at burying our fears, and we equate admitting fear with weakness, so we keep them hidden, often from ourselves into the bargain. Our brains work overtime to come up with justifications and rationales for our refusal to change, so that we don't have to recognize that we're scared.

These are some of the most common rationalizations that you're likely to hear from your leadership team when you try to move inclusion work forward… or the rationalizations that you might find emerging in your own mind.

We have bigger priorities right now

We saw in Chapter 1 how diversity and inclusion contribute to your wider business objectives. So, whilst it might seem like there are more urgent issues to deal with right now, most of those other issues will be significantly supported by a robust inclusion strategy.

If you are trying to get buy-in from senior leadership who are insistent that other business goals must take priority, the most effective solution is to map those goals to diversity and inclusion outcomes to demonstrate how they can move you closer to success.

See Table 3.1 for some examples of how to map business benefits to inclusion actions.

TABLE 3.1 Business benefits mapping

Business goal	Inclusion outcomes	Evidence	Inclusion actions	Measures of success
Recruit 50 new staff members over the next 12 months	Wider talent pool Increased applications Increased opportunities for greater number of candidates	70% of job seekers look for diversity and inclusion in potential employers[i] 39% of job seekers won't even apply for a role if they don't believe the organization is inclusive[ii] Inclusive hiring makes companies 36% less likely to face talent and skills shortages[iii]	Introduce an inclusive recruitment strategy Provide inclusive recruitment training for hiring managers Track demographic trends in recruitment funnel and address any identified issues	Increase in quality applications Increased confidence in inclusive approaches for hiring managers Increased speed in filling vacancies
Increase market share by 5% over the next 12 months	Improved marketing reach and engagement Increased customer base Improved customer loyalty	Diverse and inclusive companies outperform competitors by 50%[iv] 59% of customers are more loyal to brands that stand for diversity and inclusion[v] 71% of customers expect brands to show diversity in advertising[vi] 82% of customers want a brand's values to align with their own[vii] 90% of websites are inaccessible to people using assistive technology[viii]	Introduce an inclusive marketing strategy Provide inclusive communications training for all staff, especially marketing and sales teams Look for opportunities to collaborate with broader communities Track demographics of existing customers, cross-referenced by customer loyalty, where possible to identify and address gaps	Increased sales Diversified customer base Increase in lifetime order value and customer retention

Increase turnover by 30% over the next 12 months	Increased staff engagement and productivity	Inclusion increases engagement by up to 83%[ix]	Review and update diversity and inclusion policies	Improved staff engagement and staff satisfaction
	Increased retention of skilled staff (and reduction in recruitment costs)	42% of businesses say improved diversity and inclusion policies increase productivity[x]	Solicit employee feedback on diversity and inclusion approaches and address any identified issues	Reduced rate of staff turnover
		Inclusion increases staff turnover by 50%[xi]	Define organizational values and how these are to be lived on a day-to-day basis	Increased sales
	Improved decision-making	Inclusive teams outperform the competition in decision-making and execution by 60%[xii]	Introduce behaviour guidelines and code of conduct in line with organizational values	Increased revenue
	Increased sales	Diverse sales teams are 10–15 times more successful than less diverse ones[xiii]	Introduce inclusive communications tools and meeting guidelines	
	Higher rates of innovation	Diverse teams produce 19% higher levels of revenue from innovation[xiv]		
	Increased profitability	Diverse and inclusive teams are 36% more profitable than competitors[xv]		

NOTE The references for evidence can be found at the end of this chapter

You can access a free Business Benefits Mapping Tool at www.watchthisspace. uk/the-inclusion-journey.

We don't have the expertise/resources

The fear of getting things wrong and/or a general fear of the unknown might lead organizations to feel that they're simply not qualified to do work on diversity and inclusion. There are a few simple solutions here.

HIRE EXTERNAL SUPPORT

The easiest way to get around a gap in your employees' skill sets is to bring someone in to do it for you. Obviously, as diversity and inclusion consultants ourselves, we would recommend that you get external help. But there really is a benefit to getting expert support, at least in the initial stages, to make sure you get your approach right. You can, of course, hire an in-house diversity and inclusion professional, but a third party can still provide support for this new staff member. Having impartial third-party professionals involved also signals to your staff that you're taking this seriously, and makes them feel more comfortable that there's not an agenda here. People feel more comfortable being honest and open with people who aren't in charge of their monthly pay cheque and don't have power over the future of their career. So you're more likely to get a clearer picture of what really needs to happen and where you should focus your attention in order to produce impactful results.

INVEST IN TRAINING AND EDUCATION

In the long term, you can develop the skills and knowledge of your existing workforce through a programme of diversity and inclusion training. You're not going to solve all of diversity and inclusion in a one-off workshop, and one-off sessions can often do more harm than good as they don't engage staff fully, potentially further distancing those who weren't interested in diversity and inclusion in the first place, and angering those who were by making it look as though you're not taking it seriously. A long-term programme of training, however, engages staff in-depth, provides resources for them to apply their learning practically and continue conversations with colleagues to deepen understanding, and offers insights into a wide range of inclusion topics.

HAVE A 'WHAT COULD GO WRONG' PLAN

To reduce the fear factor for your leadership team – and for yourself – create a plan for dealing with inevitable issues.

Write a list of everything that could possibly go wrong. Then, for each issue, write down actions you will take to try to prevent it going wrong, and actions you will take if it does, in fact, happen. That way, you know you're prepared to handle any difficulties that emerge. We'll talk more about this in Chapter 12.

We don't have a problem

It's not unusual for organizations to go into diversity and inclusion work with a strong view that they already have it all sorted. We once spoke to a medium-sized community organization operating nationally, who told us, 'We're the *most* inclusive organization'. But when we looked beneath the surface it turned out they had zero Black employees (and very few from any kind of ethnic minority), that women were highly represented in junior roles but virtually non-existent at senior management level, that a third of their staff had experienced bullying, discrimination or harassment and that their LGBTQIA+ employees were scared to go to work. This was genuinely a shock to the leadership team, who were horrified that there were so many issues, and hadn't realized what was happening on the ground.

No one wants to believe their workplace has a problem, particularly when they've been instrumental in building that workplace. Your business is important to you – you've put considerable sweat and tears into making it successful, and, as a senior leader, you've given your all to build the kind of culture you believe in. It can be heartbreaking to find out that your vision doesn't match reality. It's even more devastating when you discover that your actions may have contributed to a work environment where people are being disadvantaged, silenced or demotivated.

The first thing to acknowledge is that almost every organization has issues – this is not unique to you. The example above sounds serious, but it's not much of an outlier in the work that we do; we find similar issues, or different issues on a similar scale, in most of the organizations we work with. The bigger the business, and the longer it's been going without any diversity and inclusion work (or the faster it's grown, as rapid growth is often a catalyst for cracks to emerge), the more disharmony has likely built up beneath the surface.

If you're wanting to raise the need for diversity and inclusion work with a leadership team who might not want to believe they need it – or if you're a senior leader who wants to believe everything is perfect in the business you've built that matters so much to you – there are a few key things to get straight.

NOBODY IS PERFECT

If we asked you if you were perfect, you'd probably laugh and say 'of course not'. You'd think it was a silly question, because, of course, no one is. But if we then tell you something about yourself or your work that you can improve on, you'll likely feel defensive and upset, and you'll want to justify yourself. Objectively, rationally, we all know we're not perfect. It's impossible to be perfect, everyone has their flaws and their areas where they can grow and improve. Yet we hate being given examples of ways that we're not perfect. We're never instinctively receptive to being shown how we can grow and develop – although the people who *do* grow and improve the most effectively are the ones who put work into making themselves receptive to that feedback.

It's inevitable that there will be a certain amount of hurt and defensiveness when the issue of diversity and inclusion needs are raised, and we can't jump straight past that emotional reaction. We spend too much time convincing ourselves that emotion doesn't belong in business, when the people who feel strongly and care deeply about the business are exactly the people we want to drive it forward. Emotion is a huge part of who we are, and suppressing it never ends well. So we need to sit with the unpleasant feelings, and be willing to have discussions about why they're coming up, and whether those feelings are benefitting us. If you're faced with, or part of, a leadership team having these discussions, make space to acknowledge the discomfort and why that's coming up. The good news is, discomfort is a sign that you care. So, as we know that you care about this business and its employees, we can now focus on how we can channel those energies into continuing to build on the incredible work that you've already done and keep working towards making this business the best it can possibly be.

THERE'S ALWAYS ROOM FOR GROWTH

However wonderful your business is, we have to acknowledge that there's always room for growth. That's what we're all here for, right? Trying to move the business forward? No leadership team sits around planning their Q3 objectives and talking about how they want to maintain the exact status quo. We've already seen that, whatever other objectives are being set, diversity and inclusion can contribute. But there's also value in improving diversity and inclusion for its own sake, to create a positive culture that you can be proud of.

The fact that you're upset about the thought of there being a problem shows that you do care about your workplace being a fair and positive environment. So, even if you have worked hard already to make the culture as good as it can be, since we know that perfection is unachievable, there's always going to be opportunities for improvements. Maybe everything *is* pretty good right now, but, since we know your organizational culture means a lot to you, it's got to be worth doing everything you can to keep getting better.

THE DATA NEVER LIES

You can argue endlessly over whether or not there's an issue, but the only way to know for sure is with clear data. If you're really confident that there aren't any issues, you should be willing to prove it. If you can demonstrate that everything is brilliant, it will go a long way to improving your reputation, internally and externally, and strengthening your team's trust in you.

But, since we've already established that there's always going to be room for growth, once you examine your culture in more detail, you're likely to find some opportunities for improvement. That can only ever be a good thing if your goal truly is to make your business the best it can be.

We don't have the budget

All lofty ideals and big visions aside, often what it really comes down to is the practicalities. Money is one of the biggest barriers to diversity and inclusion work, as business leaders see it as an unnecessary cost compared to the seemingly more urgent investments needed. We've already talked about why investing in diversity and inclusion can support other business goals, but there's a more direct pay-off in investing in this work. Diversity and inclusion might have costs attached, but these are nothing compared to the costs of *not* doing the work:

- **Employment tribunals** cost, on average in the UK, £8,500[12] to defend, and there is no cap on the amount of money that claimants can be awarded if your organization is deemed to have acted in a discriminatory way. The biggest award for discrimination in 2021/22 was £228,177, and the average award was £24,850.[13] So, given that you could be paying out an average total of £33,350 for *every instance* of unfair behaviour, it has to be worth investing now to stop those behaviours from happening in the first place.

- **Hiring new staff** has some obvious costs, and some hidden ones. Some 81 per cent of employees[14] would consider leaving their role if their employer demonstrated a lack of commitment to diversity and inclusion, so that's potentially a lot of jobs you'll need to fill. You'll have to consider costs for recruitment agencies, the cost of time taken up for staff involved in the recruitment and interviewing process, the salary for the new staff member (what do you want to bet that they'll negotiate for an increase on what you were paying the previous person who'd been there a while?), the costs of training the new person and the cost of losing the skills and experience of the former employee. There's a loss of productivity while the outgoing employee is waiting to leave and then while the new employee is getting up to speed that will also cost you. Altogether, you can expect to pay an average of £62,890[15] *per employee.*

- **Disengaged staff** are potentially even more dangerous than staff that are leaving. We've already seen how diversity and inclusion improves engagement, so you know that failing to work on your diversity and inclusion strategy is going to leave many staff mentally checking out or 'quiet quitting'. Disengagement increases absenteeism and decreases productivity. It also stands to reason it will reduce the quality of output. On average, it's estimated that disengagement in an employee costs the business between 18 per cent and 34 per cent of that staff member's salary.[16] Quite an expense to maintain over time.

There are always going to be resistances to doing diversity and inclusion work, and someone will always find a reason not to do it. However, as we have shown, the benefits are so high, and the costs of *not* doing it are so great, that it's worth taking the time to examine where resistance is really coming from, and being prepared to have the difficult conversations to understand what actions will truly benefit the future of the business, so that you can all move forward together.

Notes for Table 3.1

i   70% of job seekers value a company's commitment to diversity when evaluating potential employers, PR Newswire, 18 June 2020, www.prnewswire.com/news-releases/70-of-job-seekers-value-a-companys-commitment-to-diversity-when-evaluating-potential-employers-301079330 (archived at https://perma.cc/T34R-8SU7)

ii   Not inclusive? You're losing 39 percent of job applicants, McKinsey & Company, 29 June 2020, www.mckinsey.com/featured-insights/sustainable-inclusive-growth/chart-of-the-day/not-inclusive-youre-losing-39-percent-of-job-applicants (archived at https://perma.cc/QT85-W7DM)

iii   Joseph Fuller, et al. How leaders can improve hiring practices to uncover missed talent pools, close skills gaps, and improve diversity, Accenture, 4 October 2021, www.hbs.edu/managing-the-future-of-work/Documents/research/hiddenworkers09032021.pdf (archived at https://perma.cc/5BM8-ZARM)

iv   Scott Clark. 3 ways diversity improves CX, CMSWire, 9 February 2023, www.cmswire.com/customer-experience/3-ways-diversity-improves-the-customer-experience/ (archived at https://perma.cc/2YJT-24NN)

v   Kirsten McCormick. 76 perspective-broadening stats about diversity and inclusion in marketing for 2024, WordStream, 25 January 2024, https://www.wordstream.com/blog/ws/2023/02/27/diversity-inclusion-marketing-statistics#:~:text=Some%2059%25%20of%20consumers%20polled,in%20online%20advertising%20(Facebook) (archived at https://perma.cc/F3CW-YYWB)

vi   Kirsten McCormick. 76 perspective-broadening stats about diversity and inclusion in marketing for 2024, WordStream, 25 January 2024, https://www.wordstream.com/blog/ws/2023/02/27/diversity-inclusion-marketing-statistics#:~:text=Some%2059%25%20of%20consumers%20polled,in%20online%20advertising%20(Facebook) (archived at https://perma.cc/KZ5J-RPS2)

vii   Giusy Bounfantino. New research shows consumers more interested in brands' values than ever, CGT, 27 April 2022, www.consumergoods.com/new-research-shows-consumers-more-interested-brands-values-ever (archived at https://perma.cc/AB2Q-9ZKT)

viii   33 accessibility statistics you need to know, Monsido, 16 November 2022, https://monsido.com/blog/accessibility-statistics (archived at https://perma.cc/FN2V-FP4A)

ix   Inclusive mobility: How mobilizing a diverse workforce can drive business performance, Deloitte, 2018, www2.deloitte.com/content/dam/Deloitte/us/Documents/Tax/us-tax-inclusive-mobility-mobilize-diverse-workforce-drive-business-performance.pdf (archived at https://perma.cc/M8MR-KW6R)

x   Over two-fifths of UK businesses agree D&I policies increase productivity, Employer News, 11 October 2022, https://employernews.co.uk/news/over-two-fifths-of-uk-businesses-agree-di-policies-increase-productivity/ (archived at https://perma.cc/C9XM-S5TE)

xi   Evan W Carr, et al. The value of belonging at work, *Harvard Business Review*, 16 December 2019, hbr.org/2019/12/the-value-of-belonging-at-work (archived at https://perma.cc/MVL5-DC8H)

xii Kathy Sucich. Why diversity matters in decision-making, Dimensional Insight, 15 February 2022, www.dimins.com/blog/2022/02/15/diversity-matters-in-decision-making/ (archived at https://perma.cc/YKK9-M68A)

xiii *American Sociological Review*, 2009, 74, www.asanet.org/wp-content/uploads/savvy/images/journals/docs/pdf/asr/Apr09ASRFeature.pdf (archived at https://perma.cc/WCD8-3FWH)

xiv Stuart R Levine. Diversity confirmed to boost innovation and financial results, *Forbes*, 15 January 2020, www.forbes.com/sites/forbesinsights/2020/01/15/diversity-confirmed-to-boost-innovation-and-financial-results/ (archived at https://perma.cc/3SM2-VZDC)

xv Sundiatu Dixon-Fyle. Diversity wins: How inclusion matters, McKinsey & Company, 19 May 2020, www.mckinsey.com/featured-insights/diversity-and-inclusion/diversity-wins-how-inclusion-matters (archived at https://perma.cc/V3D6-CG36)

Notes

1 Harver. 7 benefits of diversity in customer service at your company, 7 February 2024, https://harver.com/blog/diversity-in-customer-service/ (archived at https://perma.cc/K8BS-L66A)

2 S MacNaught. Startup Statistics UK 2022/2023, Micro Biz Mag, 23 February 2023, www.microbizmag.co.uk/startup-statistics/ (archived at https://perma.cc/5VSX-A2UD)

3 Mayor of London Assembly. Greater London Authority response to 'Ethnic disparities and inequality in the UK: call for evidence', www.london.gov.uk/publications/greater-london-authority-response-ethnic-disparities-and-inequality-uk-call-evidence (archived at https://perma.cc/VY9D-5CQD)

4 Universitat Pompeu Fabra Barcelona. Women are 30% less likely to be considered for a hiring process than men, 7 March 2019, www.upf.edu/en/recercaupf/-/asset_publisher/RVNxhLpxnc9g/content/id/223062374/maximized?_ga=2.193246254.281252703.1655976527-1329092305.1655976527#.YrQynXbMLIV (archived at https://perma.cc/L7RC-ART9)

5 T H Schwadron. Why did so many white women vote for Trump?, Salon, 11 November 2020, www.salon.com/2020/11/11/why-did-so-many-white-women-vote-for-trump_partner/ (archived at https://perma.cc/TWT8-226P)

6 E Wrenn. The great gender debate: Men will dominate 75% of the conversation during conference meetings, study suggests, MailOnline, 19 September 2012, www.dailymail.co.uk/sciencetech/article-2205502/The-great-gender-debate-Men-dominate-75-conversation-conference-meetings-study-suggests.html (archived at https://perma.cc/Z9DA-2T43)

7   Advisory Board. How often are women interrupted by men? Here's what the research says, 7 July 2017, www.advisory.com/daily-briefing/2017/07/07/ men-interrupting-women (archived at https://perma.cc/2RM2-MESN)

8   A Adamczyk. Why women talk less than men at work, Money, 12 August 2016, https://money.com/men-interrupt-talk-more/ (archived at https://perma. cc/3KAW-DWK7)

9   rawmeatcowboy. New report shows market share and more between Nintendo, Sony and Microsoft, gonintendo, 28 February 2023, https:// gonintendo.com/contents/16868-new-report-shows-market-share-and-more-between-nintendo-sony-and-microsoft (archived at https://perma.cc/ M4C4-26RM)

10 Statista. L'Oréal - statistics & facts, www.statista.com/topics/1544/loreal/ (archived at https://perma.cc/6GLF-36QZ)

11 W Huang, J Mitchell, C Dibner, A Ruttenberg and A Tripp. How customer service can turn angry customers into loyal ones, Harvard Business Review, 16 January 2018, https://hbr.org/2018/01/how-customer-service-can-turn-angry-customers-into-loyal-ones (archived at https://perma.cc/72DN-RWBZ)

12 Peninsula Group, HR and Health & Safety Experts. Employment Tribunal Costs, Peninsula, 18 May 2022, www.peninsulagrouplimited.com/resource-hub/employment-tribunal/tribunal-costs/ (archived at https://perma. cc/3E22-6DC2)

13 Dwf. Employment tribunals: What is the cost to employers?, 4 May 2023, https://dwfgroup.com/en/news-and-insights/insights/2023/5/employment-tribunals--what-is-the-cost-to-employers (archived at https://perma.cc/ GBF5-TQKG)

14 businesswire. Most employees would quit over lack of company commitment to DE&I Efforts, says new GoodHire survey, 26 July 2022, www.businesswire. com/news/home/20220726005410/en/Most-Employees-Would-Quit-Over-Lack-of-Company-Commitment-to-DEI-Efforts-Says-New-GoodHire-Survey (archived at https://perma.cc/MJP9-EGGR)

15 C Campbell. What is the cost of hiring someone in the UK?, nerdwallet, 5 April 2023, www.nerdwallet.com/uk/business/cost-of-hiring-someone-uk/ (archived at https://perma.cc/V3XG-KV9N)

16 M Postelnyak. Calculating the cost of employee disengagement, contactmonkey, 21 April 2022, www.contactmonkey.com/blog/cost-of-employee-disengagement#:~:text=The%20average%20cost,a%20 disengaged%20employee's%20annual%20salary (archived at https://perma. cc/8TTK-QCX6)

4

Getting everyone on board

Often you find when there's an issue in a team, it's because someone doesn't feel included. And as leaders we want to be well ahead in our thinking and how we work, so that doesn't happen.

DR HELEN CURR, CEO AT HERE – CARE UNBOUND[1]

Hopefully by now you are convinced this is the direction you need to take, and you have most of your leadership team on board with the idea too. The tricky bit is how to engage people across your organization to get involved and want to do the work. People need to understand why it matters, and why it affects them. Diversity and inclusion work will only go so far without buy-in from all teams. We see that, where people fail, the common thread is that there has not been broad enough engagement, and, often, not enough effort put in to really connect with people in different ways.

Like any journey, everyone must commit to going together. Everyone has to *want* to move and change direction. Dr Helen Curr, CEO at Here – Care Unbound, a healthcare social enterprise, says that getting everyone on board with the importance of this work is crucial. Often when there are issues in a team, investigation uncovers that someone did not feel they were included in some way, or that a decision was made without considering biases at play and without taking account of different perspectives. Curr believes that to create a sense that there is inclusive leadership, there has to be different perspectives considered and included and a shared sense across the organization that this is a priority.

To really lead on this work is to create teams where there is not only one way to do things. Where your leaders are keen to work on inclusion before issues arise. There needs to be an inherent value placed on inclusion being core to leadership styles. This does not happen overnight or after one train-ing session. There needs to be discussion, learning, understanding and also disagreements along the way.

Getting everyone on board requires different approaches for different groups of people. Different roles, and the people in those roles, are affected and engaged and interested in this in different ways. Each group needs a different communication style, message and method. As Advita Patel and Priya Bates say in their book *Building a Culture of Inclusivity*,[2] there has to be a strong element of listening too. Listening carefully means that actions move beyond performative box-ticking, into meaningful actions.

Let's take a look at the different groups you need to engage to take this journey.

Leadership team

The people leading the business have a lot of priorities to juggle. There are targets to hit, goals to achieve, compliance, governance, strategy and more. Without buy-in from the leadership team, the journey will struggle to make a start, so it's crucial that they see inclusion work as worthy of their attention.

We have seen many organizations where some of the leadership team are on board and ready to go; it might be someone in the leadership team who has stressed the need to prioritize this. But perhaps the *whole* team isn't there yet. If the majority of the leadership team is not clear on why this work matters and is not fully behind it, then everyone else will also struggle to prioritize the work, or really value it. It will always be at the bottom of any lists.

For leaders, the key is to connect with their priorities and goals. As we have seen in previous chapters, there is a compelling case for the benefits of diversity and inclusion (Chapter 1), which can be mapped to your specific business objectives (Chapter 3). There are many who will still need help, however, to see how it relates directly to them. A technique we have found works with leaders is to show them a range of business challenges they might be facing. Encourage discussion and the sharing of ideas around this. And then tell them how those things are all linked to inclusive teams. Make the link with what their challenges are and how this relates to working on diversity and inclusion.

FIGURE 4.1 Typical business challenges

Are you struggling with...

Engagement

Productivity

Recruitment

Innovation   Crisis management
          Results   Decision-making

Communication

Diverse, inclusive teams will help with all of this!

We typically use versions of Figure 4.1 with clients as a starting point for discussion. We listen to what their challenges are and then relay that back to them using words they recognize to describe the struggles they are facing. We can then link this to working on diversity and inclusion. We have found this method works well with large groups, as well as at conferences and events.

Then what makes any data and links to business challenges even more compelling is your own data about your own organization. We quickly learnt that leadership teams need to see the internal data to be truly convinced. People usually like to see charts, graphs and numbers to bring the data to life. So, to help with this, we created a simple way of showing people their current situation. Leaders fill in a free quiz to identify where they are on the diversity and inclusion journey, and several people from an organization can do this. If different people fill it in, it's an opportunity for a good discussion about the results, and any differences in perception. This takes them through Level One of our Inclusion Journey Mapping process[3] and gives them scores, graphs and suggested actions, revealing the key gaps and opportunities on which to get started. Figure 4.2 shows how this initial

FIGURE 4.2 Inclusion journey accreditation

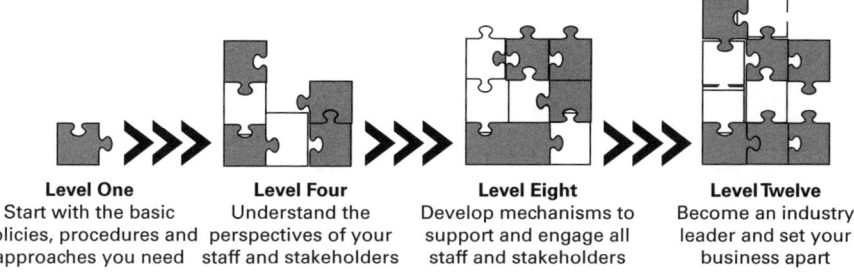

Put the building blocks in place to create a truly inclusive workplace

Level One	**Level Four**	**Level Eight**	**Level Twelve**
Start with the basic policies, procedures and approaches you need	Understand the perspectives of your staff and stakeholders	Develop mechanisms to support and engage all staff and stakeholders	Become an industry leader and set your business apart

work lays the foundations for much greater growth as you progress through the journey.

Your data, together with research data, will tell a story about the need to focus on this as a priority, and how that will impact your wider business goals.

Leadership teams are often inspired by seeing what can be done and the impact it can have. Take recruitment and retention as a business goal, for instance. We talked in Chapter 1 about the value of diversity and inclusion for recruitment, and, rather than simply pointing this out as an issue, we've found it powerful to look with leadership teams at examples of inclusion statements that show a different way of communicating about the commitment to inclusion work. Some examples of effective and distinctive inclusion statements that reflect the company's unique values and culture are shown in Figure 4.3.

Seeing what's possible, and how powerful it can be, is a great motivator.

The most compelling way to convince your leaders, though, might be through a story. Have a look at the end of this chapter at the work we did with Richmond Hill Hotel. They focused on how to engage people across their teams and bring people together to talk about subjects that are often challenging. They encouraged people to come together to raise ideas and concerns, so that they could all learn how to work better with one another.

FIGURE 4.3 Example inclusion statements from job advertising

Textio embraces diversity and equal opportunity in a serious way. We are committed to building a team that represents a variety of backgrounds, perspectives and skills. The more inclusive we are, the better our work will be.

Come as you are
Your gender, your gods, your sex life, your skin colour or your bigshot uncle don't make a difference here. Workable is a progressive and open-minded meritocracy. If you're smart and good at what you do, come as you are.

NETFLIX

It takes diversity of thought, culture, background, and perspective to create a truly global storytelling ... As we grow globally, we know that we must have the most talented employees with diverse backgrounds, cultures, perspectives and experiences to support our innovation and creativity.

Employees

To convince the people working for you that they need to come on this journey with you, there are some different approaches and tactics to think about. Your employees will be at different stages themselves on the inclusion journey, with their own perspectives and ideas about this work. You will need to think about different methods and ways to engage them depending on where they are.

Employers need to think about who gets involved in this and the different skills and reach needed. This is not about automatically going to those with protected characteristics, or those who are the most vocal and quickest to say yes to new projects. A lot of this work is about listening, analysis and project-managing, so think about who is best suited. This type of work is a good opportunity to encourage people who don't normally put themselves forward. Broadly speaking, you can break down your employees into three groups.

Ready to go

There will be employees who are already keen to do this work. They might be the ones who have been pushing you and asking questions about what you are doing on diversity and inclusion for a while. Some of those people might be driven by experiences they have had themselves. They might have experienced exclusionary behaviour, or felt they are being held back from progressing their careers. There are those who might already focus on related campaigning or activism in their lives outside work, and this is an opportunity to get involved in something they feel strongly about.

Anyone who has experienced discrimination or exclusionary behaviour themselves will need to consider their mental health in taking on this type of work. This work will require listening to people's stories and hearing what might be uncomfortable truths.

With this group, the messaging around business benefits like profitability will not sit well. Tailor your messaging around how this will improve equity of opportunity, communication and collaboration. And, most importantly, listen to them; let them talk to you about their concerns and their ideas.

Curious but busy

Many employees might feel that diversity and inclusion are intrinsically good things but lack motivation to work on them in the context of competing priorities because inclusion doesn't feel relevant or pressing to them. Data around profitability and top-level business needs also may not feel relevant to those not in senior roles, so, for them, the key is to demonstrate how this will make their working lives better.

There's a concept called Universal Design, which essentially shows that making the world inclusive benefits everyone. If a website is made accessible, with clearer information, subtitles on videos and clear calls to action, then it's a better website all round – easier to navigate and engage with for everyone, therefore driving a higher rate of conversions. If flexible working is introduced, then more opportunities are created for parents and people with disabilities, but productivity increases amongst all staff. If people are given job interview questions in advance to prepare better, then that makes the experience better for neurodivergent people, but also enables more considered answers from everyone.

Show this group that the changes you plan to make will improve the working environment, structures and processes for them, as well as everyone else.

Detractors

Then there will be those who don't see the point at all. We have to face the fact that many people are actively opposed to diversity and inclusion work. They may see it as divisive. They may think that it's a waste of time, or they might feel threatened that their place or status may be affected in some way. If someone has never experienced discrimination, they may not be aware of their position of privilege. For these people, it is worth taking the time to listen to them and understand their concerns without being defensive or pushing them into anything. As we saw in Chapter 3, they may well be struggling with fear.

In our anti-racism work, we often use a diagram created by a surgeon in the USA to talk about fear. It shows how most of us, from time to time,

FIGURE 4.4 Becoming anti-racist diagram from Surgery Redesign

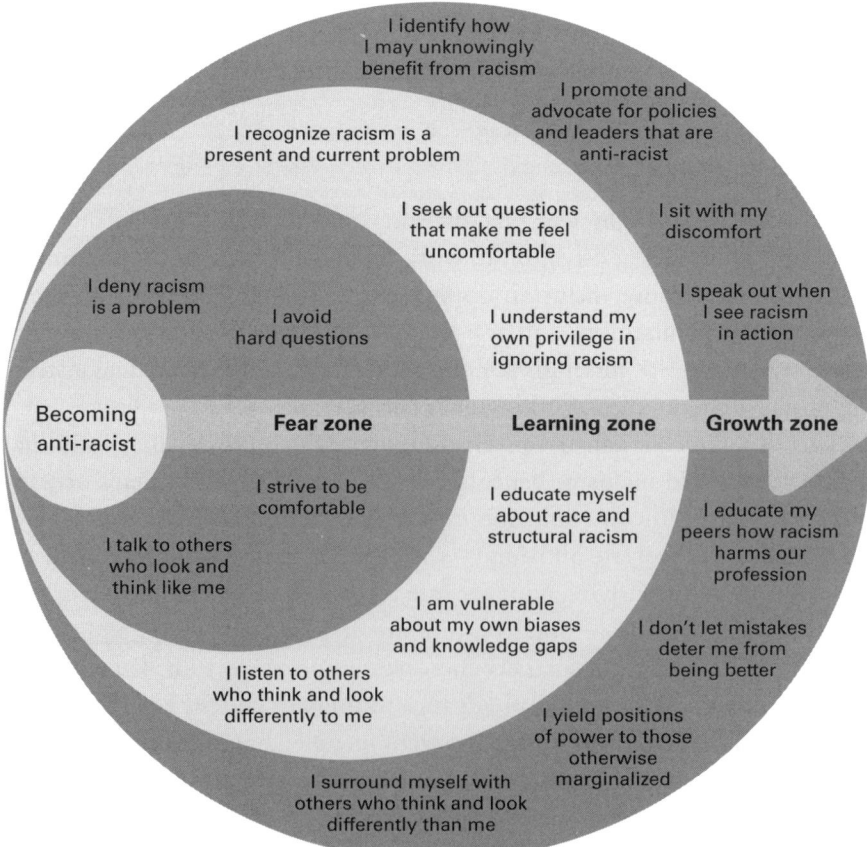

experience the fear zone, and that, through open conversations, we can aim to spend more time in the learning zone, and then progress beyond. This diagram can be adapted for different subjects around diversity and inclusion to help engage people in conversations that they find uncomfortable. Figure 4.4 enables people to voice their fears and talk about how they're feeling.

This group will take longer to convince. There may be a need to start moving forwards before they are all on board with this work; then, as they start to see the results, the positive impact might help to convince them. Show them any quick wins along the way to demonstrate how this work benefits them.

With all employees, think about ways to engage them in the process along the way. When you have mapped out the work you are going to do, show employees the plan – you can simplify as you need to, so you don't overwhelm people. Involve them in workshops to understand what areas they want to focus on. Be curious, and give them the opportunity to ask questions. Create a sense that this is something exciting to work on, and that, although there will be challenges along the way, there will be great benefits for everyone.

To engage people, consider the different ways in which people work and process information. Meetings and workshops will suit those who are happy to talk openly and share ideas. For your employees who are not comfortable doing that, online collaboration tools, smaller group or one-to-one discussions, or information they can read and absorb in their own time, will be more beneficial.

Your employees will be key to delivering on this work, so taking the time to engage them matters. You want people to *want* to get involved. If there are detractors, you want their concerns voiced openly where you can address them, not whispered quietly to whip up resistance, or festering silently and building resentment. This stage of the journey needs clear communication about objectives, timings and involvement to keep things moving along.

External audiences

We are often asked what people should communicate externally about their diversity and inclusion journey. And our response to this is, as much as you can. Tell people this is an area of focus and a priority going forwards. There is no need to present a complete roadmap until you are ready, but talk about where you are, gaps you have identified, actions you are taking and your vision for the future as you progress along this journey. Talking about it externally will show your different stakeholders that you care, and that you are taking action.

For clients, partners and other people you deal with, it shows them that you're one of the organizations they should continue to talk to. It might give them ideas for things they can do themselves. There are many companies evaluating their suppliers and looking for those focusing on diversity, inclusion, sustainability and social value. For some, it's part of the evaluation criteria for tenders. For others, they may be looking at regulatory compliance, or just wishing to protect their own reputation. And there are those companies keen to collaborate specifically with businesses who share their values.

The other key external group to consider is potential employees. They may be sizing up employers to see who they want to work for. So communicating what you're doing will show those people you're worth considering. You can be creative in how you do this too. You can be open and talk about the need for change, the work you need to do and show people why they might want to work for you and get involved.

We have worked with companies who have been prepared to be very open and communicate externally that they are at the very start of this journey, and they found that people responded well to this. If you look at some of the big brands, those who have been brave enough to be open and talk about what they are doing have had a great response, for example:

- Dove's 'Real Beauty' campaign, showing real women in their advertising[4]
- The Bias Cut 'I Look My Age' campaign, showing how women actually look at different ages[5]
- Accenture's 'Inclusion Starts With I' campaign, showing how people are perceived at work[6]
- Bumble's unlimited leave policy for employees[7]

Being open shows people that this is something you're committed to, even if you haven't nailed it yet. That you know you have work to do, and will communicate your progress along the way. Your audiences know as well as you do that your business isn't perfect in this area, but at least this shows that you've made a start.

Case Study: Richmond Hill Hotel[8]

Richmond Hill Hotel is a luxury hotel on the outskirts of London, a beautiful Georgian-style building in an idyllic setting with a view of Richmond

Park. It welcomes a variety of guests seeking accommodation close to the UK capital, as well as hosting corporate events, weddings, parties, celebrations and meetings. The hotel is also very popular with those attending the Wimbledon tennis tournament each year.

Where did they start their journey?

The first thing that the leadership team at Richmond Hill Hotel knew that they needed was a clear picture of their current situation. They had a sense that the large team that makes Richmond Hill such a sought-after and enjoyable venue are a highly diverse group of people, but they lacked the data to confirm this, or to understand how representative they were of the wider communities they serve. They were aware that the apparent diversity amongst the team did not seem to be reflected within the leadership, and wanted to better understand any discrepancies. It was also felt that some roles attracted a greater variety of people than others, and they wanted clearer insight into this issue. By arming themselves with data and clear information, the senior team wanted to identify their gaps and the actions that would drive meaningful progress.

They also felt that there were a lot of inclusive approaches being taken organically in the business, but, since most of this wasn't documented, they knew they were relying on the personal approaches of individual staff members. They wanted to cement inclusive processes and behaviours within the fabric of the organization so that these would be consistent across the hotel. Given the wide variety of customers they come into contact with, they also wanted to ensure that their staff were equipped with the knowledge, skills and confidence to understand and deal appropriately with a range of situations.

They did not want this work to stay with the leadership team. One of the key objectives was engaging all of their staff, and gaining inputs from across the business. It was vital to the senior team that everyone could feel safe and appreciated, that everyone had a voice and was not afraid to speak up. They knew that building a safe environment was critical in order to gather the honest inputs that would enable real change, and to make everyone feel comfortable and included – both in this project, and in their wider work.

Ultimately, their focus was on building a positive culture. 'We spend so much of our time in the workplace,' HR Manager Liva Jones told us, 'it should be a safe and welcoming environment.' And that culture has a knock-on effect that can destabilize the whole business. 'If we get this wrong,' Liva continued, 'we won't have staff. Retention will go down, morale will go down, and stress and absenteeism will go up. It's good to get that right from the beginning.'

They knew they needed to take a good look at everything about their company, communications and people, and get some help before embarking on training and further work. They wanted to set themselves up for the future with a good foundation and long-term plan. They were also highly aware of what a huge topic diversity and inclusion is, and the importance of navigating it effectively. 'You can get a bit lost on where to start from, unless someone guides you,' Liva Jones commented. Watch This Sp_ce were very happy to provide the expert guidance the Richmond Hill team were looking for.

How did they move forward?

Watch This Sp_ce worked with Richmond Hill Hotel on a full Inclusion Journey Mapping process, taking them through all of the steps from discovery and analysis, to planning and implementation. We helped them to create their roadmap, putting timescales and milestones in place to track their progress, and worked with them to engage everyone in the process.

Their Inclusion Journey Mapping work included:

- full audit on policies, frameworks, processes and organizational culture
- Discovery Workshops with their leadership team and employees to set the vision for the future and explore how to get there
- employee survey to understand staff needs and concerns
- data analysis to really understand the organization, customers and other stakeholders
- internal and external communications assessment

When we had the data from the initial stage of the journey, we worked with them on how to communicate these ideas to all their staff. We held separate sessions with the leadership team to talk them through the findings and agree on next steps. And we helped them get the message out to staff internally with different methods of communication, including Activation Workshops. These sessions took staff through the findings of our analysis, and gave them an opportunity to input on the roadmap for change. We talked to them about how they could get involved, and what would be needed to turn their collective vision into a reality.

One of the priorities we identified from this work was a need for a diversity and inclusion learning programme. We developed a bespoke training plan to deepen their understanding, and the initial phase took all of their staff through training on challenging assumptions and unconscious biases, as well as exploring challenging conversations and how to work with different types of people. We worked with them on examples of behaviours they might encounter and their own learning requirements. Each session included actions for each person to take, and encouraged them to work in groups with their colleagues.

The next phase of training moved on to specialist areas, such as inclusive recruitment and developing inclusive leadership behaviours, as well as supporting a wide variety of people to progress into more senior roles. They are keen to continue to work on employee feedback, and are actively engaged in creating a culture where people feel they can progress their careers.

What has been particularly positive is how well attended the training sessions have been. It is often difficult to gather together staff from across a varied and busy organization for group training, but the diversity and inclusion sessions have grown in popularity, with attendance increasing each time. Towards the end of the programme, almost every single member of staff was attending a training session – not an easy feat in such a large and complex business, and something the HR team say is rarely achieved.

How is it going?

The leadership team at Richmond Hill Hotel now has a great understanding of their data, their priorities when it comes to diversity and inclusion, and the opinions of their staff. They have already implemented some great mechanisms for staff to share their thoughts and ideas, and had open discussions with their teams throughout the journey. The training sessions are mixed, with their leadership team attending sessions alongside employees from different departments. This has given them the space to explore ideas and challenges together. Crucially, their leadership team has been open in these sessions in sharing their own questions and areas for improvement with their staff to create a positive culture of learning.

They are working on clarity around language, communication and behaviours to help them really connect with, and be inclusive to, the guests that visit the hotel. They have worked through how to handle challenging situations, and how to navigate being as open as possible with guests to show they are inclusive. Those in senior leadership positions have also had a focus on inclusive recruitment, which has inspired them to develop their approach. This project has changed their perspective on nurturing talent, helping them to think about how they encourage and support promotions and growth. They want to see a diverse spread of people progressing careers within the business.

They have seen their teams open up about the need for change in some areas, and they can see that they have people in their teams who want to lead on some of the areas of work. Their staff can see the leadership team are listening, and are open to new ideas and new ways of working.

The team are all very aware that this is a long-term project, and that it will take time to become fully embedded. They don't want to be performing tick-box exercises – they are all united in a desire to take the time to do the work properly and meaningfully.

Not everyone was this on board in the beginning, though. Diane Tapner-Evans, General Manager at Richmond Hill, told us: 'There was a job to do in the beginning to demonstrate why we were focusing on diversity and inclusion as a priority, as opposed to other areas that some people might have wanted us to focus on instead. Some people didn't understand, at the start, what we were trying to achieve. But the benefits are clear now: it's part of how we retain our team, it's part of how we engage our team, so it's just part of what we do now. And as people have become more familiar with the topic, they've become more comfortable, it's become less scary or confusing, and that has encouraged engagement.'

What went well?

Diane and Liva are clear that the collaboration between Watch This Sp_ce and Richmond Hill has been key to their success. Being able to use external experts to provide objective analysis and deliver tailored training has taken them further than they could have gone by themselves. They also appreciate the fact that the Watch This Sp_ce team were able to adapt training sessions to make it practically relevant to staff in different roles, so everyone could see why they should care about this work. We also regularly sought feedback from attendees, and adjusted our approach accordingly to meet their needs. 'It's the teamwork between Watch This Sp_ce and us that is making it impactful,' Diane Tapner-Evans told us. 'You're not just coming in and delivering a fixed slide. We're able to make it more meaningful and tangible to the team on the floor, and then it makes it more effective.'

Richmond Hill is an organization with strong values – and a willingness to stand behind them. They are prepared to lose customers or staff if those people can't respect their values. Diane shared an example of an anonymous comment from a staff member in a survey some time ago where they expressed displeasure at the hotel flying the rainbow flag in support of Pride. They haven't had any similar comments since, so Diane believes this person must have either concluded that their values are at odds with those of the organization and left, or they have realized that this isn't a place in which they are welcome to express views that make others feel uncomfortable and so they are keeping any anti-LGBTQIA+ sentiments to themselves. Diane is happy with either outcome – everyone is entitled to their personal beliefs, but at Richmond Hill Hotel it is not acceptable for them to make anyone else feel excluded or unsafe.

Diane also makes a clear distinction between blatant discrimination, bullying or harassment, and misguided behaviour or actions that stem from a lack of knowledge or understanding that simply require education. Most people, Diane believes, don't mean to be unkind or unpleasant, and greater awareness and guidance can help everyone create a positive environment. If people are not willing to take on board these learnings and come on this journey, they are welcome to go elsewhere. But there are lines in the sand that are not acceptable to cross, whether it comes from a member of staff or a paying customer.

That can be a scary position to take, to turn down paying customers. Diane remembers a guest who was asked to leave because of racist behaviour, who left a comment on a review site to say that he wouldn't be bringing any of his company to the hotel. This was an important lesson in considering how they can handle tricky situations with guests. Diane remarks: 'If that person is taking his team to another hotel where that type of behaviour is tolerated, then that will fill spaces with them so the people who can't get in with them will come to us. It's only going to displace business; there are more than enough customers to go around.'

'And people like that can damage our team,' Liva adds, 'because if we allow that behaviour, they won't feel safe in the workplace, they won't want to be here and be treated like that.'

'We don't take losing business lightly, of course,' Diane agrees, 'but you have to stand by what you believe in. And, ultimately, if you tolerate discriminatory or abusive behaviour from guests to our employees, it costs you more in the end. Employees leave, your reputation suffers, and then that word spreads both to employees and potential guests. Standing by your values is always going to be the right thing to do.'

This clear commitment to belonging and to inclusive values certainly has helped with the organization's staff retention. In the 12 months since this work began, **Richmond Hill's retention rate has increased from 46 per cent to an incredibly impressive 72 per cent.** They attribute this improvement largely to this work on diversity and inclusion, as they have clear data to show how important it has been to the team.

It is also beneficial to be aligning with the values of current and potential corporate partners – diversity and inclusion is becoming increasingly important as a criteria for selection, and Richmond Hill can now talk with confidence about the work that they are doing in this area, with the data to back it up.

Diane and Liva say there is more positive energy in the team, stronger relationships across the organization and a more powerful sense of team spirit. They loved their workplace before this project started, but they have no doubt that it has become an even better place to work. 'A diverse workplace is a more interesting place to work, and more fun,' says Liva. They advise any other organizations embarking on this journey to be open-minded and willing to learn. 'You'll be surprised at the benefits of taking this journey,' Diane says, 'but it is a process of constant change, and we're all here to learn every day. You do need to be prepared for some brutal truths, but don't take that personally, or as a reflection on you. It's not that, it's an opportunity to grow and improve. We can all, always improve, but we need to be willing to learn.'

Final words...

'Our partnership with Watch This Sp_ce has been incredibly enlightening. It has empowered us to delve deeper into the concept of inclusion within our work environment, inspiring us to adapt our working methods and communication to embrace a wider spectrum of guests who frequent our hotel.

'Our entire team has enthusiastically embraced the insights gained from the training sessions, and each member is actively contributing to driving change and creating a positive impact, with the ultimate goal of making our workplace as inclusive and welcoming as possible. We understand that this is an ongoing journey, and our collective commitment to learning and collaboration with Watch This Sp_ce will continue to shape our inclusive workplace.'
Diane Tapner-Evans, General Manager

Notes

1 Interview with Dr Helen Curr, CEO at Here – Care Unbound, October 2023
2 P Bates and A Patel (2023) *Building a Culture of Inclusivity: Effective Internal Communication For Diversity, Equity and Inclusion*, Kogan Page, www.koganpage.com/responsible-business/building-a-culture-of-inclusivity-9781398610392 (archived at https://perma.cc/Y93E-CCLR)
3 Watch This Sp_ce. The Inclusion Journey, www.watchthisspace.uk/the-inclusion-journey/ (archived at https://perma.cc/475Y-83TU)
4 Unilever. Dove, www.unilever.com/brands/beauty-wellbeing/dove/ (archived at https://perma.cc/D3VD-AHEU)
5 The Bias Cut. Ageism Is Never In Style, www.thebiascut.com/pages/ageism-is-never-in-style-welcome (archived at https://perma.cc/3UFU-DX5Z)
6 Accenture. Inclusion Starts With I, YouTube, 23 June 2017, www.youtube.com/watch?v=2g88Ju6nkcg (archived at https://perma.cc/63CS-5FAW)
7 Bumble. London Benefits, https://team.bumble.com/benefits/london (archived at https://perma.cc/J2QQ-5NCU)
8 Interview with Liva Jones, HR Manager, and Diane Tapner-Evans, General Manager, Richmond Hill Hotel, November 2023
9 Interview with Liva Jones, HR Manager, and Diane Tapner-Evans, General Manager, Richmond Hill Hotel, November 2023

5

Setting the wheels in motion

So now you're ready to go. You've identified a need, and you've made enough space in the barriers keeping you confined to create a door that opens out towards progress. Now you need to walk through it, but it's no good doing that alone. In the last chapter, you got your team to support you, but we don't just want them waving you off joyfully as you set out on this journey by yourself. This needs to be a journey that the whole organization is taking together, in order for the culture, processes and behaviours to change in a meaningful way. There is also only so much that one person can do, and this is a long and complex journey – one person by themselves is likely to get lost in the woods and bogged down in the mud. You need a team driving forward together, and resources to sustain them on the way. It's time to assemble your band of adventurers.

The team you need

Like a crack team in any movie centred around a quest or challenge, you need a group composed of different people with a variety of specialist skills and abilities. For this quest, you will need the following:

The changemakers – people within your organization who are willing to make diversity and inclusion work happen. They will form your working group who will take ownership of the strategy and will be responsible for making sure actions are taken (although they won't necessarily be the people taking all the actions themselves).

The coordinator – whilst you need a team to make change happen, the team all have busy days and a pile of other priorities to sort through. It's best to have one person who takes on the role of coordinating the action, to make sure that it actually happens, that the team are all pulling in the same direction and that everyone knows the plan. As you're reading this book, this could well be your role.

The expert – someone with in-depth knowledge on diversity and inclusion, who can advise on what is needed, provide guidance on legal obligations and potential pitfalls, and who knows best practice approaches for moving forward. This could be someone within your organization who has (or to whom you will give) the necessary training, or it could be a third-party consultant.

The sponsor – someone at a very senior level who will clear a path for the changemakers. They will make sure that they have what they need to be able to make progress and, crucially, that the rest of the organization knows that this work has support from the top and is to be respected.

Now let's look at all the team members in more detail.

The changemakers

There are people across your organization who care deeply about its success, and the way that its culture and behaviours contribute towards that. They might have been considered 'difficult' in the past, because they are frequently raising questions and issues, but this desire to make the business better and the willingness to ask tough questions make them perfect for this task. The people who care enough about the way your organization works to fight to make it better, instead of just walking away and getting a different job, will be highly motivated to drive real change.

Not everyone who raises issues, however, will be ideally suited for this work. What you don't want are people who are willing to be actively disruptive or who are engaged in a personal vendetta. There's a delicate balance to be achieved in finding people who are willing to challenge the status quo and rethink the way things are normally done, and who aren't afraid to see the situation as it really is and how it could be improved – and, crucially, then share what they see with those in power – but who aren't motivated by anger and who know how to raise issues in a constructive way. You need people who are looking forwards rather than backwards.

We once worked with an organization that knew it had a challenge ahead of it. For many years, the culture had been quite toxic, and a number of unpleasant behaviours had become part of standard practice. A new CEO was determined to change this and assembled a working group to lead on diversity and inclusion. They chose a group of people who had been particu-larly vocal in pointing out the need for change, but there was a problem. One of those people had previously experienced horrible treatment from colleagues, which had been very poorly dealt with by the organization. She was angry – understandably so – and was motivated primarily by a frus-trated yearning for a kind of justice that was never going to be possible. Her anger and frustration boiled over into disrupting meetings about diversity and inclusion to push her own agenda, and making unfounded accusations about people in the organization trying to drive diversity and inclusion work forward if they weren't following her demands. People who have had nega-tive experiences might be able to shine a light on what's needed in the organization, but, if their experience is still very raw and they're still hurting, it is probably best that you work with them to process what they've been through and understand what will help them to heal first, so that they can channel their feelings into positive progress, rather than emotional attacks.

A good changemaker is someone who asks difficult questions in a sensi-tive and productive way. Someone who looks for solutions instead of focusing on problems. Someone who is willing to look at considerations from multiple points of view and to listen to people who think differently to them. You want someone who can engage others in the work ahead, under-standing how to hear the concerns of those around them and then show how this work will address and even support those concerns. You need someone who cares about the organization and their colleagues, and also has the energy and enthusiasm to make this business the best it can be.

The changemakers don't all need to be senior people – in fact, it helps to have people from all levels of the organization. You might also find that more junior staff have more time and headspace, and are more ready to get started on this work, than more senior people with more competing respon-sibilities.

The coordinator

Someone needs to take overall responsibility for making sure the work gets done, otherwise, chances are, it just won't. The coordinator is the person who will bring together the changemakers to form a working group and then organize how they work. They will identify the expert and be responsi-ble for sharing their learnings and translating them into action. They will liaise with the sponsor to keep them informed and make sure they're provid-ing the working group with what they need to get the job done.

This is, largely, an admin role. It's organizing meetings, taking minutes, circulating actions, keeping on top of deadlines, tracking progress, sending reminders, sharing updates and ensuring everyone is on course. But don't be tempted to give this role to a junior person who's good at details. The coordinator is a vital role, and someone who will need authority to make sure people do what they're supposed to be doing, and to appoint and manage experts. They will need to have honest and open conversations with the sponsor – who will be in a very senior position – and will therefore need to feel they are on a relatively equal footing with them.

This person will also need an overview of the whole organization. Whilst the working group of changemakers will take overall ownership of the strategy, they won't be able to do it all themselves. When the group identifies actions that need to be taken, the coordinator will help them work out who is best to take that action, and they will then need to know that when they ask that person to do something, they will do it. Ultimately, the coordinator needs to be someone who has the power to make change happen.

Whoever is designated as the coordinator must have time in their schedule for this work. This is true of all members of your team, but it's most vital for the coordinator. They are the pin that holds everything together, and around which all the work revolves. If they don't have time and space to prioritize this work, it won't happen. And then everything falls apart.

It's likely, as you're reading this book, that you will be the coordinator in your organization. (You might also be the sponsor or a changemaker, in which case, once you have a coordinator in place, you might want to lend them your copy when you're done reading.) If the coordinator is you, please know how important this role is. It might be a challenge, especially in the beginning, to get buy-in from everyone and to get things moving – you might encounter resistance and negativity (we've talked about some of this already, and we'll look at some more in later chapters), and you might feel like you have a bit of an uphill battle on your hands at first as you try to push the heavy vehicle of your organization forward. But, once you gain some momentum, the wheels begin turning on their own, and the weight is lifted, a little, off your shoulders. Gradually, as you make progress, it gets easier. There's no doubt it's a tough role, though, and one that you'll need to care about to make all the effort worthwhile. What you're doing means so much to so many people, and it could be instrumental in the survival and future growth of your organization. So, thank you for your hard work.

The expert

To hire an internal diversity and inclusion lead, or not to hire an internal diversity and inclusion lead? It's a difficult question, and one that organizations worldwide have been grappling with in recent years. The number of internal diversity and inclusion roles skyrocketed in the wake of the Black Lives Matter protests of 2020, increasing 123 per cent in the three months following the murder of George Floyd.[1] However, once the impact of a global economic downturn began to be felt, and businesses were looking for staff to make redundant, new diversity and inclusion hires were hard hit. Listings for diversity and inclusion roles now appear to be declining.[2] Partly this is owing to a 'last in, first out' approach to redundancy where the last people who have joined are often first on the list to be let go. This could also be a result of many of these people being hired in a panic, without the necessary foundations being laid for the roles' success.

If you are going to hire a diversity and inclusion lead, you will need to make sure that they have everything they need to perform at their best. This means clearly defining the scope of the role and understanding what you want it to achieve. The role needs sufficient seniority to be able to challenge and influence the senior leadership team, and to be able to drive change in the organization. They need the right skills and experience to be able to fully understand what is needed and how to make it happen. They will need to be able to align diversity and inclusion objectives with wider organizational objectives so that they can measure and demonstrate the impact of their work. Above all else, they will need the budget and resources to allow them to do their job effectively. It's possible, if you do have an internal lead, that they could also take on the coordinator role.

However, there's also an element to which diversity and inclusion needs to be seen as everyone's responsibility, not just the business of one member of staff or one department. You will want everyone to feel part of the process, so that they see this work as relevant to them, so that they are engaged and invested in what is happening and in ensuring the best possible outcome, and so that they feel that their voices and input have been heard. Once a diversity and inclusion strategy has been developed and staff across the organization are engaged in making it happen, it might turn out that there simply isn't enough work to justify a salary for a specialist full-time role. There's also a lot of work to do in training and educating an internal expert, and enabling them to keep up-to-date with the latest developments and requirements in this field.

Instead, you might consider appointing an external diversity and inclusion expert. The benefits here are not just that you only need to pay project fees, not a full-time salary, where you can dial costs up and down to suit your needs and budget over time, and that you will often get a whole team of experts within a consultancy for less than the cost of one internal member of staff. But the major benefit is that external experts instil a greater degree of trust in the process. If the person leading on diversity and inclusion is answerable to the boss, staff might struggle to believe that their work isn't being influenced by what the people at the top want rather than what the organization needs. Any fear or resistance already felt at a C-suite level, or any issues that staff already feel that the leadership have allowed to build up or haven't dealt with effectively, will be seen as unlikely to change. Whether that is true or not, perception often shapes reality. This work will need honest inputs from across the organization, and the team, especially the more junior members, are unlikely to feel comfortable being completely honest if they think the leadership are looking over the diversity and inclusion lead's shoulder at what's being said. Someone who is objective and without personal agenda within the business, and who doesn't have the power to fire anyone whose opinions they don't like, will often have an easier time getting buy-in and engagement.

It doesn't have to be an either/or choice though – you might choose to hire an internal diversity and inclusion lead, and also appoint an external consultancy to support them. They might provide training and resources to your internal staff member, or simply act as their colleagues to help shape the strategy and get work done. They can also provide that sense of trust and objectivity when seeking inputs or presenting plans to back up the internal lead's ongoing activity.

The sponsor

The sponsor doesn't have a huge amount to do, but their role is absolutely crucial to success. This needs to be someone with serious clout in the organization – a member of the C-suite or senior leadership team. It could be the CEO or MD, but the most important thing is that their word carries weight.

The sponsor's role is to give authority to this project. They make clear to the rest of the team that this work is to be valued and respected, and that it has the backing of those at the top. They will also remove, as far as possible, blockers and challenges that the changemakers come across. They will need the power to allocate budget and provide resources to get work done. They will have regular meetings with the coordinator, so that they can keep up to date on progress and be aware of any issues.

The main role for the sponsor, though, is to be visible. They should support the coordinator in communicating progress to the wider team and making clear why this work matters. They need to send a message that this work is sanctioned at the highest level, and that supporting it is a requirement. They will also underline the fact that this work relates to the wider organizational objectives, and that it's therefore something that impacts how every member of staff's success will be measured.

The resources you need

For any long journey, you need provisions to sustain you. But many businesses set out on the diversity and inclusion path without packing properly. Here are a few things that you'll need to prepare.

Budget

Your team will need money to make the vision a reality. Whether it's hiring external experts, arranging training, creating resources, staging events, introducing new HR or measurement tools, working on accessibility projects, changing processes and policies, or whatever your particular areas of need might be, getting this work done will require investment. How much you can afford to spend will vary, but be aware that the more you invest, the more you will achieve.

Time

Too many organizations bolt diversity and inclusion work on to the responsibilities of existing staff members without taking anything out of their existing workload. If someone already has a list of responsibilities that take up the entire of their allocated working hours, how can they get additional work done in that same time? Something will have to come out to make space for diversity and inclusion, and you need to make sure that everyone's workload is realistic. For real progress, there should be space carved out in a role to focus on diversity and inclusion, without simply overloading the staff member. This work should also form part of their objectives, as we all focus on what we measure.

Policies

Your policies and processes form the foundation of your organizational culture, so ensuring inclusion is embedded within them is vital. This is where having an external diversity and inclusion expert, who also understands policy creation, can be an important first step. Get all of your existing policies reviewed and updated, and create new ones to fill any gaps and provide the support and guidance your team needs to build an environment of inclusion and belonging. A clear statement within each one of the value of diversity and inclusion also helps to set staff expectations – this statement shouldn't be bland copy-and-paste corporate wording that ticks the boxes in terms of compliance but actually says very little; it should be an inspirational and motivating statement that sets out the vision for what kind of organization you want to be and excites your staff about the possibilities that diversity and inclusion bring.

Terminology

Clarity around diversity and inclusion terminology is an area that a lot of businesses find worrying. There are no clear 'right' terms, and language in this space is changing and evolving all the time. To avoid that fear of saying the wrong thing – which often leads to saying, and therefore doing, nothing – your organization can agree on a glossary of terms that you use internally. We have shared a glossary of terminology at the end of this book to help you with this. This should be informed by people within your organization and wider communities who are represented by these terms, and should be a collaborative exercise. You won't get universal agreement on every term, but you can demonstrate that you have taken an overall consensus and then make adjustments for individuals who want a different approach on a case-by-case basis. The way we recommend doing this is by running workshops and using collaboration tools to discuss and agree definitions. We do this as part of the Discovery phase of the journey. Ask people what terminology they find difficult. Then facilitate discussions to agree on definitions and words people are happy to use. This helps everyone feel more confident.

Learning

Diversity and inclusion is a broad subject with a lot of complexities. If your team is going to work together to build a culture of inclusion and belonging in your organization, they're going to need training to develop the knowledge and skills that will allow them to understand this intricate landscape and how best to move through it. An organization can only build an inclusive culture if every member of staff is working towards that goal, so every member of staff will need training. There's been a lot of talk in the media in recent years about how 'diversity and inclusion training doesn't work' – that's because a lot of organizations have tried to solve all their inclusion issues in a one-hour workshop, and, shockingly, it hasn't done much good. One-off, tick-box exercise training sessions run the risk of alienating and disengaging everyone. Most people need to think about what they are learning, and come back for more sessions to discuss. What you need is an ongoing programme of training, backed up with ongoing discussions and practical activation. Listening to real people's stories to understand lived experiences can also be a valuable learning tool.

Research and best practice

Diversity and inclusion is an ever-evolving field, where knowledge and understanding are changing all the time. You will need to have a mechanism in place to keep up with the latest research, stay on top of new ideas and ensure you're in line with legal requirements and best practice as these develop. Reading the latest books, attending conferences, joining webinars and networking groups will help with this. There are a lot of articles and posts written around these subjects too, so there is a lot of information out there to help you stay up to date.

Data framework

In Chapter 7, we'll talk more about data and the role it plays in your inclusion journey. For now, just know that you cannot move forward unless you know where you're starting from. Data is the key to understanding your existing gaps and opportunities, and measuring your progress. You will need a clear framework in place for measuring different kinds of data across your organization – from tracking demographic trends in your recruitment funnel, to assessing pay gaps, to measuring staff engagement, data is key to your success.

Ready to go

Diversity and inclusion isn't just one person's responsibility – the whole organization needs to be involved and engaged in building an inclusive culture. But you will need specific people to drive it forward: changemakers, a working group to make things happen; a coordinator, to organize the work and keep on top of everything; an expert, to supply best practice guidance, legal requirements and insight into what is needed and what actions will make an impact; and a sponsor, to demonstrate to the organization that this work has authority from the very highest level. This team will need budget and time made available to them in order to get the job done. In order to ensure that all staff can engage with this work, the organization will need to ensure the right policies and processes are in place, that there is clarity around how everyone should approach inclusive terminology and that there is a programme of training and learning in place. Finally, there will need to be a mechanism in place for at least the coordinator to stay on top of the latest research and best practice in the field of diversity and inclusion, and that there is a framework in place to allow the diversity and inclusion team to track the data that will inform what needs to be done and whether it's working.

Once you have all that ready, the journey can begin.

Notes

1 McKinsey& Company. Unlocking the potential of chief diversity officers, 18 November 2022, www.mckinsey.com/capabilities/people-and-organizational-performance/our-insights/unlocking-the-potential-of-chief-diversity-officers (archived at https://perma.cc/P4FX-5TZB)

2 C Symonds. DEI teams hit by tech layoffs: a lesson to be learned, factorial, 28 November 2023, https://factorialhr.com/blog/dei-teams/ (archived at https://perma.cc/W3SE-8Y2W)

PART TWO

Drawing the map

6

Where do you want to go?

Any journey starts with a destination in mind. Unless you're one of those brave types who rocks up at the airport with a bag packed and just looks to see what flights are cheapest. Most of us set out on a journey because we know there is a place we want to reach. The downside with the inclusion journey is that you will probably never reach that exact location (sorry to break this to you, maybe we should have mentioned it earlier). There is no such thing as a perfectly inclusive organization, and it's highly unlikely that you're about to be the first. Inclusion, and belonging, are ongoing processes of learning and growth; and, the more you learn, the more you see what there is to do.

However, having a point to work towards is what enables us to set the path. We might never reach an end, but we can move ever closer to where we want to be. If we know what our ideal destination looks like, we can keep checking that we're heading in the right direction. That's why, at Watch This Sp_ce, our starting point for every inclusion journey client is the Discovery phase.

In the Discovery phase, we examine the organization's core values, and clarify the culture that they want to build. We use these to help them define what inclusion means to them – because it means something different to every organization. We can then work with the staff and other stakeholders to visualize what this inclusive workplace would look like in practice, which in turn enables them to identify shifts in approach that will be needed to make this a reality.

Normally, our clients pay for this as part of their Inclusion Journey Mapping process, but we're going to show you how to do it yourself for just the price of this book. Don't tell anyone!

Why are you here?

The first stage of the Discovery phase is to clarify why your business matters. Every organization in the world was set up with a particular aim in mind, whether that was to solve a problem, fulfil a need or bring joy to people's lives. Sometimes, though, we lose sight of the point in the day-to-day grind and the need to keep the lights on. So it's good to take a step back every so often, and remember why you're doing all this.

Mission

Your mission, or purpose, is the reason your business exists. It's the change you're setting out to make in the world, the thing that wouldn't happen (or wouldn't happen as effectively or for as many people) if you weren't bothering to do the work you do.

Your mission statement should inspire your team, but also give them direction, helping them understand what it is they're supposed to be doing, and why their work matters. It should help your potential customers, partners or other future stakeholders understand why your work is relevant to them, and why you are the people they should choose for that work. It should also govern the decisions and choices you make as a business.

There are three components to a good mission statement: what, how and why:

What is your organization setting out to achieve? What need are you responding to? In what way are you making change?

How do you do it? Why are you the right people to do it? What makes your approach special?

Why should anyone care? What's in it for your audience? What's the lasting impact of your work?

If you want to clarify your mission or purpose statement, use the space below to break it down into three sections.

1 What does your organization want to achieve?

. . . .

. . . .

. . . .

2 How do you do that? Why are you the right people to do this?

. . . .

. . . .

. . . .

3 So what? Why should anyone else care? What's the impact?

. . . .

. . . .

. . . .

EXAMPLE

At Watch This Sp_ce, our full mission statement looks like this:

1 What does your organization want to achieve?

Watch This Sp_ce makes diversity and inclusion work in a meaningful way in organizations. We want to transform talk into actions, and make sure those actions have lasting, valuable impact in creating spaces that work for everyone.

2 How do you do that? Why are you the right people to do this?

Our team combine industry expertise, and decades of experience in business strategy, with lived experience to support powerful insights and inspiration, combined with practical action plans and ongoing learning.

3 So what? Why should anyone else care? What's the impact?

We are building a world of work that enables everyone to fulfil their potential and give their best, and we know that this benefits everyone. Diversity, inclusion and belonging drive higher innovation, better decision-making, improved results, increased productivity and greater profits, as well as increasing happiness, wellbeing and equity. We all work better together.

Values

Underpinning your mission should be your core values. These are less about the what, the why and the how of your work itself, but more about the way in which you show up to that work. Your values are what you stand for, what you believe in, the line in the sand that you won't cross. They give your team something to unite behind, something to believe in. No matter how different your team members are in terms of perspective, approach and identity, the business' values bring them all together. They are a flag to fly to tell potential employees and potential customers whether you are their tribe – is this somewhere they can belong?

Your values should set you apart from other businesses, and they should be meaningful. I cannot tell you how many times we have run workshops with teams who have told us that one of their core values is 'customer service'. That's not a value. It doesn't set you apart, and it doesn't mean anything. Are any businesses setting out to provide terrible customer service? No. Good customer service isn't something to be proud of, it's a minimum requirement that your customers should be able to expect. Maybe you go the extra mile in some special way, and that might be related to an element that *is* a core value, but when 'customer service' comes up in workshops we always ask clients to dig a little deeper. What's special about your customer service? Why do you do it that way? Why does it matter to you that it's done that way? These are some of the questions that might unearth a value that underpins your customer service… but usually we urge our clients to take customer service off the list entirely.

Other things I'd urge you to remove from your list of values include:

- excellence
- innovation
- quality
- teamwork
- value

These are all good things, and just because they're not on your list of values doesn't mean you shouldn't be doing them – but that is rather the point. You should be doing them as standard. They don't really say anything – they're not telling us anything about what makes your business special or how your staff should show up on a day-to-day basis. They're bland and empty corporate words that are more likely to demotivate your team through their lack of impact than they are to rally anyone behind your cause.

The following are some examples of brand values that are really powerful.

1 Ben & Jerry's

Ben & Jerry's manufactures ice cream, but its values have nothing to do with its product or its business strategy. They are core beliefs that inform everything about the way the brand shows up in the world:

- Human rights and dignity
- Social and economic justice
- Environmental protection, restoration and regeneration

2 Everlane

This clothing company wanted to do things differently and disrupt the fast fashion industry, and its values clearly set it apart from the competition:

- – Ethical approach

- – Designed to last

- – Radical transparency

3 NerdWallet

Describing itself as 'not your typical finance company', NerdWallet's values set out a clear approach to company culture:

- – Consumer, company, team, self

- – Relentless self-improvement

- – Open, candid, and constructive

- – Informed risk-taking

- – Ownership

And, because it's only fair that we put our money where our mouths are, here are Watch This Sp_ce's core values:

Challenge: We want to encourage our clients to step outside their comfort zones, to confront some potentially tough truths and engage with some often challenging subjects. It's in the discomfort and the uncertainty that learning and growth take place.

Compassion: But, while we want to challenge everyone, we also recognize that this work can be tough, for a variety of reasons. Everyone comes to diversity and inclusion work from different places in terms of understanding, experience and positivity. We want to meet everyone where they are, and make sure that everyone feels heard and supported so that we can all move forward together.

Impact: A lot of diversity and inclusion organizations just deliver off-the-shelf products without any strategy behind why they're doing the work, and without a measurement framework to review whether the work made any difference. We don't like that. We don't believe in tick-box exercises, and we're not here to just enable organizations to say they did something about diversity and inclusion. We're here to make a tangible impact. So strategy, analytics to identify areas of need and measurement to understand results are key to the way we work. We won't take on work if we don't believe it will make an impact.

You only really need three core values. Five at the most. Don't over-complicate the matter. Keep it simple and focus on what you really believe in and what you really won't compromise on.

You need to be prepared to stand behind these values. They can't just be words in a document that sits on a virtual dusty shelf. You need to back them up with action. Take the case of Barclays bank, who changed its logo to rainbow colours as a gesture of solidarity with the LGBTQIA+ community during Pride month in 2019. Some saw it as a rather tokenistic gesture to begin with – dressing your logo up in different colours means very little unless you're prepared to put effort into actually supporting the community in question – but at least it was a gesture. As should probably have been expected with the taking of any values-based stance, there were people who disagreed with this show of support, and a number of people complained on social media that they didn't want to see their bank supporting Pride. Barclays didn't appear to have adequately prepared for this, as its social media team didn't seem to know how to respond. The Barclays Twitter account began apologizing to the complainants, saying it could 'appreciate' their views and that it was sorry for any upset. It also reassured its followers that it would be changing the logo back very soon.

Understandably, this caused outrage amongst the LGBTQIA+ community and allies, who were furious that the bank had apologized for supporting basic human rights. Twitter user @irishwol commented:

> if Barclays makes [its social media team] apologize for flying the rainbow then they've no business flying it in the first place. The whole POINT of [Pride] is to not apologize for our existence.

The bank was accused of simply using Pride as a marketing opportunity and attempting to profit from the cause without genuinely wishing to be allies to people who are routinely subjected to abuse, harassment and violence because of their sexuality or gender identity. Barclays then attempted to rescue the situation by issuing a statement to say that it was committing to supporting the LGBTQIA+ community and standing against homophobia or transphobia, but, by now, most people believed these were just empty words. Barclays ended up in a situation where it had alienated both those who opposed LGBTQIA+ rights *and* those who supported them. Not a good day at the office.

By contrast, look at Yorkshire Tea's response to the Black Lives Matter protests in 2020. While a number of brands were rushing to show their support for the movement to bolster their reputation, Yorkshire Tea hung back, unsure that it was well-positioned to comment on the situation. One YouTuber, well-known for racially charged videos, posted on Twitter that they were pleased Yorkshire Tea wasn't supporting Black Lives Matter. Yorkshire Tea responded with a tweet that clearly set out its values and took a firm stand for what it believes in:

> Please don't buy our tea again. We're taking some time to educate ourselves and plan proper action before we post. We stand against racism. #BlackLivesMatter

The tweet gained huge amounts of support, clocking up more than 73,300 likes and being shared extensively. Many people said they were going to start buying Yorkshire Tea from now on because they were so pleased to see a brand standing so resolutely by its values. Of course, there were also negative responses, with some people saying they weren't going to buy Yorkshire Tea again. When one user said they were going to switch to PG Tips, that brand then replied to say it didn't want them either: 'If you are boycotting teas that stand against racism, you're going to have to find two new tea brands now.'

There's no doubt that some customers won't have liked the stance these two businesses took against racism, but they were clear – this was a line in the sand, this was something they believed in and that mattered. Not every customer is your customer, not every potential candidate is right for your team, and that's OK. As we saw in Chapter 3, scarcity mentality drives us to think there is a finite number of opportunities and that we must grasp as many as possible. But that's simply not the case. There will always be more customers, more potential employees, there will always be new opportunities for growth. By trying to please everyone, as Barclays did, you end up losing everyone. But by clarifying who you are and who you are right for, you attract those people to you in their droves, and strengthen their loyalty to you.

Be clear on your values, be clear on how you act on them, and make sure your staff are given the necessary training and support to follow through on those actions on a day-to-day basis.

What does inclusion mean to you?

Being an inclusive organization isn't just about accessibility and representation. It's also about how you can enable everyone to perform at their best. It's about creating an environment in which everyone feels engaged and motivated, and where they know their voice will be heard. There is no one way to do inclusion, though. There are lots of different methods and practices that can support inclusive environments, and different ways to implement them. Every organization has its own unique mission, values, culture and approach. Therefore every organization will also have its own unique definition of inclusion.

In order to uncover how your unique business can build an inclusive environment, we need to work out what inclusion means to you. This shouldn't be an exercise undertaken by just one person. This is a collaborative discussion across your whole team. At Watch This Sp_ce, we hold workshop sessions for staff across an organization where we ask for people's personal reflections, and then help them to explore shared ideas together. We then take the common themes that emerge from these sessions and collate a definition that we ask everyone to give their feedback on.

Here are three examples of definitions our clients have come up with.

1   A UK business service provider

'Inclusion means creating a safe environment for people to be their full selves, and providing tailored support and opportunities to ensure they can flourish and thrive as such.

'In this environment, differences are celebrated, understood and accepted. The way of doing things doesn't favour a certain way of operating or behaving, and everyone is able to challenge the status quo. Everyone can be confident that their voice will be heard, and they will be treated with respect and without judgement.'

2   A UK membership organization

'Inclusion means proactively empowering staff and the organization to be equitable, even if/especially if it makes us uncomfortable sometimes.

'It means crafting an environment that comforts the needs of all staff, empathy that transcends equality, and places equity at the forefront of proactive, actionable steps. With the willingness to deepen their understanding, staff have the ability to hold themselves accountable, without immediate defence nor justifications, and to be attentive to barriers that permit discriminatory treatment to others. Staff undergo consistent training and digest information in order to accommodate different lifestyles, needs, beliefs and characteristics, without judgement nor assumptions. Staff feel empowered to advocate for others, and themselves, when they witness or experience exclusion, and simultaneously are proactive in the sight of injustice, implementing long-lasting laws,

EDI [equity, diversity and inclusion] policies, as well as informal (but mandatory) opportunities. In the delivery of all operations, all people are considered, and staff are receptive, malleable and strive for change, for the impact of all voices.'

3   An international technology company

'Inclusion means that everyone has an equal opportunity to contribute, and that contribution is welcomed and treated with respect. We combat groupthink and embrace healthy conflict because that will lead to better outcomes.

'We recognize the value of our differences, so everyone can be their authentic self without fear of judgement, and colleagues treat one another with compassion and empathy. We work to tackle bias so that we can create a safe and nurturing environment where everyone has equal opportunity and support to succeed. We recognise that this is an ongoing process of continual learning.

'We want to break barriers for diversity and inclusion in the markets we operate. We are devoting time and resources to achieving this goal, and providing tools and processes to enable full participation in a way that works for each individual.'

These are all very powerful, and they all certainly reflect what the impact of an inclusive environment should be. But they're all different – they all reflect the unique culture and values of those particular organizations. This means that those staff members will feel bought into this vision, because they helped to create it, and because it aligns with the overall approach they're familiar with. Everyone feels more motivated to make it a reality, because it feels tangible, it feels aligned with the organization that they believe in. And that is very exciting.

What does an inclusive organization look like?

Another question that we ask participants in those workshops is: What does an inclusive organization look like? What does it feel like? If your workplace was perfectly inclusive (and we know perfection isn't truly attainable, but we can dream), what would you hear? What would you see? What would you experience?

Our participants create a variety of depictions of inclusive workplaces – they draw pictures, they create comic strips, they write scenes, they make word maps or sometimes they just write lists. Whatever form that they feel comfortable working in, together as a team, they co-create a vision of the work environment that perfectly aligns with their definition of inclusion.

Some other questions that support this vision-building include:

- What environment enables you to perform at your best?

- What behaviours or outputs would make you proud of your workplace?

- How do you know that other people are happy to work at your business?

What do you need to do to make that a reality?

So now we know:

- what your business is setting out to achieve

- what your business stands for and what informs your company culture

- your big vision for inclusion within the context of the points above

- how that should work in practice

Now you can figure out what you have in place that's supporting you to move in that direction, what might be holding you back from moving that way, and what you don't have that you will need. The final stage of a Watch This Sp_ce Discovery Workshop involves listing every single element that a business wants, and doesn't want, in order to get to where it wants to be, and then plotting them on to the chart in Figure 6.1.

The best approach to this exercise is to get every single element down on Post-it Notes – one Post-it per element – then draw a large version of that chart and ask people to put their Post-it Note at the right point on the scale. This allows you to take a top level view of all the elements you need to develop, create, guard against or remove. It's also often eye-opening to find out to what degree staff feel you do or do not have certain elements in place already.

Your pins in the map

By the end of this process, you will have a very clear idea of where you want to get to. By defining the mission and values that underpin your business,

FIGURE 6.1 Inclusion needs matrix

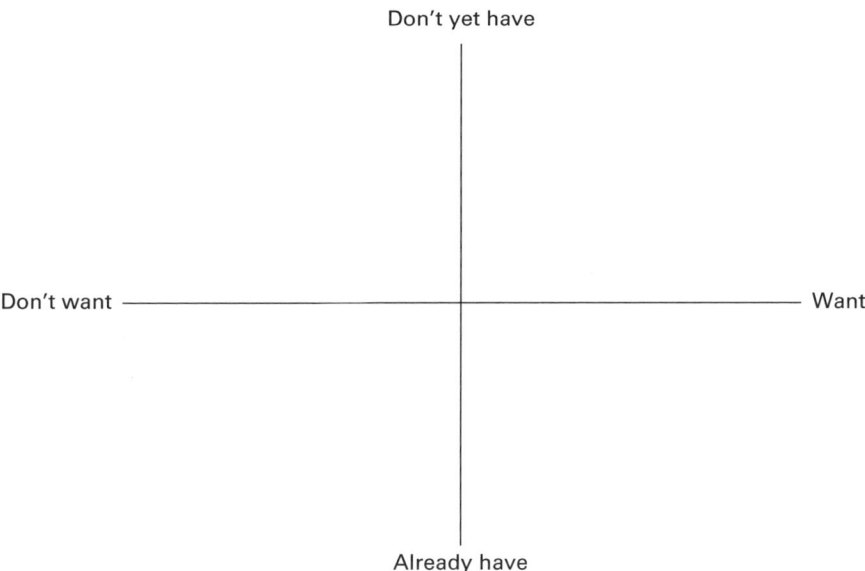

you have come to understand the foundations of your company culture and therefore what inclusion should look like for you. You now have a concrete concept of what it is you are trying to achieve. Diversity and inclusion are no longer woolly buzzwords; they are meaningful, tangible ways to unite, engage, motivate and get the best from your team. You also now have a clearer understanding of what will help you move forward and what might hold you back.

Having clarified your destination, you can now get to grips with your starting point. How far away are you from your goal? How are your team feeling about taking this journey? How long is it going to take you to make progress? So, in the next chapter, we'll show you how to examine your current situation and identify the steps you will need to take to reach the vision you outlined here.

Case study: London-based technology company

A tech company approached Watch This Sp_ce because it was getting constant questions from its teams, asking what it was doing about diversity and inclusion. We've seen in previous chapters how important diversity and inclusion is to employees, and this business' employees had made that very clear. Diversity and inclusion were beginning to be raised at every company meeting – even when it wasn't on the agenda.

Watch This Sp_ce worked with the company on its inclusion journey, and the Discovery phase was an important first step. Gathering together staff from across the business was a valuable opportunity for them to share why this was important to them and what their key needs, wants and focuses were. This process allowed the staff to feel heard and that they were truly part of driving this work forwards. It set them up with a solid foundation for their audit and action plan, and ensured that, when these were shared, the team felt it accurately responded to the needs of the organization and they bought in to helping make it happen.

Now the company doesn't get questions about diversity and inclusion from its team anymore. Everyone knows exactly what they are doing in this area, and can see a tangible action plan and measurable progress. Not only are they mindful of the action plan they have, they have even hired internally to ensure they have the resource to fully commit to taking it forward and seeing further growth as a result.

The whole team has been highly engaged with the diversity and inclusion work, and there is a real sense of positivity about its future.

This example shows that companies do not have to have all the answers, or resolve everything immediately. Showing employees that this is a priority and starting to take action on this will have an impact in itself. Employees can be engaged in the start of the process, and talk about their ideas for how to progress. Then even if there is a lot of work to do, everyone knows what the starting point is, and how they can get involved in the journey.

7

Where are you now?

Before you get carried away racing off towards your destination, we need to find your starting point on the map. Otherwise, you run the risk of taking wrong turns and getting lost along the way. From the Discovery process in the previous chapter, you now have an idea of what elements you need to work on, and what you need to work to get rid of. But in order to fully plan out the steps of your journey, and to be able to measure your progress once you get started, you'll need a detailed and accurate picture of your current situation, informed by data.

At Watch This Sp_ce, we conduct a full audit for our clients that takes a holistic view of the whole organization. There's the technical stuff, like policies, processes and demographic data. Then there's the more qualitative, intangible elements, such as staff engagement, company culture and reputation. There's a lot to consider, and all of the different parts intersect and impact one another. So in order to break it down into manageable chunks, we divide this work into six sections: people, communications, engagement, culture, methods and performance.

There are a lot of questions that we ask in each of these sections, and a lot of different facts, data points and input opportunities that we assess. We couldn't possibly give you all of them – partly because it would take up most of the book, and partly because it's a trade secret. But below we will summarize the main elements that we look at, and the most common gaps and opportunities that our clients uncover at each stage.

Translating your findings

Before we get stuck into the areas you need to look at, a quick word about how to interpret what you find. In order to translate what you discover into a tangible action that can be measured against an overall target, you will need to work through a process like the one in Table 7.1.

TABLE 7.1 Translating findings into actions

Finding	Questions	Goal	Actions
What have you discovered? What gap or issue have you found? Where have you identified an opportunity for improvement?	What questions does this raise? What more do you need to know to fully understand the situation? What assumptions might you be making about this finding, and how can you challenge these?	What would the ideal situation/outcome look like if this finding was addressed? Where would you like to be with this in 6/12/36/60 months?	What steps can you take to reach those goals?

We'll see this in action in a moment.

You will see that many of the questions in each category impact one another, and an answer in one group of questions may inform your understanding of a question that was raised in another group. That's why it's best not to look at these sections in isolation, so that you can get a full picture of what's really going on in your business, and why.

People

In this section we are looking at the way that your organization brings together different people. This part of the audit looks at your recruitment process, your staff retention and the reasons that people leave. It examines the demographic make-up of your organization, and how that is distributed. It also asks questions about how accessible you make entry into your business.

Demographics

How representative is your organization of the community/ies that you serve? This requires not only data collection within your business, but an awareness of the wider context that you work in. For example, let's imagine that you are a company based in Brighton & Hove, UK, but that your customers are UK-wide. You will need to look at your staff within the context of the city that you predominantly recruit from, but also within the context of the people that you want to attract and support as customers. This might look something like Table 7.2.

TABLE 7.2 Example demographic data comparison

	Gender	Ethnicity	Age	Sexuality	Religion	Disability	Neuro-divergence	Born outside the UK	Primary/first language other than English
Company X	63% female 37% male	85% White, 13% Asian 2% Mixed	20–29: 10% 30–39: 35% 40–49: 40% 50–59: 15%	20% lesbian/ gay/bisexual/ other	52% Christian 45% no religion 1% Muslim 1% Hindu 1% other	7%	18%	5%	2%
Brighton and Hove	50% female 49% male 1% other	86% White 4% Asian 2% Black 5% Mixed	20–29: 13% 30–39: 12% 40–49: 13% 50–59: 15% 60–69: 11% 70–79: 10%	10% lesbian/ gay/bisexual/ other	59% Christian 27% no religion 1% Jewish 1% Muslim 2% other	19%	Unknown	20%	11%
England and Wales	50% female 49% male 1% other	82% White 9% Asian 4% Black 3% Mixed 2% other	20–29: 13% 30–39: 13% 40–49: 13% 50–59: 15% 60–69: 10% 70–79: 8%	11% lesbian/ gay/bisexual/ other	46% Christian 37% no religion 7% Muslim 2% Hindu 1% Sikh 0.5% Jewish 0.5% Buddhist 0.6% other	24%	20%	17%	9%

Please note that this is a *highly simplified* breakdown of the data that you need to look at. You'll also want to collect your own data in line with how your country's national statistics are measured so that you can compare your organization to the country as a whole. In the UK, we use the national census as our benchmark, which separates data for England and Wales from the rest of the UK. This data might not necessarily align with how your staff identify or give you the complexity that your staff want to see, and you will need to explain this to them. There's nothing to stop you measuring at a deeper level internally, but you will need a top-level way of drawing a meaningful comparison.

It's also not as simple as the overall demographics of your staff. Diversity might, on the whole, be in line with your community, but is that diversity evenly distributed? Going back to Company X above, on the face of it, it appears that they have attracted a high percentage of women and that it is in fact men that are in the minority. However, on closer inspection, we find that 82 per cent of those women are in junior roles, and that women make up just 12 per cent of the leadership team. This means that, not only is the leadership team not representative of the community the business serves, but it's not representative of its own organization.

It also turns out that 65 per cent of female staff have been with the business for less than three years. Are female staff leaving at a higher rate than male staff? Have a high number of women recently been recruited? These are questions that we can answer by examining any data that is collected on new recruits, staff leavers and exit feedback.

This is how we identify gaps and opportunities, and can then translate that into action. In this example this looks as follows:

Finding: Women are over-represented in the organization as a whole, but significantly under-represented in management and leadership positions.

Questions: Why are women not progressing within the organization?

How can we support more women to take on management and leadership roles?

How can we make our senior roles more attractive to women?

Goal: Increase representation of women within management roles within the next three years.

Increase representation of women within leadership roles within the next five years.

Increase representation of men within junior roles.

Actions: Introduce talent development programme to support women in junior roles to build their careers.

Introduce flexible working and other family-friendly policies.

Review input from female staff to understand barriers or issues that they experience.

Review exit data and feedback to understand reasons that female staff leave.

Introduce inclusive recruitment processes to mitigate the impact of (un)conscious bias on recruitment.

Introduce promotion, development and performance review processes to mitigate the impact of (un)conscious bias.

Recruitment

When it comes to your recruitment, it's important to look at every stage of the process, from role design, to how you market your vacancies and try to attract candidates, to the recruitment policy and how that seeks to mitigate bias, to how you onboard new staff members and set them up for inclusion and success. Key things to think about are:

- What are the perceptions, internally and externally, of your employer brand and your organizational reputation?

- Do you have a consistent job advert template that sets out important information (such as salary – salary secrecy is one of the key drivers of gender and ethnicity pay gaps, and a major reason that a number of candidates choose not to apply for a job) and does so in a way that is accessible, engaging and gives a clear idea of the culture and values you want people to sign up to? (You can download a free job advert template at www.watchthisspace.uk/resources.)

- Are you advertising your job using job boards, networks and communities that actively target people from under-represented or marginalized backgrounds and identities?

- Are you using accessible materials and methods?

- What proactive steps have you taken to reduce the impact of bias and to ensure equity of opportunity at all stages of the recruitment process?

- How do you support different needs throughout the process?

- Are you collecting demographic data at each stage of the recruitment, development and exit funnel so that you can identify and address any trends?

- Do you have an onboarding system that supports different needs and working/learning/communication styles?

- What is your staff turnover rate like, and what are the most common reasons people give for leaving?

- What mechanisms do you have in place for setting salaries and role level, and how do you mitigate the impact of bias on these decisions?

Communications

It's not going to come as a shock to you what this category involves, and there are two major components: internal and external. With both of these, we're looking at how effectively you communicate with different types of people.

Neurodiversity and communications styles

These are huge topics in themselves, worthy of their own book, but the essence that you need to be aware of is this: everyone's brains work in different ways. Neurodivergence includes things like autism, ADHD, dyslexia, dyspraxia, dyscalculia, OCD, depression, anxiety and many, many more. It's a very wide range of ways in which the human brain can operate outside the parameters expected by our society. Then, beyond this, there are also a range of ways that human brains can absorb, interpret and organize information. You may be aware of visual, auditory and kinaesthetic learners, and different models suggest further learning styles. To be good communicators, we need to cater to the varied needs and approaches that will shape how our message is received and interpreted. We also need to make space for other people to formulate and share their information in the way that most enables them to give their best. For example, some people communicate best verbally, some through writing. Other people need time before a discussion to consider their thoughts, some think better when they talk an issue through with others, while other people want to hear inputs first and then reflect on the discussion before they're clear on their views. Some people are extroverts who are energized by being around other people, whereas introverts need plenty of time alone or in small groups to recharge. There's far more to this, and a topic worth learning about in depth. But the big question to ask yourself when you look at your communications is: are you communicating, and enabling others to communicate with one another and with you, in a way that works for different learning, communications and information processing styles?

Internal communications

Essentially here, we're looking to see whether everyone is being given an equitable opportunity to both receive and interpret important information and to share their views, ideas and inputs with the organization.

TOOLS

There are a huge variety of internal communications tools available to businesses, and many companies have fallen into the trap of adding more and more as new shiny things come along until their staff are thoroughly overwhelmed. Take an audit of the communications channels that you use internally and ask yourself what the purpose is of each one. Does it do something no other channel can do? Do you need it? How is it supposed to be used – and do your staff understand that? Are they using your channels in the ways you intended them to? Are they receiving clear guidelines and direction on how to do that? Is someone responsible for supporting staff to use all these tools effectively and keeping track of what tools you have and what you need?

Even reviewing your most basic communication tools – like how your teams use email, and what your process is for meetings – can reveal a great deal. Meetings are a serious sticking point when it comes to inclusion. They favour a very specific type of person – one who is happy to hold forth publicly on their ideas and opinions, one who doesn't mind interrupting people and will hold their ground if someone tries to interrupt them, and one who enjoys thinking on their feet. Most meetings are also actually very badly run. Do you need as many meetings as you have? Are there other ways that you can enable people to share ideas or make decisions without using this particular method? Can you combine meetings with other mechanisms to give opportunities for a wide range of working and information styles, and personalities, to offer their best inputs? You can find a guide to creating inclusive meetings at www.watchthisspace.uk/resources.

COMPANY INFORMATION

When it comes to your internal communications, how much are you actually sharing with your team? We're looking for regular updates on strategy, progress, any changes and developments, and any achievements for the team to be proud of. There should be a process in place for these updates to go out on a scheduled basis – say, monthly or quarterly – otherwise they have a tendency to only happen when someone thinks of it. We want to see staff being kept in the loop, and everyone, across the whole organization, feeling that they're part of the bigger picture because they're kept informed and their contribution is acknowledged.

We're also looking at how this information is delivered. Is it accessible? Does it work for different types of people? Lengthy texts are unlikely to be particularly easy to process, or especially engaging. Including different types of media in your communications – videos (making sure they're subtitled), images (such as graphs and charts to get information across) and interactive features – makes your messages more accessible to people with different needs and information processing styles, and also makes them more interesting for everyone. Where you do use lengthy text, breaking it up with clear headings and providing summaries at the beginning very much helps.

External communications

Here we're looking at the information you present on your website, your social media channels, any external publications or materials that you produce... essentially anything you use to talk to people outside your organization about what you do and why they should care. There are some fundamental elements that a number of organizations neglect:

- Is there alt text on all your digital images? And are you using it for its intended purpose – to enable people using assistive technology to understand what's in the image – rather than to try to game your search engine optimization (SEO) rankings?

- Are all the videos you share subtitled? This isn't just important for people with hearing impairments (about 20% of the global population),[1] but also for the 75% of people who consume videos on mobile devices, 92% of whom do so in silent mode.[2]

- What's the colour contrast like on your website? Is it suitable for people with dyslexia or visual impairments?

- Does your website use clear headings and a well-defined and accessible navigation structure?

- Are calls to action clear and well contrasted from the rest of the information?

- Do you include a variety of people in your images and videos? Otherwise, you could be inadvertently suggesting that your business is only for a certain type of person.

- Are there clear tone of voice guidelines in place that tell your staff how to communicate in a way that is accessible, inclusive and in line with your brand values?

Engagement

In this section, we are looking to see how engaged and motivated your team are, and what opportunities they have to make their voices heard. We're also interested in how engaged they are with your inclusion journey, and whether they see the value of the work you are doing, as well as having confidence that you will actually do it.

When it comes to the latter point, this will become clear during the Discovery process that we spoke about in the previous chapter, and in the survey that we will come to at the end of this one. We're looking at overall engagement rates and levels of participation, as well as the inputs and feedback that are being shared. It's always worth diving deeper into findings that this brings up – it's easy to assume, if engagement with the Discovery phase is low, for example, that your team isn't interested in diversity and inclusion, or doesn't feel that it's necessary. When we have explored this further with clients, however, we've often found that staff passionately believe in diversity and inclusion, but they don't see the point in engaging because they don't have any faith that the leadership team will act on any inputs they provide, and that makes them angry before the work even begins. It might be that diversity and inclusion work has been done before, but it wasn't taken further, or wasn't delivered very effectively, and so staff no longer see the point in taking part. Maybe a previous incident was mishandled and staff now don't have confidence in the leadership team supporting under-represented staff. Or it might be that they feel their voices have been ignored in the past on other topics, so they don't expect to be listened to this time. Sometimes staff really don't see the value in diversity and inclusion, and some further work needs to be done to show them why this will benefit them. Whatever is going on, it will need a targeted response, so you need to ensure you have the whole picture before you act.

A great deal of understanding how engaged your team are with your business and each other will require you to talk to them. A survey (see below), focus groups, interviews and reviewing any previous staff feedback you have received are all valuable ways to understand what's really going on beneath the surface. Beware, though, simply putting out a few simple survey questions and then taking the answers as definitive. Your staff might not be completely honest on a survey that you send out – they might worry that they'll be identified from their answers, however much you assure them it's confidential, because subconsciously they still feel they're responding to a question that *you've* asked them. They also might want to please you and tell you what you want to hear – 49 per cent of people (and 56 per cent of women)[3] identify as people pleasers, and many more of us are hardwired to give people the answer we think they want. Using an external company to send out the surveys and conduct the interviews can help – people are more willing to be honest with them as they know these people can't fire them or discipline them, and they view them as more neutral and not someone they need to placate. You should also use multiple questions to dig beneath the surface of large considerations like 'are you motivated in your role?' so that you can tease out how much of those responses are truly genuine.

Another important factor to look at is what mechanisms you have in place to enable staff to contribute their ideas, raise issues, ask questions and challenge the way things work. Do you ask for input into decisions? Do you encourage challenging feedback – actively asking your staff to try to find a problem with a decision or a plan so as to test if it really is the best it can be? Do you encourage debate and discussion, or are you anxious about disagreements and constantly pushing for straightforward agreement? How visible are your leadership team – do they regularly make themselves available to share information and ask questions? Are they approachable and accessible for staff at all levels? And with all of these considerations, we're looking to support people with different information processing styles, different communication strengths and different needs, as well.

Culture

The work on your mission and values is essential in building your culture. In this section we need to assess whether your values are clear and meaningful, whether everyone understands them, and whether they set out how the organization should work on a day-to-day basis. This is also an opportunity to review what you use to proactively shape your culture. Do you have behavioural guidelines and/or a code of conduct in place? Do you have a committee or working group that is responsible for things like social events, cultural celebrations and other ways to bring people together? Are managers and leaders regularly reminding the team of the kind of culture they want to build and how everyone can work together to build it?

Social events might not seem like the most important part of your business, but if the only team bonding opportunities all take place at the pub, you're alienating people who don't drink. You're also risking the possibility of a fairly toxic environment – a lot of women and staff from marginalized groups have been subjected to unpleasant or even dangerous behaviour when everyone's had too much to drink.[4] Social events should give staff an opportunity to get to know each other, to meet people outside their teams, and to connect on a deeper level with the mission and values of the business. These events need to be accessible to everyone, and should involve activities that everyone can, and feels comfortable to, participate in. Going for a spa day, where everyone will need to strip down to their swimming costumes, could be deeply uncomfortable for many reasons, and asking everyone to trek around a golf course for an afternoon when some of your team have mobility issues isn't encouraging a positive and productive team environment. Taking input from your staff on what they would like, and what they need, in a team event is a great first step to taking a more inclusive approach. Likewise, only celebrating Christian events like Christmas and Easter can make a lot of people feel like outsiders. Having a calendar of different cultural celebrations and key awareness days (like Pride and Black History Month) that you can mark with your team (with their involvement) is an easy win when it comes to showing that you want to build an inclusive culture.

The hardest part of this section involves taking a look at the worst of your organizational culture. When we work with clients on this audit process, we will ask staff whether they have experienced or witnessed incidents of bullying, discrimination or harassment. Our clients are always shocked by the results. No one wants to believe that this sort of behaviour occurs within their company, but unfortunately it happens everywhere. It's inevitable, when you bring together a group of human beings, that some of them will act negatively towards one another. To what extent this behaviour occurs is important to know so that you can deal with it – this is not a time to bury your head in the sand, or the problem will only get worse. Also, it is vital to know how far your staff have faith in you dealing with any issues that do occur, and how comfortable they would feel reporting this behaviour. This may well lead staff to disclose times that they have reported behaviour in the past that wasn't dealt with, or was mishandled, or times that they felt they couldn't report it because the process made it difficult, or they were too afraid of retaliation. If this kind of behaviour is able to continue unchallenged, you will never be able to build an inclusive organization, and you will never be able to gain all the incredible benefits of diversity and inclusion that we have seen are possible. You will end up with low levels of motivation, high rates of turnover and potentially catastrophic decisions in an environment where no one feels able to be open and honest. Time to face the hard truths and take practical steps to weed this behaviour out now before it becomes so embedded in your organization that it chokes everything else.

Methods

This is a very practical section – a chance to evaluate what policies and processes you have in place to support diversity and inclusion, and how well your staff are able to engage with these. We're looking at policies that are specifically relevant – such as an actual policy on diversity and inclusion, and policies on elements like bullying, discrimination and harassment, modern slavery and behavioural expectations – as well as policies that provide for different needs and experiences (parental leave, carer's leave, transitioning at work, menopause, bereavement, emergency leave, etc). We also want to see how core behavioural policies, such as your grievance policy and your disciplinary policy, take account of different needs, power imbalances, the potential impact of bias and life challenges.

There are also very basic considerations here, such as whether your policy documents are all stored in one, easy-to-find location, and whether staff are all informed from the very beginning of their time with you (preferably before they commit to working for you) and then regularly reminded throughout their time with the company about what those policies are and where to find them. Staff may not always want to ask about potentially sensitive policies – like parental leave, for example – but this is vital information that might inform some big decisions and actions in their lives. It's also easy for staff to forget about policies over time, and these shouldn't just be tick-box documents that are ignored – they need to be living documents that are regularly reviewed and interacted with, otherwise they become meaningless. Documents should also be checked for spelling and grammar (by someone other than the person who wrote them – no one can accurately check their own work); we regularly see policy documents with multiple

spelling and grammar mistakes and, whilst these may be fine for the majority of staff members to navigate and recognize the intended meaning, staff
for whom English is not a first language or who are neurodivergent could
lose the meaning altogether. Then we need to assess whether your documents use inclusive language – are you avoiding gendered terms, jargon,
acronyms, assumptive or stereotypical language and terminology that might
be alienating? Simple things like recognizing that not every employee who
gets pregnant will be female, and not every partner of a pregnant person will
be male, in the language of your parental leave policy are very easy to implement but make a substantial impact on the staff who need them.

For a real gold star in this section, we want to see that your policies and
processes all state a firm commitment to inclusion, and that this isn't just a
copy and paste corporate-speak paragraph, but a statement that brings to
life the vision for an inclusive future that you outlined in your Discovery
phase. We also want to see that you're looking beyond the scope of your
legal obligations, and considering inclusion at its broadest, supporting areas
that might not be protected by law, such as neurodiversity and parenthood.

In addition, this section offers an opportunity to reflect on how well you
are enabling different people to work within your organization on a practical level. How accessible are your physical spaces, your tools, your ways of
working? How many staff feel able to request adjustments, and how many
of these feel their needs are being met? How proactive are you in encouraging staff to ask for adjustments and monitoring how well these are working?
Do you offer (truly) flexible working, and support staff to work around
considerations like caring responsibilities and lifestyle needs? In your
Discovery process that we discussed in the previous chapter, you outlined
your vision of how an inclusive organization should work in practice – this
is your chance to look at how you are practically supporting that implementation and what more you can do.

Performance

There are two elements to this – your diversity and inclusion performance,
and the performance of staff themselves.

Diversity and inclusion

This is often quite a short section for many businesses. For questions such as,
what diversity and inclusion targets do you have in place, and how much

progress have you made on diversity and inclusion so far, the answer might well be: none. Don't worry – this process is going to put targets in place for you, and enable you to measure progress in the future. So it's all under control.

Staff performance

Assessment of staff performance should start with how objectives are set. This means first looking at organizational objectives, and then how a line is drawn from these to team objectives and then to individual objectives. All staff should understand what is expected of them personally, and how this relates to the wider business. This also needs to be consistent for *all* employees, and to take account of different needs and ways of working. If this is done effectively, then you can ensure that the mechanisms by which staff progress is assessed are also consistent, inclusive and effective.

A note here that annual appraisals, in our opinion, are, by and large, terrible, owing to them being once a year only. We are all massively impacted by recency bias, which means we are incapable of reflecting back on an entire year – we will, at most, look at the previous few months. Other biases, such as the halo effect, mean our assessment of performance (our own or other people's) will often be skewed by any single very good or very bad event. It's also a bad idea to ask a staff member to provide a numerical reflection of their own performance (such as a score out of 10) before their manager gives their own view. The anchoring effect means that the manager will be dragged up or down by the employee's own evaluation, removing objectivity from the scoring process. Taking a coaching methodology – where managers and employees regularly reflect on objectives, progress and blockers together – is a much more effective approach and is less susceptible to the impact of bias.

This section also takes into account training and development, and career progression opportunities. Questions like whether staff are satisfied with the opportunities available to them and whether they receive enough support to engage with them, whether proactive steps are taken to encourage staff members to take up opportunities, whether there are clear plans in place for staff to move forward and whether steps have been taken to remove bias from decision-making processes are all important here. Another consideration is whether your organization actively seeks to create development opportunities for underrepresented staff.

Similarly, we want to look at how salaries, pay increases, promotions and bonuses are awarded. Does your organization have any pay gaps, and are you taking steps to address them? If you don't know, this is a good time to find out! Have you made proactive efforts to remove bias from these decisions? Do you have processes in place that are applied consistently? Do these take account of different needs or personality types?

Then there's the question of how you reward and celebrate success, beyond simple financial incentives. Salary increases and bonuses aren't necessarily the best ways to motivate employees – in fact, they could be detrimental.[5] In a truly inclusive organization, everyone already feels that they are fairly compensated for the work that they do, and their motivation to give their best lies more in their feeling of being part of the mission and values of the business, and wanting to deliver for the team to which they feel they belong. Therefore, finding ways to recognize hard work, celebrate when the organization as a whole, as well as particular teams and individuals, reach key goals, and make clear that the range of different contributions that have made this success possible have been noticed and valued, is a vital component in creating the inclusive environment you're working towards.

Stakeholder survey

In addition to all the work you're doing above to look into how you do things, you will need to ask for input from your staff, and any other key stakeholders (such as members, partners, service users, as appropriate), to give you a deeper understanding of all of these elements.

At Watch This Sp_ce, when we begin an audit for a client, we simultaneously send out a survey that asks a number of questions that relate to each of the six sections above. This gives us quantitative and qualitative data to help us test some of our findings and answer some of the questions that they have raised.

For example, it might well be that there are mechanisms in place for staff to provide feedback to the leadership team, but 67 per cent of staff feel that they are not able to provide input. Why don't people feel able to use what's in place? When we discuss it with the leadership team, they might say that they hold Q&A sessions, but no one submits questions; or that they ask for input on a particular decision, but no one shares any inputs. When we look into the comments the staff have supplied, or conduct further interviews with staff members, we discover that they have inputted in the past, but they feel that their views were ignored, or that they are scared to share their views because they fear the leadership team will react negatively. We can then recommend to the leadership team that they create a process by which all inputs will be responded to, and reasons for not taking forward suggestions will be carefully explained – and that they communicate the creation of this process to the team. They should also introduce mechanisms by which staff can share inputs anonymously, and they might consider coaching to help them solicit and respond to feedback more effectively.

You also need to include demographic questions within your survey, so that you can cross-reference the answers you receive. It's all very well to report that 78 per cent of your staff feel highly motivated in their role, but if you break down that data to discover that only 22 per cent of your staff from ethnic minority backgrounds feel motivated, then there is a clear issue there that needs addressing. If you haven't been collecting demographic data on your staff so far to inform your findings in the People section, this is also a useful way to start!

Where to now?

It's clear that there is a great deal to consider when you look at your current situation. Be prepared for it to take time, and be ready for some tough truths. It may be that your business doesn't look quite how you thought it did, but that's OK. Now you can clearly see the gap between where you are and where you want to be – and you can set a course to get you there. Once you have reviewed all of the data points we've considered above, you can set tangible targets and put an action plan in place. We'll talk more about action planning in the next chapter, and more about goals and measurement in Chapter 10, and all the hard work you put in here will be invaluable in understanding what you need to do, and then being able to review and report on how well it's working.

Bonus materials

If you're finding the thought of navigating all these data points alone rather daunting, you can be guided through them in manageable step-by-step levels by using the Inclusion Journey Tracker at www.watchthisspace.uk/the-inclusion-journey.

Notes

1 World Health Organization. Deafness and hearing loss, 2 February 2024, www. who.int/news-room/fact-sheets/detail/deafness-and-hearing-loss (archived at https://perma.cc/92XS-UFGR)

2 S Roberts. Sound on? Sound off? 64% marketers using video see benefit of captions, verbit, https://verbit.ai/sound-on-sound-off-64-marketers-using-video-see-benefit-of-captions (archived at https://perma.cc/UF5D-5PHF)

3 J Ballard. Women are more likely than men to say they're a people-pleaser, and many dislike being seen as one, YouGov, 22 August 2022, https://today.yougov. com/society/articles/43498-women-more-likely-men-people-pleasing-poll (archived at https://perma.cc/H4SW-YRKN)

4 N Nanji. Firms told to cut down on alcohol at work parties, BBC, 9 May 2023, www.bbc.co.uk/news/business-65468218 (archived at https://perma.cc/YHC9-HYPD)

5 A Kohn. Why incentive plans cannot work, Harvard Business Review, September–October 1993, https://hbr.org/1993/09/why-incentive-plans-cannot-work (archived at https://perma.cc/X2UD-RSSN)

8

How are you going to get there?

What we learnt we need to do, through our analysis, is to show a connection between good leadership engagement, good staff engagement and good patient outcomes. That's what makes people want to get involved and take action.[1]

PAUL DEEMER, HEAD OF DIVERSITY AND INCLUSION AT NHS EMPLOYERS

With a workforce the size of the UK National Health Service (NHS), there is a lot we can learn about how to engage a large number of people with an inclusion journey and encourage them to take action. With 1.4 million employees, the sixth largest organization in the world, the NHS shows us the importance of clarity in communications, and setting clear and measurable actions that people can track. This chapter looks at how you are going to make progress on your inclusion journey, and how you can encourage others to take the journey with you, and we'll be using the NHS as an illustrative example.

The NHS and the power of data

Paul Deemer heads up Diversity and Inclusion at NHS Employers. After a career in local government and charities, he worked with the Department of Health on policies and then moved to NHS Employers. He talks about how being very clear on priorities shows people what actions they need to take, whatever department they are in. Everyone can then see how and where they can get involved. Diversity and inclusion priorities need to be linked to the top-level priorities for the NHS, so staff understand that working on inclusion leads to better patient outcomes.

The organization leads on working with data and using that to inform priorities and actions. The NHS Staff Survey is completed by 600,000 people, which means they have a lot of data to work with. These insights show them where the greatest needs are, and they then publish their areas of focus,[2] with six 'High Impact Action Areas'[3] laid out and targets set. This plan is made available publicly, and then NHS Employers support NHS organizations to implement the plan.

One area they are focusing on currently is the experience for staff recruited internationally. Their data shows that people who join the NHS from overseas have a worse experience than domestic recruits, and they know that many more staff will need to come from outside the UK in future. By carefully assessing the data, they can understand key ways to improve the experience for people from overseas, and specific actions are being undertaken to work on how these staff are recruited, onboarded and treated at work.

Another area of focus is disability, which links to several of the high-impact priorities. Paul works with the Disability Pioneers Supergroup, a group of around 50 people across the country who are passionate about the rights and wellbeing of staff with disabilities across the NHS. They work in different areas of the health service and have formed this group in the same way that many companies form Employee Resource Groups or Working Groups. They meet quarterly to exchange knowledge and ideas, and progress key actions.

Now some people reading this might think, how does this relate to me and my work? There are not that many employers working with 1.4 million staff members and 600,000 survey responses. How can such a huge employer be relatable to your inclusion journey?

Well, like many inspirational journeys, we can take learnings from the NHS Employers' experience that we can apply on a smaller scale to our own organizations. They achieve their goals by breaking down data, strategy and engagement into very clear actions. They plan and resource areas of focus and link these to objectives for teams. Crucially, they communicate clearly and regularly to make sure they move forwards with actions and results and that people can see this. The six identified high impact areas are documented, communicated and tracked so that they are relatable and accessible to everyone. The data is published on a public website, so it's widely available and they are accountable. And the actions they are taking could be applicable to lots of companies, whatever their size and reach. The action plan is shown in Table 8.1.

TABLE 8.1 National Health Service equality, diversity and inclusion improvement plan

NHS equality, diversity, and inclusion improvement plan:

Action number	Action	Success metrics
High impact action 1	Chief executives, chairs and board members must have specific and measurable EDI objectives to which they will be individually and collectively accountable	Annual chair and chief executive appraisals on EDI objectives Board Assurance framework
High impact action 2	Embed fair and inclusive recruitment processes and talent management strategies that target under-representation and lack of diversity	Relative likelihood of staff being appointed from shortlisting across all posts Access to career progression, training and development opportunities Year-on-year improvement in race and disability representation leading to parity over the life of the plan Year-on-year improvement in representation of senior leadership Diversity in shortlisted candidates
High impact action 3	Develop and implement an improvement plan to eliminate pay gaps	Year-on-year reductions in the gender, race and disability pay gaps
High impact action 4	Develop and implement an improvement plan to address health inequalities within the workforce	HEE National Education and Training Survey (NETS) Separate Indicator Score metric on quality of training
High impact action 5	Implement a comprehensive induction, onboarding and development programme for internationally recruited staff	Reduction in instances of bullying and harassment from team/line manager experienced by (internationally recruited staff)
High impact action 6	Create an environment that eliminates the conditions in which bullying, discrimination, harassment and physical violence at work occur	National Education and Training Survey (NETS) bullying Year-on-year reduction in incidents of discrimination from line managers or teams

SOURCE www.england.nhs.uk/long-read/nhs-equality-diversity-and-inclusion-improvement-plan/#high-impact-actions

Looking at this action plan shows us the principles many organizations can use to provide clarity for their team on what's needed:

- Use data to identify your needs
- Focus on key prioritized areas to define the journey
- Describe the success metrics for each area, so people know what success looks like

Paul Deemer says that they collaborate with health services in other countries too, so they can share learnings, actions and understanding. For example, they have talked to international health services to understand the impact on staff from different ethnicities during the Covid-19 pandemic. In the UK, it was very quickly clear that employees from minority ethnic backgrounds were dying or getting very ill at alarming rates.[4] Understanding the situation at home, and then discussing this with other countries has been a vital element of the learning from the pandemic. They collaborate to see what other countries experienced, what they learnt, and what actions they have taken. Similarly, at Watch This Sp_ce, we encourage employers we work with to share learnings, challenges and successes with other organizations, too, and we often bring together inclusion journey clients for that very purpose, so that people can learn from and support one another. Sharing paths, roadblocks and destinations can help people to figure out what is going to work for them.

Now let's look more closely at how *you* are going to take things forward on your inclusion journey.

Getting moving

All good journeys need signposts and milestones, so that you can plan your route, and move towards future destinations with stops along the way. Each stage of the journey will move at different speeds, have different obstacles on the route and take you in some different directions. But now that, from Chapters 6 and 7, you have a strong understanding of where you want to go and where you're starting from, you can work out what steps are needed and in what order they need to be taken.

We saw, from the example of the NHS, how important data is to inform action. From your work in the Discovery phase, you have gained insights into the gaps that need addressing and the opportunities for improvement.

You know what actions need to be taken. So now it's time to plot those actions on to a roadmap, with clear timescales, being realistic about what can be achieved at different times.

Since you've begun to engage your team from the start, there will be people already getting their bags packed for this journey, wanting to know when you're setting off. This is a key time to be energizing others, too, as you'll benefit from a variety of perspectives and personalities along the way. If you haven't already assembled the team we talked about in Chapter 5, you need them now.

Now is the time to work out, together, how things are going to move forwards. There are a few things to think about here:

- **Ways of working** – not everyone works well in group workshops and meetings, so consider different ways to get people involved, including online collaboration tools, one-to-one discussions and multi-input workshops, so that a variety of voices can be heard.

- **Variety of people** – as we have seen in earlier chapters, any project needs a variety of people to benefit from different perspectives and ideas. Consider how you open this up to encourage a range of contributions, rather than simply allowing the people who shout the loudest and put themselves forward the most forcefully to take the lead.

- **Time and money** – as we saw in Chapter 4, everyone who is going to work on this will need time allocated for this work, and you'll need to consider what budget you need to secure for training and tools to work towards your objectives.

Time and money are often an afterthought for many organizations. But all those actions you've listed out can't possibly happen unless people have the time, training and tools to make them happen. Without considering these things your journey will be slow to start, get stuck in traffic and potentially grind to a halt.

With action planning, there are lots of methods you can use, but we suggest going for something that everyone can understand clearly and easily. We like SMAART goals:

Specific – defining what you will do, and using action words

Measurable – using clear indicators to measure progress and success

Achievable – making sure actions are within scope and possible to achieve

Assignable – giving every action an owner who is responsible for delivery

Relevant – making sure the actions make sense and are relevant to the project

Time-bound – being clear about when things will be achieved

If you can keep these clear ways of defining actions in mind, it becomes easier to communicate them, track them and engage people in working on them. There are some great ways to help people visualize the actions too. You can track them in a spreadsheet, or similar, and share the document. We have found that online collaboration tools work best, so that everyone can access it and contribute their ideas. Look for online collaboration tools that give you visual ways to display actions and track progress – there are many free and subscription-based options out there, including Google Sheets, Trello, Miro, Asana and monday.com.

One of the things that has worked well for NHS Employers is making the action plan publicly available. Everyone can see what needs to be done, and how they can contribute to it. Managers are encouraged to discuss the action plan with staff and stakeholders regularly, so that everyone is engaged with it and aware of progress.

Prioritizing actions

Your big list of actions might be starting to feel overwhelming. How on earth are you going to do all these things as well as everything else you have to do? This is where prioritization comes in. Planning any journey requires knowing the best order to take your route in, and which sections will take different times. Are there any emergencies? Are there any accidents to attend to? Are there any traffic problems or roadblocks you need to be aware of along the way?

Prioritization is a balancing act between the tasks that will have the biggest impact in terms of results, and the tasks that can provide you with some quick wins to boost your momentum. Increasing the diversity of your management team might be a high priority, but it also could take years. So, whilst you need to make a start on it now, you might also get going on a simpler task, like subtitling all your videos, to show some progress you can all be proud of. You also need to maintain an awareness of where one thing has to happen before another can start. You won't know if you've increased the diversity of your management team, for example, until you've got your data framework in place to accurately record diversity across your organization.

You will need input from across your organization to help define the order of your action plan, and to ensure those actions can be delivered. Bringing people together in group sessions, sharing online information and having conversations across the business will all be valuable. Empower and encourage your leaders to communicate widely about this work and to encourage different inputs.

When you are working on prioritizing the actions, you want to take people with you and for them to feel involved and connected to the actions so they naturally want to take ownership. As we've seen already, relying solely on group meetings to engage people might mean that you miss out on a lot of valuable contributions, for example from introverts, from some people from certain cultural backgrounds, from some women (who are more likely to be talked over in meetings), from some neurodivergent people, and from people who are shy. Nadia Finer, in her book *Shy and Mighty*, finds that, although numbers vary in different countries, an estimated 50 per cent of people are shy at points in their life.[5] She writes that most organizations do not have a culture of nurturing quieter voices. It's not only that people are shy, but there can also be differences in communication or processing needs, and there are people who will not feel safe to talk openly in meetings. To make these discussions inclusive, make sure there are also online collaboration tools, ways to share thoughts in writing, opportunities to ask questions, information provided in advance to allow preparation, time for reflection after any group discussion, and opportunities to have conversations and adapt communications as you need to. An inclusion journey, by its very definition, needs to include everyone. So think carefully about how you do that at this stage so that you gain greater clarity on the direction here, and also so that you don't lose your team as you move forward.

Prioritization also needs to consider internal time factors. Are there already dates scheduled for employee surveys? Are there other reporting timelines which are significant? Are there key events which impact timelines, for example a financial year-end? These all need to be factored in so that you do not produce a set of actions that conflict with other areas of work. Link this prioritization with your business goals and objectives so that everyone can see how these things are going to help you deliver on the overall business goals as well as the inclusion journey.

You need to consider what can be achieved in the short term, the mid-term and the long term. When we work with clients to progress through the inclusion journey levels,[6] we always make sure there will be some short-term results. There will always be some quick things that people can get going on straight away which are good for morale, to show your team that progress is happening and help build momentum to get more people working on the next steps. It's also good for your reputation, both internally and externally, showing that your commitment to this work is real and that you are getting things done. Anyone who uses the Kotter[7] model of building change, which we look at in more detail in Chapter 11, will know about this. One of the steps in the process is to 'generate quick wins', because this provides hope, inspiration and confidence, as well as encouraging more people to come on board.

Someone who understands this well is Sitara Rivers[8] of the UK Civil Service. Sitara's wide-ranging career in diversity and inclusion has taken her into charities, education providers and police forces, and now to the Department for Environment, Food and Rural Affairs (DEFRA). She has seen some common themes across different organizations, and says there are always actions you can take:

> You can start by making a really small tangible step, that might just be having a conversation with someone around how to make work practices more inclusive. I think sometimes if you're in companies that are fearful of EDI, they think it will take away from the main job someone is employed to do. You can easily steer around that by thinking about what tiny fragments could be done. Like sending out an email and not using acronyms or adding my pronouns. That's a small step, and there are many like that which people can take.

At DEFRA they are writing policies that affect so many different people, so considering different needs and perspectives means they write better policies for everyone. During her time at DEFRA, where policies focus on fundamental areas like food, Sitara has been encouraged to research and learn about different people's lives. People are on different incomes, live in very different places and have different dietary needs, all of which policy creators need to take into consideration.

Resourcing actions

Now that you have worked out what actions you're going to take and in what order you are going to do them, you should hopefully have a group of voyagers ready to set off. The reality is that a lot of those people will have other priorities they need to deliver on, as well. So you now need to consider how to resource this work with the right people and tools to make sure progress is made. In Chapter 4 we looked at how the people taking this journey with you fall into different groups, and how to support them in coming on board. You'll want a range of roles, levels of seniority, life experiences and perspectives.

When we talk to people about diversity and inclusion journeys at their workplace, we are quite often met with a view that this work is over to the People or Human Resources team. This is one of the biggest misconceptions. For an inclusion journey to succeed, there needs to be commitment and involvement across the organization. This work impacts every team and needs engagement from everyone. The People and/or HR teams are key stakeholders in this, it's not that they won't be involved. They will have a lot of insight and knowledge to share, and have an interest in seeing this progress. It is often people in these roles who initiate this work, and they may have the clearest link between this work and their organizational objectives. But to leave it all on their shoulders will mean your journey will grind to a halt or be very slow to progress.

Assembling the right team for this work requires some stakeholder mapping, and ongoing conversations as you are working on engaging the team, to make sure that everyone who wants to, has the opportunity to get involved.

From Figure 8.1, an example of what your stakeholder mapping might look like, you can see we recommend reaching out as much as you can to different areas of the organization to bring in different perspectives and ideas. You also need to consider the different types of people who will bring

FIGURE 8.1 Stakeholder mapping diagram

Key players	Keep informed
Leadership team	HR operations
Diversity working group	Senior managers
People and culture team	Compliance
Recruitment team	

Advisers	Detractors
Marketing	New product engineers
Data and operations team	Some budget holders
Legal team	

rich insights to this work. In Chapters 4 and 5 we looked at some of the different types of people to consider from demographic perspectives, people's roles and their preparedness for getting involved in this work. Bringing all this together in your thinking will help you assemble that team who can take responsibility for delivering on areas of the actions.

A number of these people might be eager to take the journey without fully considering what's involved, so it's important at this point to clarify what is needed from and expected of them. You can then define who will take on what actions, and how you expect them to do that. As we saw with the NHS example, making these actions a part of people's performance objectives is important. We focus on what we measure, and if diversity and inclusion isn't on anyone's targets, it will inevitably fall to the bottom of their priorities. This is echoed by Sitara Rivers, who, as previously mentioned in this chapter, says that Civil Service employees also have objectives around inclusion.

These objectives should also align with existing targets – someone in a People role who is measured on targets around recruitment, for example, is perfectly placed to take ownership of targets related to your inclusive recruitment goals. Make a clear link between your overall objectives for the organization and your inclusion objectives, and you will be setting yourself up for a smoother journey.

Taking the first steps

There is a lot we can all learn from the approaches of the NHS and the Civil Service in the UK. To get to any destination points, think about the different people who can contribute perspectives and ideas, and make sure they can all be heard. Who will bring insights and ideas that you might not have thought of before? Who will bring those lightbulb moments of 'have you thought about this, though?' You can also look wider to external networks. If you discover that there are perspectives and experiences you do not have in your teams, consider who you can talk to at other organizations to help you bring in those insights. There is a worksheet to help you consider your resourcing needs, as well as prioritization of actions, in Table 8.2.

In your resourcing of people, look at the different skills you have in your team and how these can be matched to the tasks required. Some of the work is detailed and requires analytical approaches. For other areas of the work, you need creativity and big picture thinking. For all of the work, you will need energy and commitment to keep things moving. Get people involved and engaged, and you will find that your inclusion journey will progress

TABLE 8.2 Worksheet to support planning, prioritizing and resourcing of actions

Worksheet example with example actions

Area of focus	Business goal	Inclusion journey goal	Measure	Timescale	Priority
Recruitment	Improve employer brand to attract candidates	Introduce inclusive recruitment policy and processes	• Attract job seekers from different demographics, 40% women, 20% different ethnicities, 20% with disabilities • Offer inclusive recruitment experience for 100% of vacancies	In next 12 months	1
Representation	Create high-performing teams across company	Improve diversity and inclusion in teams across all departments	• 40% women in all teams • Ethnic diversity in all teams	In next 24 months	2
Working practices	Improve retention rate of employees and offer increased flexibility	Inclusive, accessible and flexible working practices for all employees	• Review all premises for accessibility • Introduce flexible and remote working for all teams • Produce inclusive working and communication guidelines for all teams	In next 12 months	1

much faster. In his book *Rebel Ideas*, Matthew Syed talks about the value of teams that bring different perspectives to decision-making. He says that 'teams of rebels beat teams of clones,'[9] so how can you make sure you're not generating a team of clones for your inclusion journey? You need that band of rebels ready to take adventurous steps in a journey that will have twists and turns along the way.

Notes

1 Interview with Paul Deemer from NHS Employers, October 2023

2 NHS Employers. NHS Staff Survey 2022: key findings, 9 March 2023, www.nhsemployers.org/news/nhs-staff-survey-2022-key-findings (archived at https://perma.cc/V24P-UAL6)

3 NHS England. NHS equality, diversity, and inclusion improvement plan, 8 June 2023, www.england.nhs.uk/long-read/nhs-equality-diversity-and-inclusion-improvement-plan/#high-impact-actions (archived at https://perma.cc/A9AS-RKE5)

4 Public Health England. Beyond the data: Understanding the impact of COVID-19 on BAME groups, June 2020, https://assets.publishing.service.gov.uk/media/5ee761fce90e070435f5a9dd/COVID_stakeholder_engagement_synthesis_beyond_the_data.pdf (archived at https://perma.cc/9HUM-KFE5)

5 N Finer (2022) *Shy and Mighty: How to step out of the shadows and live a bigger life*, Quercus

6 Watch This Sp_ce, *The Inclusion Journey*, www.watchthisspace.uk/the-inclusion-journey (archived at https://perma.cc/8FYU-W2FY)

7 Kotter. The 8 Steps For Leading Change, www.kotterinc.com/methodology/8-steps/ (archived at https://perma.cc/Z3XA-ZX7Z)

8 Interview with Sitara Rivers from the Civil Service, November 2023

9 M Syed (2019) *Rebel Ideas: The power of diverse thinking*, John Murray Publishers

9

How are you going to keep moving forward?

By now, you are well on the way. You have your roadmap and your actions, and you have started to assemble the team to go with you on this expedition. With journeys, it's easy to get excited at the start and feel the thrill of where you might go when you're in the planning stage. Keeping things moving forwards through the tougher bits of the journey is the challenge. How do you make sure that the journey is going to keep progressing, without people going off-course or leaving the train altogether? In Chapter 8, we looked at some elements to consider in how you bring people together for this work. This chapter will look at how you keep that team motivated and engaged, and how you can give them the support they need to move ahead.

You will see a theme emerging around communication. Communication is a key element in keeping things moving, and we will look at how you can communicate effectively to maintain momentum and support different needs.

Travelling styles

We all have different ways of travelling and different styles of doing things. Some prepare for a trip for months, and some pack their bags the night before. It's the same with working styles. We all have different ways of working and processing information. This is the context to now think about in keeping your team moving forward and making sure they have the support they need. Here are just a few differences in styles:

- **Reading vs listening** – are you a reader, who needs to absorb a lot of text-based information to understand something? Or do you find it easier to take in information if you listen to someone talking?

- **Words, images, sounds** – if you ask someone to describe something to you, it will give you an insight into whether they interpret the world, and best express themselves, through words, images or sounds.

- **Details vs highlights** – some people need to see a lot of detail to consider and analyse, whereas, for others, a lot of detail baffles and bores them, so you need a combination of levels of detail in information.

- **Understanding vs doing** – however much you explain theory or ideas, for some people, they only understand once they start doing something; that's why some people read instruction manuals, and others just get stuck in.

- **Thinking vs discussing** – some people need time and space to think things through for themselves before they're clear on their views and ready to discuss the matter; other people won't feel they have a strong grasp on a subject, or their own opinions, until they've talked it through with others and heard other viewpoints.

In all of those examples, can you see an issue? Many of these styles conflict with one another. So a person who needs to think quietly to process information will struggle with people who need to talk everything through. You will need to consider the different information processing styles and think about how you can adapt communications and processes for the different types of people you want to get involved in this work.

There are other factors to consider too: there will be differences in personality types, lifestyles, perspectives and more. It is a good investment of time to consider how you will accommodate all of the diverse people taking part in this project, which will be good learnings for how you support diversity in your organization moving forward.

This does mean taking more time to prepare, but you will make up this time in how much faster the improved engagement, understanding and collaboration will allow you to move once you get going. Some actions you can consider for how you produce communications are shown in Table 9.1.

TABLE 9.1 Guidance for preparing communications

Visual	Highlights	Details	Thinking	Discussing
Use pictures, diagrams and colours to illustrate key information	Use clear headings and bullet points so that people can skim read	Provide additional information which can be in attachments and links	Provide information in advance and offer ways to submit written considerations	Hold forums or workshops to enable idea-sharing

You will also need to consider any adjustments people need. An inclusion journey needs to be inclusive from the start. Review the accessibility of information, tools, physical spaces, and things like locations and times of day to make sure there are options to suit everyone. Ask people what works for them and get advice from experts.

Roadmap activation

Having laid the groundwork, you can now let everyone get stuck in. It's time to unveil the roadmap you built from your analysis in Chapters 6 and 7, using the methodology from Chapter 8. Make sure you present the information in a way that enables everyone to understand the priorities and what's required of them.

At Watch This Sp_ce, we hold Activation Workshops at this point in the journey. This helps to engage the working group responsible for the roadmap in planning those first steps that they need to take. Owners can then be assigned for different areas of work to start moving things forward. This is another time when a combination of tools and methods is helpful. You might hold some in-person workshops, some online, use an online collaboration tool and give those who prefer the chance to have a one-to-one discussion about their involvement.

This stage needs guidance and support from the overall project owner so that people do not feel overwhelmed by the amount of things that need to be done. Help the team break actions down into tangible tasks that they can get involved in and bring other people into as well. Continue to pay attention to different learning styles. There are people who need to see coloured Post-it Notes (or online versions thereof) to feel energized, and other people who will want a report that outlines the data. You might find it beneficial to have a discussion with the working group right at the start, to share learning styles and preferences so that everyone feels well supported along the way.

An example of how you might break down your roadmap actions is provided in Table 9.2. Please note that the priority and timescales of different actions will depend on the unique factors of your individual organization.

Planning well at this stage and making sure people understand the different actions and objectives is vital for the success of this journey. Give people the opportunity to discuss and debate ideas and shape the actions they take responsibility for. You want people to feel they are part of this. This method of engaging people is well described in the 'Fair Process Leadership' theory

TABLE 9.2 Example roadmap actions

	Priority	Timescale	Owner
Data			
Create a process for collecting and analysing demographic data.	High	Short term	HR Operations
Monitor salary data to identify potential pay gaps.	Medium	Medium term	HR Operations
Training			
Introduce an ongoing training programme covering: • The benefits of inclusion • Unconscious bias • Inclusive communication • Inclusive recruitment • Psychological safety • Challenging conversations • Neurodiversity • Allyship • Anti-racism • Inclusive leadership	High	Short term	Learning and development
Recruitment			
Create a job advert template.	High	Quick fix	Talent Lead
Analyse job adverts for biased language.	High	Short term	Talent Lead
Display salaries on job adverts.	High	Quick fix	HR Operations
Review the language around diversity and inclusion in the Recruitment Policy and Equal Opportunities Policy.	Medium	Quick fix	Compliance and HR Operations
Review the content used for recruitment communications.	Low	Long term	Marketing
External Comms			
Undertake a website audit.	Low	Long term	Marketing
Ensure that any videos have subtitles.	High	Short term	Marketing
Policies			
Introduce a statement on the benefits of diversity and inclusion and a commitment to these in the equal opportunities policy and other relevant communications.	High	Quick fix	HR Operations

by Ludo Van Der Heyden from INSEAD.[1] The concept of Fair Process Leadership is about giving everyone the opportunity to be involved in key decisions. This is not decision-making by committee – there will be overall leaders of sections of work who make decisions based on the inputs they have received. The theory of this model is that, if people are given the opportunity to say what they think should happen, they feel more bought in to what then takes place. Even if their idea is not taken forward, the fact that they have had their say helps them get on board with a new direction. We will look at this model in more detail in Chapter 11.

Support sources

Support for this journey comes in different forms. For one thing, there will be learning to do for everyone involved. Everyone in the organization will need training to help them understand complex concepts, and to share thoughts and ideas with each other. The people steering the journey will need further and deeper training and discussions to help them with this work. A culture of openness and safety will take careful planning and work to create, so that everyone's voice is heard, and people feel genuinely included.

For training for the team involved in the inclusion journey, there is no magic one-hour session which will fulfil all needs. There will need to be ongoing learning as the journey progresses. Each stage will bring different knowledge and skill needs to the fore, and these will need to be supported in order for the team to progress. Again, different learning styles and needs will have to be considered. Some people will thrive on reading and reflection, but there will be others who need interactive learning so they can ask questions and share ideas with others.

For another source of support, you may find it useful to talk to other organizations about their learning and skills development in this area. Going to conferences, events and meet-up groups are valuable ways to start these discussions. This external networking can also take the form of being mentored or supported in some way by others who have progressed a little further than you on their inclusion journey. We encourage our clients to talk to one another to learn from different successes and challenges. Talking and sharing about the experiences can help to open up ideas and find alternative ways forward. External networking also allows you to learn from mistakes others might have made, without having to repeat them yourself.

As we saw in Chapter 5, there is also an important supporting role for a sponsor. This is the senior leader who puts their weight behind this work.

They will need to engage with people, keep lines of communication and escalation clear, and generally be someone the team can go to when they need to talk things through. The sponsor is the person who will maintain communication with the wider leadership team to keep them updated. This person, or these people, will need to be mindful of when to bring in others to keep the journey moving. Dr Helen Curr, of Here, who we introduced you to earlier, advises: 'in any kind of leadership position, there is just an inherent value in really paying attention to inclusion'. The inclusion journey needs to be discussed amongst leaders so they fully understand what is being done and why, and how they can support it. Leaders need to play a pivotal role in getting their teams involved and enthused about this work.

Taking pit stops

For people involved in an inclusion journey, there is often an emotional toll which everyone needs to be aware of. By its nature, work to address systemic inequalities requires introspection, and perhaps reliving uncomfortable experiences from the past. Those raising their hands to take accountability and responsibility for delivering on actions need to feel equipped to deal with challenges along the way. The support that people need cannot be underestimated and should be considered carefully in your journey planning. Engaging with a mental health expert to support the team is something we recommend as part of your scoping and budgeting. By that, we do not mean a one-off one-hour training session – there needs to be ongoing support for the whole team along the way.

Marc Caulfield,[2] a mental health advocate, trainer and TedX speaker on the importance of mental health support, says:

> The worlds of Diversity, Equity, Inclusion and Mental Health are inextricably linked. Driving DE&I change can be a very lonely and isolating place. Nothing is more important than your own mental health; after all you can't make a difference if you are yourself not in a robust place mentally.

He goes on to offer advice for those starting an inclusion journey:

> Do not allow one group or one person to derail the journey for their personal agenda or vendetta, which may be based on their own experiences and make it difficult for them to be objective.
>
> You are making the workplace a better, healthier place for *all*; this is not about taking things away from other people.

Caulfield's point about the risk of one person derailing an inclusion journey is something we have seen in practice several times. Perhaps one person has experienced a form of discrimination which means that their pain skews their thinking. As we've said before, an inclusion journey, by definition, is about including everyone, which means it can't become about one particular issue to the exclusion of all others. Extra care needs to be taken to ensure the people involved understand this, and that they are supported well. If personal experiences are having an impact on their thinking, they need to work with an expert to process what they have been through.

That's not to say that people who have experienced discrimination should not be involved. Their experiences and perspectives will give valuable insight to your journey and roadmap. But their wellbeing, like everyone else's, must be a priority. They will face the challenge of understanding that other people will have had different, and equally valid, experiences. They will also come up against some potentially distressing views from people who don't see the point of diversity and inclusion at all, and maybe some who are opposed to equity altogether. Your organization has a duty of care to ensure everyone has support and guidance as they take this journey.

In the initial rush to get everything moving, it can be easy to forget about taking breaks and pit stops. This work is important, but it's also mentally taxing, so Marc Caulfield says that it is good to be clear with people that if they need to take a break on something, that's fine. Take the time to look after the people on this journey so that everyone arrives in good shape to each milestone along the way.

Those breaks can take different forms. For some people they may need to step away from the journey completely for a while, or altogether, and it needs to feel safe for them to do so. For others, it could be that they get to a point and then need to take a pause to re-energize themselves. Everyone should feel that taking a break is not a bad thing to do. Every journey requires pit stops to re-energize, and it's the same with this one.

Keeping you posted

Your team, by now, should be off the starting blocks and progressing with tasks and actions. You will start to see some of those quick wins delivered, and generally feel a buzz around this work progressing. Showing the changes that are happening is a good way to generate even more interest and engagement across the business, and externally.

At the start of the journey, it's easy to know about all the key actions and to see the quick wins happening. At this stage, the team involved are more likely to be talking regularly to each other and sharing progress and ideas. Maintaining this momentum and keeping sight of what's happening as the journey progresses is not something to take for granted. You do not want people to start feeling like things have gone off track or they do not know what the next stage will be. You can lose people's interest and enthusiasm if that happens.

If you are the person taking the role of the overall project coordinator, then you also need to consider how you will find time to keep track of this work. How involved are you going to be in the different workstreams? And how are you going to consider your own support and training needs? There will be an emotional toll for you, too. People will look to you for vision, progress and momentum. And any roadblocks or issues along the way are going to land at your feet. So, consider what support is in place for you, and what needs to be put in place. Where this is not considered, we have seen inclusion journeys struggle as the coordinator can start to feel overwhelmed and/or demoralized, and that has an impact on the entire project.

Above all else, you need to stay open to learning and growth as you move forward. Dr Helen Curr says, 'It's amazing what you can do if you really force yourself to stay in a curious position.' She encourages continually asking questions to understand the journey as it progresses. There is a responsibility for the coordinator, the working group and any sponsors to keep everyone updated, but if you want people to really understand and engage with this journey, don't just tell them facts, help them to ask questions. Signpost who they can ask and listen to their inputs. Make sure you're answering the questions that come up so that people maintain and grow that sense of curiosity.

Ultimately, for this journey to keep moving forwards, you need solid support mechanisms in place to make sure everyone's needs are met and their enthusiasm is encouraged. In the next chapter, we will look at how you can keep track of your progress as the journey goes on.

Notes

1 I C Woodward, E A More and L Van der Heyden. 'INVOLVE': The Foundation for Fair Process Leadership Communication, INSEAD, February 2016, https://sites.insead.edu/facultyresearch/research/doc.cfm?did=57856 (archived at https://perma.cc/PW7G-6SUY)

2 Interview with Marc Caulfield, Director and Founder of DNA Neuroanalytics, November 2023

10

How will you track your progress?

Describe what you want to achieve from both a 'vision' perspective and a 'metric' perspective.

SHEREE ATCHESON, DEMANDING MORE[1]

The inclusion journey has now picked up pace. Actions are progressing, people are moving, and those involved know what they are working on and what they want to achieve. What about everyone else though? Within your organization and externally, you need to share your goals and objectives, and how you're measuring up against the targets and timescales from your roadmap. This chapter will look at how you communicate that progress to your internal and external audiences, and how to measure your impact. Along the way, we will look at how to encourage feedback and inputs, and how to respond to them.

Sheree Atcheson, a Group Vice-President of Diversity & Inclusion and author of the book *Demanding More*, talks about the importance of setting out clearly what you want to achieve in terms of your vision, as well as the metrics you are going to track. The vision of where you want to get to will inspire people to get involved, and the metrics are how you show everyone that progress is being made. Seeing progress helps everyone to feel motivated to continue with the journey.

Mapping your vision

To keep people up-to-date with your progress, you need to first explain to them the vision for the journey. Using your learnings from the Discovery phase and the insights that informed your roadmap, the team can shape inclusive communications that outline the vision for where you are going, and then enable everyone to contribute their views. You will want to convey:

- Why you are taking this journey and the need for it
- What you are doing along the way
- Who is involved
- How people can get involved
- How people can give their inputs and feedback

This overall messaging helps to keep people feeling enthusiastic about the work, and avoids the scenario where people say they do not know what is going on. We worked with one company who said that, even though they were working hard on diversity and inclusion, their staff were constantly asking what they were doing and complaining that they didn't appear to be doing enough. Their team was passionate about diversity and inclusion, and keen to take action, but frustrated that they didn't know what the company was doing around this. Then once they started engaging people with workshops, surveys and feedback mechanisms, the questions stopped, and satisfaction on the subject increased. Even though they were still taking the same level of action on diversity and inclusion.

Why the change?

Simply that they had communicated well. They had given everyone the opportunity to get involved and feel connected to what was going on. Everyone started paying more attention to the actions that had been happening all along, and the team created an online interactive tracking board so that their colleagues could all follow the progress. So staff no longer felt the need to keep asking about it, and they felt more positive about what their organization was doing because they could see progress in action.

Measuring your steps

We looked at how to set actions in Chapter 8, using methods to create SMAART objectives. That's a good place to start, but to keep things on track you need to continually measure the progress of these actions, and whether they are on time and on budget. Like a GPS system that gives you an estimated time of arrival, you want to monitor all the steps being taken, to know when you are likely to reach different destinations along the way.

The measurement of the roadmap and actions also helps to keep people motivated, as they can see the points of progress along the way. No one person will be involved in everything, so using a clear method to provide an overview of what's happening and how it's going enables all staff to stay engaged and informed. In Chapter 8, we looked at a detailed roadmap that sets out all the actions a company needs to take. For measurement reporting, you'll want to take a more top-level overview that shows progress against the goals you set in a way that is easy for your staff and key stakeholders to understand. There are some great online tools available which help visualize measurement in the form of dashboards, too. An example of how this data can be visualized is shown in Figure 10.1.

As we've seen in previous chapters, your measurement approach should link the inclusion objectives with the overall organizational objectives. This not only supports ongoing buy-in but helps to convert any people who may have been detractors for this work.

We encourage sharing this information clearly, regularly and in different formats to maximize engagement. To really embed this within your systems, introduce mechanisms for team leaders to share progress updates in their team meetings, giving opportunities for staff to ask questions. Where this is done well, and communication happens regularly and in different formats, that's where we see organizations make good progress.

Telling people where you're going

By now, you probably feel pretty confident that everyone inside your organization knows about the inclusion journey and where to find out more about it. You'd be surprised, though. No matter how widely you think you've communicated something, there are always people who still don't know about it. They may have other priorities that have distracted them, or they might not have been so interested in it early on. Most people need to be told about something several times, and in different ways, for it to become embedded in their minds.

Use your measurement framework to keep communicating clearly and regularly. Consider those different communication processing styles we looked at in Chapter 8, and don't be afraid to repeat yourself. In *Building A Culture of Inclusivity*, Priya Bates and Advita Patel explain that you need to

FIGURE 10.1 Example actions measurement framework

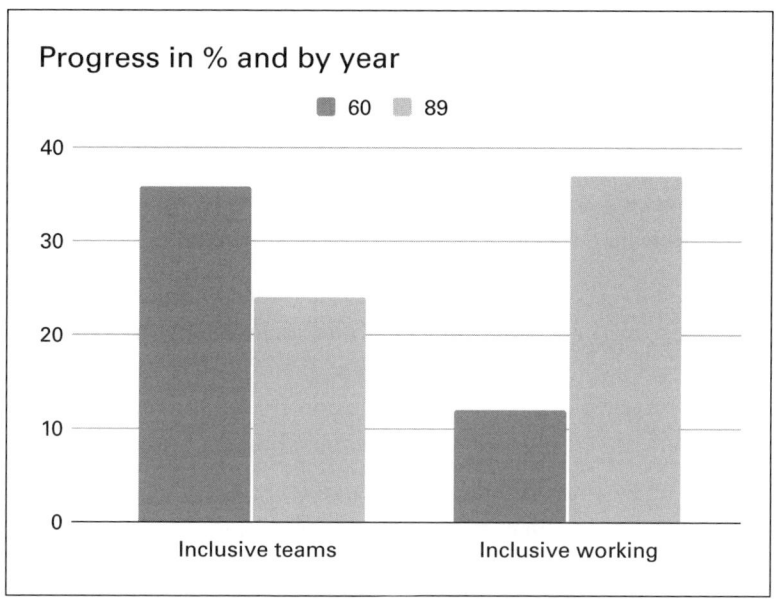

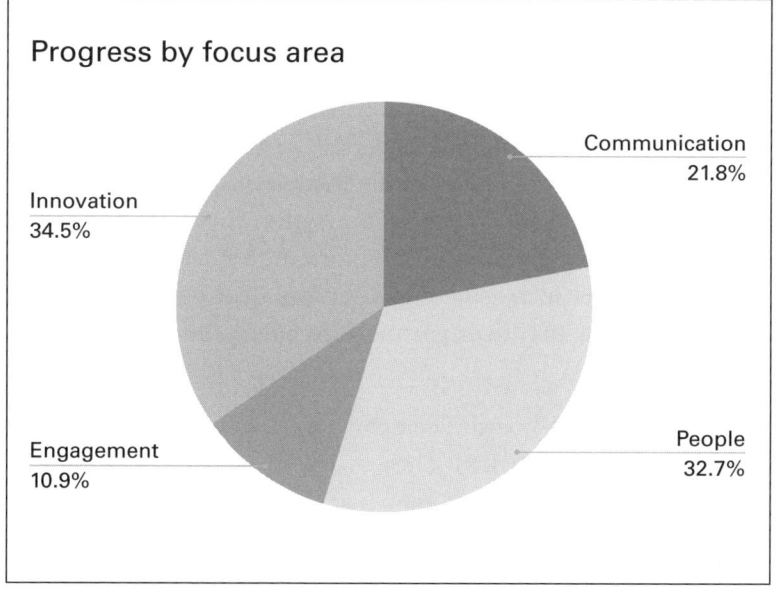

share successes as well as failures, so that the reporting is authentic.[2] They say that this helps to build a culture of trust in the work.

Regular, honest communication also benefits your external reputation. You don't need to wait until you've made a lot of progress to talk about your journey publicly – there is great value in communicating about work you are *going to do*. As with the example of NHS Employers that we looked at in Chapter 8, sharing actions that you are starting work on builds trust, gives hope and offers inspiration. There are some key audiences who this impacts:

Potential recruits – job seekers are increasingly looking for employers who are doing something about diversity and inclusion. More than three out of four job seekers[3] state this as a priority, so an employer who communicates that they have an inclusion roadmap, and talks about the actions they are taking, will be more appealing to candidates.

Prospects – when potential clients or customers are sizing up who to buy from, seeing an inclusion journey in progress could help make that decision. Increasingly, people are looking for ethical suppliers and brands, with whom they share vision and values. Diversity and inclusion actions are also becoming more and more valuable criteria when bidding on tenders.

Partners – when choosing who to collaborate with, many businesses are making it a requirement that potential partners are taking action on diversity and inclusion. This is partly because it's important to their own diversity and inclusion targets or ways that they are assessed by key parties, and partly because it's important for their own reputation. They're also under increasing pressure from their own staff and external audiences to show that their partnerships align with their core values.

At Watch This Sp_ce, we worked with an organization who needed to hire new people to join their board. Their client base was young and diverse with different ethnicities represented. Their board was not. So what they did was to communicate externally that they had a problem. They said, explicitly and transparently, in their advertising for these roles that their board did not reflect their client base and they wanted to do something about it. They asked if people wanted to join them and help in that mission.

That openness had a big impact.

Suddenly, they started to receive applications from the types of people they had been trying to recruit for a while. This showed them the value in being transparent and direct. Instead of pretending that everything was perfect, they were honest about having an issue, they stated openly what the problem was and asked people to help. It worked. Since then, we have advised other companies to follow a similar approach to attract a wider range of candidates, and it has always worked wonders.

Being open about your gaps, and telling people how you plan to address them, can have a huge impact on your reputation.

Reviewing your approach

When you decided to embark on this journey, you probably had an idea of where you wanted to go. Even if it wasn't a perfectly formed vision, you had a vague concept of what you might be moving towards. The Discovery phase will have solidified that vision into something more tangible, and shown you where the gaps are, then the Audit phase identified the actions you needed to take to move forward. You've already been on a steep learning curve.

Now, as you progress, there's more to uncover. Different approaches will be tested, and these will give you different results. As you work on new actions, you'll discover new gaps. You'll also be getting a lot of feedback from different parts of the business. This means you need to regularly review your approach and potentially change direction and agree new destinations from time to time. This is something to keep careful track of. Failure to recognize when you need to make a change can throw the whole journey off course.

Let's take the example of Plus X Innovation, who set out on their inclusion journey with Watch This Sp_ce at a time of growth for their company. Plus X Innovation is a hub for start-up and scale-up businesses; they help entrepreneurs to realize their ambitions with support to allow them to grow. They have big plans for growth themselves, so they wanted to make sure they embedded inclusive approaches early on.

They started with a Discovery phase to get people energized and engaged. They got a team together from across the business to take responsibility for the actions. Things initially progressed well with good momentum. Then they hit a roadblock. This was not owing to lack of commitment and enthusiasm, but the business plans to scale accelerated, with a new site opening, and their teams suddenly became very busy working on that. This pulled their focus from the inclusion roadmap and left them with little time to give to it.

At this stage it would have been easy for them to lose track completely. Pausing or stopping their inclusion journey would have been an easy option for them. The problem is that it would have then been difficult to pick up where they left off, and they knew that. So what they actually did was to go back to the initial vision and reflect on why this journey mattered. It was crucial to their organizational priorities, including the plans for their new site. They needed to show that they stood by their genuine commitment to progress with their action plan. They needed to instil the values and vision of their inclusion journey as they expanded to the new site and new people joined their teams.

So they got back on track.

They brought their focus back to the goals and re-prioritized the actions carefully. They streamlined what they were working on, and saw that the actions around recruitment and retention were the most important ones for this point in their journey as their team was set to expand. So they made space to address those actions and that workstream, then found that their whole journey picked up pace again.

Feedback and input

Some of the reasons Plus X were able to get back on track were owing to feedback and input. Their team felt this project was crucial for creating a sense of belonging with new team members at the new site. Staff were able to voice these views, as the business had created a strong culture of listening, and their teams knew that they could talk to leaders openly and express their concerns.

Feedback is an element that needs to be built into the journey process. As well as the rush of the initial Discovery phase, how will people give their input and feedback as you go along? Will you stay on the same course no matter what, or do you want to learn as you go and listen to people as your journey progresses? If you miss this stage out, you risk losing people's interest and engagement.

For feedback to work, consider *how* people will tell you what they think. You may already be running regular employee surveys. Or you may already have a culture where people regularly share their views. Or you may need to introduce something new. We have seen different approaches work well. At Richmond Hill Hotel, as discussed in Chapter 4, employees can give anonymous feedback for leaders to consider. They have found that, as leaders respond with respect and consideration to this anonymous feedback, their employees have begun to give feedback that is not anonymous too. They feel like they can approach leaders directly with their input and thoughts, and know they will be listened to.

At Here – Care Unbound, a healthcare social enterprise, Dr Helen Curr and the team use regular 'pulse' surveys, as well as discussions in team meetings. With the surveys, they use an online tool which allows them to respond to feedback, while maintaining anonymity, so that they can work to resolve issues. They find that this approach encourages staff to talk more openly about these things, too.

At Here, they practise the 'teal' method of working, as described carefully in Frederic Laloux's book *Reinventing Organizations*.[4] This method is about enabling people to bring their whole selves to work and share how they are feeling. Here starts all meetings with a check-in to ask everyone how they are, and they take care to check *out* with everyone, too, at the end of meetings. This creates a culture of psychological safety where people are comfortable to share their feelings, thoughts and ideas. They are constantly working to build this culture, so it's not that they never experience issues along the way on their inclusion journey. But the approach they take enables people to feel they can share roadblocks and challenges in a very open and honest way, which gives them a much better chance of effectively addressing these issues. Other methods we have seen work are 'listening circles', regularly held spaces where people talk about their work openly with other people.

Nadia Finer, author of *Shy and Mighty*,[5] encourages everyone to consider those who are introverts or who are shy in how they collect feedback. There are people who will never feel they can share their feelings in open group meetings. So ensure there are a variety of methods for people to tell you what they think. Nadia suggests ensuring that there are ways to give input and feedback that do not require speaking up in a big meeting. So you might consider surveys, online collaboration tools or one-to-one discussions to help people to contribute.

The main goal here is to create a culture where people can be open, so that you'll become aware of problems or opportunities that you might not have spotted, and to provide mechanisms to allow different types of input at regular times.

Responding to inputs

What you do with this feedback is an important factor in whether people will *continue* giving you feedback. It's one thing to receive the ideas and thoughts people have, it's another to do something about it.

All change management methodology talks about the importance of reviewing and acting on feedback. We will look at this in more detail in Chapter 11, exploring different models of change management and which ones might be useful for you. For now, take some time to think about how the team will act on feedback and input. Some of it might be difficult to hear. The types of things people might feed back about are:

- feeling excluded from getting involved in the work
- disagreement on the actions, or priority of actions
- discomfort at changes being made
- frustration at not seeing things progress quickly enough
- upset at not understanding the actions and progress being made

As you can see, a lot of these things are linked to communication. As Advita Patel and Priya Bates say in their book *Creating a Culture of Inclusivity*,[6] creating clear, inclusive communication builds employee engagement. If you openly share your action plan, and the roadmap is open and visible for everyone to see, then you minimize the risk of people feeling excluded from the journey. You also then open yourself up to feedback, which might show a need for some changes of direction.

Changing direction is not a failure of the journey. Think about car journeys and how sometimes, if you encounter roadworks or traffic or other problems, you need to change direction, but not necessarily the destination. You might need to review your approach, amend your priorities or introduce new actions to your plan.

Let's look at an example. We worked with an organization who had not prioritized looking at promotions and progression as part of their initial scoping of their inclusion journey. They felt the initial focus should be on recruitment, and that the work on progression could come later. As they moved ahead and started communicating widely to the organization, they got strong feedback that people wanted to see what was happening for employees already at the company. It was all very well to focus on new recruits, and they could see why that was important, but they were frustrated at the lack of attention to issues that directly impacted existing staff themselves.

This caused them to pause and reflect. They took a pit stop.

They looked at all their data again. The data helps, at these points of reflection, to guide your next steps. They saw that those employees were right. The data showed them that a number of employees with disabilities or from ethnic minority backgrounds had resigned, and in their exit interviews had said they were leaving because they felt they were not given opportunities to progress their careers.

The leadership team took the time to reflect on this and talk to the Inclusion Journey team to understand their perspective. Then they all decided together that one action that had originally been set as lower priority should actually be a top priority. This was creating a Future Leaders Programme (see Table 10.1).

Programmes like this are an incredibly effective way to help people progress their careers. Participants can either be put forward by a senior member of staff or they can apply to join a programme themselves. Then they are matched with a sponsor in a senior role who works with them throughout the programme. The participants receive training and coaching to help them develop their careers and build leadership skills, and the sponsors are given training to enable them to provide effective support. The participants often work on a project to help drive change in the company, but also to help them network and work with different teams. Sometimes these programmes involve reverse mentoring, and there is an element of that in the sponsor/participant relationship.

TABLE 10.1 Future leaders programme – typical elements for 6-month or 12-month programmes

Who	Element	With whom
Participants	Application and selection process	Supported by Line Manager
Participants	Welcome event	With all participants
Participants	In-person workshops	With all participants
Participants	Online workshops	With all participants
Participants	Sponsor 1:1 sessions	With Sponsor, typically once a month
Participants	Change project	With some participants
Sponsors	Sponsors volunteer and are selected	With programme facilitator
Sponsors	Sponsor workshops	Online or in person with other Sponsors
Sponsors	Celebration event	With Participants, Sponsors and Leaders
Line Managers	Support with applications	With Participant
Line Managers	Ongoing reviews	With Participant
Line Managers	Celebration event	With Participants, Sponsors and Leaders

(continued)

TABLE 10.1 (Continued)

Typical workshop subjects – Participants
What's holding you back?
What are your superpowers?
Where do you want your career to go?
Challenging conversations
Inclusive and productive working
Building your network

Typical workshop subjects – Sponsors
Allyship
Challenging your assumptions
Inclusive leadership

At this particular organization, the change really worked. The people who had given the feedback could see they were being listened to. The team working on the recruitment actions were energized by seeing retention and progression improve. And the programme became one that the company now runs regularly to help develop cohorts of participants who network with each other.

That's one example, and we have seen many others where some changes in direction have been required. Consider the impact of not doing that. Had that company not taken the time to review their data, listen to people and change course, they might have ended up with very disengaged employees. We'll look in more detail at the process of identifying a need to change direction and putting together a plan to do it in Chapter 13.

Review points are all about looking at data and going back to the core vision and goals. Link the goals to the business objectives, and it doesn't then feel like this work is taking people away from their core tasks; it's an integral part of their role. Measure progress along the way and always be prepared to listen, review and change course when needed.

Now you're really moving on this journey. In the next section, we'll look at how you can maintain this progress for the long haul, dealing with any bumps along the way. We will also look at how you share the driving so you don't feel like you're travelling alone.

Notes

1 S Atcheson (2021) *Demanding More: Why diversity and inclusion don't happen and what you can do about it*, Kogan Page
2 P Bates and A Patel (2023) *Building a Culture of Inclusivity: Effective internal communication for diversity, equity and inclusion*, Kogan Page
3 Glassdoor. What job seekers really think about your diversity and inclusion stats, 12 July 2021, www.glassdoor.com/employers/blog/diversity/ (archived at https://perma.cc/5HNM-RTS7)
4 F Laloux (2014) *Reinventing Organizations: A guide to creating organizations inspired by the next stage of human consciousness*, Nelson Parker
5 N Finer (2022) *Shy and Mighty: How to step out of the shadows and live a bigger life,* Quercus
6 P Bates and A Patel (2023) *Building a Culture of Inclusivity: Effective internal communication for diversity, equity and inclusion*, Kogan Page

PART THREE

Don't stop moving

11

Maintaining enthusiasm

At the start of the journey, when people are excited about new opportunities and bursting with ideas, enthusiasm is easy to generate. Hands are raised to volunteer for tasks, messaging groups are set up, and plans are made for the work ahead. The problem lies in maintaining that initial energy and keeping things moving so you reach those goals you all set out to achieve at the beginning. This section is all about how you keep things on track, maintain that momentum and carry your project over any bumps in the road, so you keep travelling forwards on your inclusion journey.

When you started talking about this work and introducing the idea of an inclusion journey, it is very likely that you saw initial bursts of excitement as everyone considered what might be achieved. The same is true of a lot of journeys, where the initial possibilities fill everyone with a buzz. The reality, though, is often less fun than the original concept. Travelling is tiring, and it always takes longer than you expect. As you progress, then, how do you avoid some people in the backseat getting fed up and asking to get out of the car at the next stop? In this chapter, we will look closely at how to create an engagement plan to help everyone stay connected to the overall mission. We will look at how to maintain that initial enthusiasm along the way, and how to handle the changes that need to be made as you travel, whilst keeping people interested in the journey. Everyone will have different ideas about the speed of travel, when you should take breaks and where you should head next. So we will look at how you manage different expectations about the journey and keep people involved.

Engagement and enthusiasm

To drive real change at pace, you have to generate momentum in the work you are doing, and keep that momentum going. Dee Mathieson is the UK

Managing Director at Elekta,[1] a pioneering technology company helping clinicians treat cancer and brain disorders through precision radiation medicine. Mathieson is their first female Managing Director in this international company with over 4,500 employees. In her work driving inclusion at Elekta, she talks about needing to create a movement that maintains momentum to keep people interested. The buzz of people seeing things actually happening at the start creates a ripple effect of more and more people wanting to get involved. She says that once you, as a leader, get things started, employees start to pick up tasks and ideas and run with it themselves. Elekta has thousands of employees working worldwide, so that's a lot of people to engage in driving change. Mathieson has found that, as she works with UK employees and they gain enthusiasm, they then talk about the work to their international colleagues, and that chain reaction spreads to those teams too. The more they share what they're doing in the UK, the more they see other teams asking them about the work. And that creates conversations and the sharing of ideas across their teams. The UK team also starts to learn what is working for their international colleagues too, and it creates an environment of sharing and learning.

This is all about engaging people effectively. Mathieson is a great believer in being visible as a leader, and getting involved in the inclusion journey herself to help to drive that engagement. She believes your role as a leader is to create space to enable people to get involved, to facilitate participation, to learn from other companies, and to make decisions so that things happen. She has also personally taken actions herself, like setting up Wudu washing facilities for Muslim employees at their Crawley, UK office. These are dedicated spaces for the rituals of washing before prayers for Muslims. The prayer room has been in place for a while, this was an important additional requirement. Employees were surprised to see things like this happening, and the momentum from it has meant that more people come forward to ask about changes. So they now have celebrations for different religions, and things like chat forums for people to talk and share their ideas and challenges, which keeps people feeling enthusiastic about the process of evolution.

At Elekta, the global organization started with a women's group to address progressing more women into leadership roles across the company. The success of that initial group, the changes they made and the ideas they identified didn't just drive results on their objectives, but they inspired work in other areas, and offered guidance to new groups with different focuses. There are now several employee resource groups working on a wide range of issues and ideas across the organization, with international collaboration and engagement. They now have a VP of Diversity, Inclusion and Belonging based at their head office in Stockholm, and this work is a key part of their strategy.

Elekta shows us that if leaders help people to make changes happen and talk about those changes with colleagues, it will spread enthusiasm and engagement for more things to happen. When progress begins to be made quickly, and this is clearly communicated even to people not closely involved in the work, more people want to become involved and new ideas are sparked.

As work continues, though, and hurdles get in the way, enthusiasm can start to wane as people find progress slow and other priorities they have might prevent them from focusing on this work. This is especially true for those who are not in the driver's seat. We recommend creating an engagement plan early on, which everyone sees right from the start. Spending the time working this out will help to keep your journey going at the pace you want it to.

The engagement plan does not need to be complicated (see Table 11.1). This is about setting out how you want to keep everyone connected to the overall mission, encouraging input and involvement, and tailoring your approach to your different audiences. This will form part of your overall communications strategy, which we'll look at in Chapter 14, so, when we get to that point, bear in mind the lessons from Elekta about encouraging sharing and learning.

Your engagement plan, if communicated effectively, can also be a great recruitment tool to encourage more people to volunteer to contribute to the project.

Changeable conditions

A core part of maintaining enthusiasm depends on helping people to navigate changes that happen as you make progress. And, as we've already seen, change makes people feel uncertain, which can make them fearful. Even if this change is for the better. With workplace changes, the main fears are around what they might mean for individuals, their role and their daily lives. While they are worrying about their future, there is a risk that they could become disengaged in their work, and, even worse, they could become detractors and encourage others to feel fearful and negative about the

TABLE 11.1 Example engagement plan

Audience	Interests	Concerns	Messages
Primary audiences			
Staff	• How will I be supported? • How will this help me do my job (better)? • How will I be given support to develop my career? • Will I be protected from negative behaviour? • What changes will there be to the working environment? • What changes will there be to the organizational culture? • Will this help me collaborate more effectively with my colleagues? • How can I make my voice heard? • How can I improve my knowledge and skills in diversity and inclusion? • What are you doing to benefit people like me? • Are the leadership team committed to this work?	• Is this going to lead to real action? • Is this going to affect my role or my job security? • Are we going to have time to do this work? • Is this going to mean more work for me? • What if I get something wrong? • How might this impact my mental wellbeing? • Will this make me stand out (as a minority)? • Will this make me unwanted (as a member of a majority group)? • How will leaders perceive me?	• Why we chose to start an inclusion journey • What an inclusion journey is • What we have learnt • How you contributed to the output • What our Inclusion Journey Roadmap is and what goals we're working towards • What actions we will be taking • What this means for you • How you can be part of taking this work forward • How we will make space for you to take part in this work • How you can feed back on how this work is progressing • How we will update you on the progress of this work • What results we will be able to share and when we will share

Customers	• What are you doing to support people in our networks? • How can I improve my knowledge and skills in diversity and inclusion? • Will this change how we work with you? • How will this be perceived by our audiences?	• What an inclusion journey is and what it does • The results of the inclusion journey and what these mean • What we've learned from the Inclusion Journey Mapping • What our Inclusion Journey Roadmap is and what goals we're working towards • How we will update you on the progress of this work • What results we will be able to share and when we will share them

Secondary audiences

Potential staff	• Will this be a positive environment to work in? • Will I be welcomed into this environment? • Will I be supported to develop my career? • Are there other staff members like me? • Have there been issues before? • What if I get something wrong? • Will I stand out or be hired as a token (as a minority)? • Will I be unwanted (as a member of a majority group)?	• The results of the Inclusion Journey Mapping and what these mean • What we've learned from the Inclusion Journey Mapping • What our Inclusion Journey Roadmap is and what goals we're working towards • What actions we will be taking • What results we will be able to share and when we will share them
Media	• What tangible impact is this having? • What are you doing differently to other organizations? • What lessons are there for others? • What positive stories are there? • How will this be perceived by our audience?	• The results of the Inclusion Journey Mapping and what these mean • What our Inclusion Roadmap is and what goals we're working towards • What actions we will be taking • What results we will be able to share and when we will share them

project. Of course, some people do enjoy change and will be ready for it – there will be a mixture of responses. But, since research shows that 63 per cent of people fear uncertainty in their future, we need to consider carefully the conditions we want to create to help people feel comfortable with the journey as it unfolds.[2] The best way to reduce uncertainty is to plan carefully for implementation.

Those doing the driving also need to create an environment ready for change in the work that they are doing. Nothing in the roadmap is absolute. Plans and actions can be moved and changed as you progress and as the conditions change. You will learn new things, and have different ideas along the way, and you need to be able to flex appropriately. You will also need to adapt to issues outside the project itself. There could be a change in the organizational structure, for example, or a new CEO, or economic fluctuations which require a new approach. Consider the drastic changes brought about when the world went into lockdown during the 2020 pandemic. Most businesses had to change everything they were doing at a rapid pace. The most flexible organizations fared the best and were able to continue operations with less disruption than those who were more rigid in their approach. People need to know that changes can, and probably will, be made.

On the flip side, those who are not so closely involved in the work need to see that change is happening to believe in the journey. Regular progress updates encourage confidence and help everyone to recognize the value. Checking items off a list gives people a real sense of moving forward, and provides them with a surge of dopamine that an achievement has been made. This encourages them to keep moving, and keep making progress. This also helps you collect more people who want to join you in your travels and help drive things ahead.

With all of this discussion around change, it is useful to look at some change management models to help you manage this. There are several different models which are widely used across different organizations, and which can be used to frame your inclusion journey. Some of them have been mentioned briefly already in other chapters. To help you consider which method is best for you, we will look at each one in a bit more detail here.

The 8 Steps For Leading Change – John Kotter[3]

The change model developed by John Kotter, a leader in change management theory, '8 Steps For Leading Change', is used by a number of companies all around the world. The diagram (see Figure 11.1) is often spotted on

FIGURE 11.1 Kotter's 8 Steps For Leading Change framework

SOURCE www.kotterinc.com/methodology/8-steps

office walls. The success of this method lies in the fact that it is easy to implement in a variety of organizations and it is not dependent on a particular industry. It's visual, so the diagram can be displayed for staff to see and use in their work. It's a simple process, which explains how to drive change and keep the momentum going as you do so. To create this model, Dr Kotter observed leaders who were trying to drive transformation across different organizations. He noted what he saw working well to sustain change, and he used this to create the framework. He also recognized that change needed to be ongoing, and so designed his model to be circular.

Each stage in this framework has a definition to help people understand how to drive changes effectively. There is a book[4] that accompanies the model, which provides more detail about each stage, but the following is a summary of the key points.

GIVE A REASON

It starts with telling people about the need for change to happen. The principle is that there must be a need for change in the first place. We must create a sense of urgency. Why is this important? And why is it important now?

What data and other evidence can you use to convince people of the need for change? Work on clearly articulating a compelling reason, or perhaps several reasons, why this change must take place now. Examples we have seen work well are talking about gaps in strategy. Perhaps you are struggling to recruit right now? If you are, data about the need for new staff and the challenges being experienced, the costs of not recruiting the right people, and sector-wide issues around recruitment or competition for roles, as well as about the impact of inclusion on recruitment, would create a compelling sense of urgency for this work.

TAKE ACTION

Then, once those wheels are in motion and people have seen there is a need for change, you can move on to building a team of enthusiastic people, and to enabling action by removing barriers which might slow down any progress. So there might be processes you need to change, or budgets to allocate to allow change to happen. The method describes the importance of generating quick wins early on to show people that progress is being made. This builds momentum. Then you need to sustain acceleration to keep things moving after the initial successes.

CHECK AND EVALUATE

The final stage in this model is about evaluating and making sure that changes, replace old habits to become how you work now. The new mindsets and behaviours maintain that environment where change can happen. This means that there is no slipping back on the progress that has been made, and that there is an organizational culture of assessing strengths and opportunities and taking appropriate action.

Fair Process Leadership – Ludo Van Der Heyden

The model developed by Ludo Van Der Heyden at INSEAD Business School[5] emphasizes transparency in communication about change. There is open engagement with all stakeholders, who can get involved in sharing their ideas about what changes could happen. This requires leaders to engage and connect with their teams. It is a model about listening more than telling people things, and asking what they think should happen. The steps to the process are shown in Figure 11.2.

Changes are framed and communicated to people as an idea that something needs to happen, and people are told the reasons why. So, for an inclusion journey, this can be framed with data that makes a compelling case. Then the work focuses on listening to what people think. This can be done in a variety of ways, including group discussions, individual conversations, surveys, polls and listening groups. Van Der Heyden encourages pushing people to really consider different perspectives in this engagement. He advocates methods like groups wearing different hats to consider what another group might think about something in order to consider all options. This model is about reaching out and considering a range of perspectives and options before making any decisions, so it is well suited to an inclusion journey.

This model is not about decision-making by committee. It is about gathering all the possible ideas and options from a wide range of people before making decisions. With this model, people are asked what they think, and time is taken to hear from people. Then a leader or leadership team (or perhaps the inclusion journey project team) takes the ideas and inputs from everyone to decide on actions and a way forwards.

This approach means that people see they have a voice and that they will be listened to if they speak up. They can see that there is value being placed on their opinion and people want to hear from them about their ideas. Even if, in the end, their particular idea is not taken forward, they still feel valued. And this sense of being valued and listened to means that they get on board with new ideas, including the ones that weren't theirs.

FIGURE 11.2 Fair Process Leadership model (diagram adapted from the Fair Process Leadership Model at INSEAD)

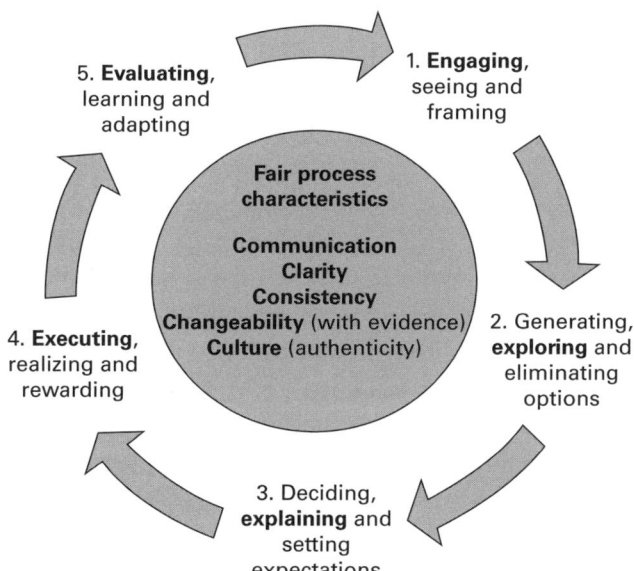

This model also has a phase for evaluation so that there is learning along the way to embed changes and to see what other approaches need to be considered. The evaluation phase can involve going back to people to find out more about what they think to help shape the way forward. Continuing to engage with people, telling them about changes and asking for feedback along the way is a core part of this model.

This model requires strong levels of trust to give people space to work as they choose to, and also the patience to allow people the time to consider ideas and have their say. We are often asked if this means decision-making will be slower. The answer is yes, gathering all these inputs will mean that the decision-making process takes more time. However, when you get on to taking actions, everything will be quicker. Employees are quicker to mobilize and get involved in the changes as they already know they will be happening. They are already engaged, so they are quicker to contribute and take action. There are also fewer questions and concerns raised to hold progress back. This method is all about trust, openness, justice and a fair process for change.

Teal Leadership – Frederic Laloux[6]

The third model is for leadership rather than focused specifically on change, but it does enable changes to happen in a different way as it empowers people to work in a different way. Frederic Laloux wrote his book *Reinventing Organizations* to describe how businesses were developed with leaders making decisions for employees to implement, and how this traditional approach can be disrupted and changed. People in traditional types of organizations expect leaders to tell them about changes, and they go to leaders to ask for decisions about changes they want to make.

This model uses colours to describe models of leadership: 'red' organizations focus power and control around a leader; 'amber' organizations have layers and hierarchies to manage people; in 'teal' organizations, instead of 'command and control' style leadership – where leaders tell employees what they must do and monitor how they work – people are empowered to take ownership themselves. People are asked to work in the way that suits them, and make decisions based on what they think is the best way to deliver on the purpose. This enables faster decision-making as people take responsibility for change and progress themselves. In this model there is no 'typical' way of working. Difference is valued, so if someone has a different way of doing things, they are welcome to follow their approach. People are encouraged to bring their whole selves to work, and not hide who they are and how they think things should be done.

For this method, the initial work is on creating a clear purpose, mission and values. Then time is spent to make sure that all employees understand the purpose and how it relates to their role. And then people are empowered to make their own decisions, work as they choose to and report back as they feel they need to. People are encouraged to ask for support if they need it, but if what works best for them is to work more independently, in a different way, at different times, or using different technology or approaches, then that is all fine. The key thing is to stay true to the overall purpose. If there is uncertainty, people can check back to the purpose and see if they are making a decision that fits with that.

In organizations that use this model, leaders have a coaching relationship with their team. They trust their employees and do not need to control them and check on everything all the time. The coaching relationship is about asking people questions, helping them to seek answers and supporting them to feel they can make decisions themselves.

This way of working is a good one to look at for inclusion, and especially so for driving change. If decision-making is more distributed and not held by a leader or group of leaders, it means that different voices can be heard and different people can take responsibility for actions. The responsibility for leaders becomes to create a strong purpose and communicate that to people. And to consider what will help people to take responsibility themselves for taking action.

So that's three models we have seen work well in engaging people and creating the conditions and momentum needed for change. Consider if any of these models will work well for you in moving your inclusion journey forwards.

Acceleration and momentum

Whichever change model you use, or if you use your own model of change, you are seeking to drive acceleration and maintain momentum. This has to be front and centre of discussions about strategy and the future. The momentum will only be maintained if it is a priority area for all departments in the organization. Without this focus you may see that things start to slow down or fizzle away.

Dina Knight is Chief People Officer at Datatec and Logicalis Group,[7] an international multi-skilled solutions provider of digital enablement services. She has had a varied career in technology and telecoms in several global organizations, leading the people teams with a focus on driving change. She has experience in changing the talent pipeline and changing the demographics of leadership teams across large organizations. In her roles, there have often been specific challenges to address, such as an ageing workforce or needing more women in senior roles. She talks about driving change with acceleration. So when she is talking to leaders she asks them to consider: who is the next CEO? Which people in the organization are ready to replace them? Who can progress to a more senior role right now? She asks leaders to consider taking some chances. Which people may not be 100 per cent ready, but with coaching and help could take responsibility for a senior role now, and be supported to make a success of it?

This approach of asking leaders to think creatively and take risks has driven positive results in every role Knight has had over her varied career. She has created award-winning apprenticeships, and talent schemes to develop future leaders, and at Datatec she surprised her colleagues with how quickly the People team can make changes in how they work. She believes in helping people to make decisions and make changes, and supporting them along the way, which drives change at a faster pace and accelerates momentum.

She encourages all leaders to see that areas of focus such as diversity, inclusion and sustainability are part of the overall business goals, not separate things. In her role at Datatec, she reports on inclusion goals to the board regularly, which keeps the roadmap on the agenda so it does not get forgotten. It is front and centre of discussions for all leaders in the company.

For employees, what they see is the support and engagement of the People team and the leadership team in the work they are doing. They see decisions being made and they see communications about what the priorities are for inclusion. There are several employee groups focused on these priorities, so that staff are involved in the work. Employees see the difference in who is appointed to new roles, and they know about training and talent programmes for those who want to progress into more senior roles.

This creates a culture where people are not afraid of change, and they are able to make those changes happen. There will be hurdles and there will be different courses to navigate, but showing people what is happening and why, and helping them to get involved will mean you create an environment ready for change. Encouraging leaders to make bold decisions about promotions makes change happen faster at the highest levels. When you see organizational change stalling, it is often because the ideas behind it have not been thought about carefully enough. Taking the time to learn about methods of driving change will keep your journey moving at the pace you want it to, even when there are bumps in the road – and we will look at how to navigate challenges in the next chapter.

Notes

1   Interview with Dee Mathieson, MD Elekta Ltd, December 2023
2   T Bauer. Adapting to change: How to master it, personally and professionally, www.fingerprintforsuccess.com/blog/adapting-to-change (archived at https://perma.cc/QDA2-UCPX)
3   Kotter. The 8 Steps for Leading Change, www.kotterinc.com/methodology/8-steps (archived at https://perma.cc/34G7-C4QA)
4   Kotter. The 8 Steps For Leading Change E-Book, www.kotterinc.com/8-steps-e-book-download/ (archived at https://perma.cc/H84V-2J89)
5   I C Woodward, E A More and L Van der Heyden. 'INVOLVE': The Foundation for Fair Process Leadership Communication, INSEAD, February 2016, https://sites.insead.edu/facultyresearch/research/doc.cfm?did=57856 (archived at https://perma.cc/GY38-WDHN)
6   F Laloux. *Reinventing Organizations*, www.reinventingorganizations.com/ (archived at https://perma.cc/6JEJ-WR6N)
7   Interview with Dina Knight, Chief People Officer at Datatec and Logicalis Group, November 2023

12

Bumps in the road

You've now put in a huge amount of work to plan this project and get it off the ground. It's tempting to think that, with all this effort, everything should just run smoothly. Unfortunately, with something as complex as inclusion work, that's rarely the case. That can be a tough fact to face, given that you're probably already feeling tired and like you've had to push a boulder up a hill to get this far. Don't worry, though. In this chapter we're going to look at how you can keep moving even when the road gets bumpy. As we saw in the previous chapter, being adaptable in your approach is key if you want this work to go the distance – remember that this is a long-term, perhaps permanent, project, not one that will be finished and ticked off neatly, so it needs to be able to flow alongside, and as part of, everything else the business is doing as standard. In short, we need to be ready for anything.

Common setbacks

These are some of the most common issues we see organizations facing as they progress along their journeys, and guidance on how you can deal with them.

Backlash

We've already discussed the fact that, not only will some of your team not be entirely enthusiastic about this work, but some might be actively opposed to it. We talked in Chapter 4 about how to get some of these people on board in the first place, and how the results produced as you go along will start to win them round. Attitudes to diversity and inclusion tend to ebb and flow, however, often inflamed when a media storm arises, or provoked by particular actions taken by the business. We've seen clients suddenly face backlash from staff when they've introduced a programme to develop underrepresented staff, for example (grumbles of 'Why are *they* getting special treatment? What about people like me?'), or when they've moved a regular staff party from the normal, popular venue to one that was accessible for wheelchair users ('But we *always* have our staff party there, this new place is rubbish!').

At Watch This Sp_ce, we ourselves get a flurry of angry emails and social media messages every time right-wing news outlets run stories on the perils of inclusion. It's a Yuletide tradition for us, now, to wait for one right-wing outlet in particular to dig out one of our blogs on how workplaces can make their festive celebrations inclusive for everyone and slap a headline on it claiming that we're cancelling Christmas – the emails we get then are quite something, but it usually results in a spike in website traffic that does wonders for our search engine visibility! Sadly, the media will periodically run stories claiming that inclusion is here to destroy us all. These stories are written to stir up fear, and they work, so you may see staff who had previously been fairly disinterested in your inclusion efforts suddenly becoming resistant or even actively antagonistic when this sort of negative feeling is provoked. You might find also members of your external audiences starting to voice opposition to your work. You may even get your own social media trolls popping up. Don't worry, though. It's never fun dealing with these kinds of messages, and you need to make sure your staff have the appropriate training and mental health support to deal with it. But, if you've been clear on the why behind your actions from the start, then these incidences present opportunities for you to talk to your staff and wider audiences about the reasons for this work, the impact it will make and the way in which it is rooted in your mission and values. Difficult conversations can be worrying – that's why we provide training specifically on handling challenging conversations, because so many people find them stressful and confusing – but if you have laid the solid foundations for your choices, then you will have the confidence and skills to have open discussions about the benefits for everyone.

GETTING IN FRONT OF THE STORY

You can do a lot to mitigate the chance of backlash occurring in the first place by communicating effectively. We'll cover your ongoing communications strategy in more depth in Chapter 14, but people are far less likely to feel fearful or resentful of changes if they know exactly what is happening and why.

The *why* behind your work should be a major focus of all your communications. Go back to the data that you gathered in Chapter 1 and the business benefits you mapped in Chapter 3 to remind everyone of the practical value of this work and how it will be good for everyone, and regularly return to the link with your organizational mission and values that you set out in Chapter 6 so that *everyone* is reminded, frequently, that this is a core part of what you stand for as an organization. With regular discussion and ongoing sharing, this should become embedded within the collective psyche of your team, and people are more likely to then come to see it as part of the status quo rather than something threatening. When dissenting voices do speak up, you are standing on solid ground from which to explain the point of all this, referring them back to the objectives and values that you're working towards.

Any new changes or implementations should be communicated widely before they occur, to help people feel informed and to give them greater understanding of what is happening and why – this will vastly decrease the likelihood of people becoming upset by work that's taking place. When changes come as a shock, or people aren't clear on how they will be impacted, it tends to trigger a feeling of panic. If everyone is clear on the what, how and why, and on any changes that affect them directly, they are usually much more comfortable.

It's also worth keeping an eye on the media for any news stories that might provoke reaction. Not only will that mean you can take a proactive approach to supporting staff where they need it (more on that in Chapter 13), but you will be prepared for any negative emotions that might be stirred up amongst your team or wider audiences, and you can prepare a response just in case one is needed.

HAVING THE CONVERSATION

No matter how prepared you are, however, some pushback is bound to occur at some point. If particular concerns are raised – let's say someone is worried about you putting in a gender neutral toilet, for example – then you will need to be willing to have a conversation with the person who has brought it up, and, depending on the nature of the issue, you will likely need to put out communications to your wider audiences to explain the situation. The important thing is to acknowledge the concerns of those involved, without compromising on your values. Remember the example of Barclays Bank in Chapter 6, who apologized for taking a stand on what they believed in – there's a fine line to walk between recognizing where some people might be experiencing fear or uncertainty, *and* staying firm in your values. You can welcome people to share their concerns with you, listen with empathy and compassion, tell them that you've heard their views, share any steps you might have determined are appropriate to mitigate or support them *if* that is in line with your commitment to inclusion, and then explain to them the benefits of this work and why it is right (in terms of business benefits and values) that it goes ahead.

With the example of concerns about toilets, this might involve sitting down with people who have raised concerns to ask them to explain clearly exactly what they are concerned about. They may say that they are worried about the safety implications of toilets being open to different gender identities. You can then tell them that you have heard their concerns, and that you don't want them to feel unsafe. You can either share with them any risk assessment that you have undertaken, or commit to performing a risk assessment, and ensuring that safety features – such as gender-neutral toilets (and, ideally, any other facilities) having floor to ceiling cubicles, or being self-contained, single-occupancy, lockable rooms, and not being in isolated locations. You could also take this as opportunity to look at the safety of all spaces where staff might feel vulnerable – after all, there's nothing to stop a cisgendered man walking into toilets that are designated as female-only if he is intent on assaulting a woman, and it's important to have an honest conversation about these issues with people who have safety concerns, rather than pretending that gender designation is going to magically protect everyone. You could also point out the number of trans or gender-non-conforming people who are assaulted, harassed or verbally abused in single-gender bathrooms if their outward presentation is perceived to not align with the gender identity stipulated by the facilities, and clarify that their safety also needs to be protected.

The important thing is to leave any conversation about concerns with an acknowledgement that voices have been heard, assurance that any legitimate worries have been taken into consideration, and clarity on what the next steps are and why.

DON'T FEED THE TROLLS

You need to be able to distinguish, as well, between what you consider a legitimate concern, and what is an unreasonable viewpoint. A question about safety, for example, is worth reviewing to ensure that any potential problems have been identified and dealt with. Whereas, if you begin offering return-to-work coaching for birthing parents coming back from parental leave, and someone complains that this support shouldn't be made available because those new parents 'belong at home with their children instead of returning to work', then this complaint can be confidently dismissed as not in line with your organizational values. You need to come back to your unique values and your definition of inclusion to be clear on what is open to discussion and what is not.

If someone is simply 'trolling' – making inflammatory comments or accusations in a deliberate attempt to cause distress and/or provoke anger or upset – you need to end the conversation swiftly, and not allow their rhetoric any air time. Trolling is most common online, usually where people can be anonymous with their attacks; in this environment, the best course of action is to just block their account and delete any posts or comments that occur within spaces you control. Engaging with them will only make the situation worse, and could cause distress to people affected by their messages.

This kind of 'trolling' behaviour can occur in real life, too. It appears to be less common, as people rarely want to be visible in openly discriminatory or aggressive views, but it has been known for staff members or other stakeholders to use forums, Q&A sessions or meetings to make a series of unpleasant comments or inferences. If you have the behavioural guidelines in place that we discussed in Chapter 7, these incidents should be reasonably straightforward to deal with. For staff, this behaviour should be a clear instance of misconduct, and you will have a procedure in place to deal with that. For other stakeholders, too, you will want to have a clear process for dealing with behaviour that contradicts your policy.

In the same way as we don't want to give discriminatory and/or abusive comments attention online, we want to avoid giving these views oxygen to build and spread in real life as well. If this behaviour occurs in an in-person format, or an online meeting, the person should be removed from the space immediately and told why. The remaining attendees should be told that these comments are in breach of your organization's behavioural guidelines and not in line with your values, and so the person has been removed. If comments have been submitted via digital methods, they should be deleted from public view, with an apology issued to anyone who might have seen those comments. If the comments have not been publicly shared, they should remain private, but your behavioural guidelines and disciplinary process should still be followed.

For this to work effectively, everyone needs to be clear on those behavioural guidelines and your disciplinary process. These should be living documents that are regularly interacted with – ways you can bring them to life include:

- regular team-building days that explore your values and associated behaviours, referring staff back to the guidelines
- periodic team meetings that reflect on the values and behavioural guidelines
- reminders during leadership business updates about the culture you are trying to create and how that works

These are useful ways to keep bringing attention back to how staff are expected to treat one another – and to make them aware of what will happen if they breach that trust you have placed in them.

Errors and complaints

We've said it before, but it bears repeating – mistakes will be made. We are all flawed human beings, and it's inevitable with something as sensitive and complex as inclusion work that someone (or the whole team) will get something wrong or inadvertently cause upset.

We spoke in Chapter 3 about the process for dealing with these missteps:

- Acknowledge the problem
- Apologize, unequivocally
- Listen to where you've gone wrong and how you could do better
- Learn from the mistake
- Communicate about how you'll put that learning into practice

When there's a complaint or mistake, it can panic senior staff, and sometimes make them want to cancel the whole project. This is where your crisis plan (we mentioned this in Chapter 3, but we'll come back to it in a moment) comes in handy – remind your team that you planned for this, and that this was always supposed to be a journey of learning. Gather data to show that this hasn't negatively impacted the business – from following up with complainants to demonstrating that you've resolved the issue to their satisfaction, to reviewing changes in staff engagement or external audience approval. Remind your leadership team of the examples we saw in Chapter 3 that demonstrate that 'cancel culture' isn't really a thing, and that complaints can actually be *good* for business, if you handle them effectively.

Changes in personnel

Probably the factor we've seen create more issues for inclusion journeys than any other, is changes in key personnel. There are two major ways that this can impact a journey – change in leadership and change in the inclusion team.

CHANGES IN LEADERSHIP

You did a lot of work at the beginning of this process to get the leadership team on board – so when someone who was a major advocate for this work at C-suite level moves away from the business, it can be a huge blow. Perhaps their replacement doesn't see the benefit of inclusion work, or is actively against it. Perhaps this person was the main reason you got board level buy-in for this work in the first place, and, now that they've gone, the rest of the leadership team are wondering if they can just drop the whole thing. Don't panic – it's time to go back to basics.

PLANNING AHEAD

Relying on just one member of the leadership team to be your champion puts you on dangerous ground. Maybe you can only get one of the leadership team to back you at first, and that at least gets the wheels in motion, but you shouldn't rest at that one person and then sit back. Make it your aim to win over more of the C-suite as time goes on.

Take opportunities to sit down with different members of the leadership team and discuss the results you're seeing from the work you've done. Ensure that you're presenting to the leadership team as a whole on a regular basis to show them results. Always relate the results you discuss to the wider organizational goals (remember the business benefits mapping exercise we did in Chapter 3?) so that they can see the benefits *for them.*

Provide the champion that you do have with the tools to talk to the rest of the leadership team about the progress of the project, the results and the benefits. If they are armed with the information they need, they will be able to have honest and open conversations to encourage their colleagues to share concerns or misgivings so that they can address them.

SUCCESSION PLANNING

When you know that your key member of the leadership team is leaving, work with them on a plan for what happens next. If they have been the sponsor for this project, how can they help you recruit a new sponsor? How will they make clear in their handover to their replacement that this work is valuable and is to be supported? What steps can you both take to safeguard the upcoming stages of the project, whether that means securing budget and/or sign-off for key activities now, or getting agreement for plans going forward?

A smooth handover does wonders for the success of a project – an incoming member of the leadership team is much more likely to just allow work to continue if it's moving along smoothly rather than taking the time and effort to dismantle it. However, if effort is required on their part to make it work, they might not want to bother. So make sure that, before the outgoing person leaves, everything is lined up as carefully as possible to continue with minimal effort on the new person's part. This includes getting the data and evidence you need to show that your efforts are working and that continued work will yield worthwhile results.

Demonstrating the reputational value of the project is important, too. A new member of the leadership team is unlikely to want to be the person to pull the plug on inclusion work if they think it will look bad publicly. So gathering data on staff, customer and wider audience satisfaction with this work, and making sure your commitments for the future have been outlined publicly (so that it's difficult for the leadership team to back down from them), could help carry momentum forwards.

Changes in the inclusion team

If the coordinator leaves the business – or has to step away from the role of coordinator owing to workload – this can leave the project without clear guidance. If members of the working group leave or step away, this can also destabilize the project and reduce morale.

HAVING A BACK-UP

In any major project, it's a good idea not to be entirely reliant on one person. If all knowledge, skills and power are held by one person, you're asking for trouble. That person could become ill, they could get head-hunted elsewhere or they could win the lottery and leave work altogether. It's always good to have a few deputies, and a central store of all necessary information. Whilst one person holds the main role of coordinator, a couple of members of the working group might support them in this role and fill in for them from time to time, so that they know the ropes and they're able to step in if there's an emergency. When the working group is up and running, take a look at who the most enthusiastic and committed members are, and invite them to get a little more involved and support with the coordination. It also helps to spread the load, so that no one person is taking on too much.

Similarly, whilst you have a core working group who are responsible for the delivery of your roadmap, you can look around to see who else across the organization is really interested in this work and is a champion for inclusion in general. They might not be part of the main working group right now, but they might be given smaller tasks and asked to help encourage enthusiasm for the work more broadly, and they might also be invited to share their thoughts and feedback on how things are going to show that you value their support. If you keep these people engaged, they could be future members of your working group when new recruits are needed.

Some organizations rotate membership of the working group, changing who attends meetings on a quarterly or bi-annual basis. This means that a much wider variety of people get involved with the work and means that there's less reliance on particular people. It does mean, however, that there is less continuity in terms of the knowledge and understanding in the room. The role of coordinator then becomes even more essential to maintain that thread throughout the process. It also becomes even more valuable to have a central store of information.

Any project needs a digital 'brain' – a place where all information and resources are stored, where careful records and plans are kept, and where staff can access facts and learning that they might need along the way. This could be a shared drive, document portal or project management system. We've all been in a situation where the one person who knew everything about a project was suddenly ill or quit, and everyone else was left completely in the dark. As coordinator, in particular, getting as much of the information that's in your head into some sort of organized system is vital.

Training and learning should be consistent across the organization as well. It can be tempting to only provide certain training to key members of staff, because they're the ones that will be working on the project (and because it's cheaper to provide training to fewer people), but then, if they leave, the skills and knowledge leave with them. And, although it costs more to train your entire staff body, you don't want to be in a position where only a select group of people understand what inclusive behaviour looks like and how to implement inclusive practices. The more understanding of inclusion and inclusive practices that you can embed across the organization, the better – not only do you avoid losing that person who knows everything, but you build a company culture where *everyone* is skilled at including everyone else.

SUCCESSION PLANNING (AGAIN)

Just as with your member of the leadership team, you need a clear succession plan for your coordinator. If someone else needs to take over the role – even temporarily – you want them to be able to pick it up smoothly so that you can continue on your journey without too much waiting around or confusion.

Keeping documentation about your roadmap up-to-date – including what actions are required, timelines, responsibilities and measurements, as well as any course corrections or re-forecasting (we'll be looking at these in the next chapter), is crucial. The data that shows what objectives you're working towards, how these relate to organizational goals and how you're making progress against these is vital to keeping everything on track, so the more straightforward that you can keep the recording and displaying of this data, the better.

MAINTAINING MORALE

The biggest challenge when people leave is the impact this has on the people left behind. When someone who has been pivotal to the success of a project is suddenly gone, the rest of the team can feel anxious or dispirited about the future. At this point, it's a good idea to celebrate the work that this person has done, and the successes that you've all achieved together. You can use that important data to show how far you've come, and look back at the roadmap to see how far you've travelled. We'll talk more about celebrating success in Chapter 17, and it really does wonders for a team that have their head down for long periods of time, trekking over tricky ground.

Then you will want to regroup the team, go back to that vision you outlined at the beginning and why this matters to you all, and look at what steps are next in the roadmap and how you're going to tackle them. Renew the sense amongst the team that you've done hard things before, you can do them again – and the end result is going to be so worth it.

Business challenges

Another big hurdle is when the organization as a whole hits some turbulence that pulls focus from this work. If the business is facing crisis or disruption (such as supply chain issues or an economic downturn), you might find that the powers-that-be – and maybe the wider team in general – lose their faith in this project. They might feel there are bigger problems that require attention (not to mention budget), or they may simply feel that it's not a priority right now.

We've been here before – in Chapter 3 we talked the leadership team through why this work would support those bigger problems and priorities, and we mapped the business benefits accordingly. This is a good time to go back to that benefits mapping exercise, and look at what the organization needs to achieve now in order to navigate this new challenge. You can then demonstrate how progress on the inclusion journey will directly contribute to the bigger picture.

You can also go back to the data we highlighted in Chapter 1, about how diverse and inclusive teams are far more effective at spotting, surviving and learning from a crisis, as well as how much more successfully they make decisions. Your sponsor will come into their own here, in championing how important maintaining the inclusion journey will be to overcoming the difficulties the organization is currently facing. If the inclusion journey has had a chance to make some decent progress, you will be able to use results you have already generated to prove just how valuable this work has been to the wider business objectives.

There is also the reputational value to consider – as we saw in the case of new leadership personnel, maintaining an awareness of how this work is perceived across the team and externally can make clear the dangers to the business of giving up on this work.

Funding and resourcing issues

Another, likely related, challenge is when the business runs into financial or resourcing problems. Sometimes, although everyone in the organization might fully recognize the value of the work and be completely committed to keeping it going, the money or the staff or the tools they were relying on using are suddenly, for whatever reason, not there. This can sometimes be the biggest challenge of all, because it's not about changing anyone's mind or proving the value of your work, it's about actions simply not being possible on a practical level.

We've witnessed this in action a few times, and we'll share an example of how it can be navigated.

CASE STUDY: CHARITY FUNDING

We worked with one large charity, who were strongly committed to their inclusion journey. They threw themselves enthusiastically into the journey mapping process, and worked hard to engage their huge group of geographically disparate volunteers in the Discovery and Implementation processes. Work was just getting underway on their roadmap, when they hit a blockage on the path.

The UK's cost-of-living crisis was drastically impacting the costs involved in delivering their services, and they'd also seen a drop in donations. This was painfully squeezing their budgets. As the impact of this was beginning to be felt, their Chief Executive had to step away from the organization for personal reasons. They were facing a very difficult time, trying to keep the charity itself on course, and delivering the services people were relying on, without key personnel and with reduced resources.

It would have been easy to put inclusion aside completely. But, for them, that was never an option. They were dedicated to the vision they had set out during their Discovery process – and they'd communicated this vision to their volunteers, many of whom had been heavily involved in shaping it, and there's no doubt that there would have been a highly negative reaction if the work had been abandoned. Yet they knew they couldn't deliver at the scale they had originally hoped for.

So we sat down with the leadership team, and we formulated a plan. We looked at the key priorities that had been identified during their Discovery process, and the actions that sat alongside them. Then we asked ourselves, "What one thing can we do that will make the biggest impact for each of these priorities?" For each priority area, there were many actions that would be valuable, but not all of them would be possible in the current situation – however, of those that were still possible, we identified the ones that would make the biggest impact. And we focused on those.

We put together a much smaller, more cost-effective and less time-intensive roadmap, that would be achievable in the next six months, whilst the leadership team worked on steadying the ship as a whole. We then worked on communicating to their volunteers and wider audiences that, whilst work had to be scaled down for now, it wasn't stopping; that this was a journey that they were committed to for the long term; and that this was only the beginning. It might be a slow beginning for now, but they were determined to do what they could. We also shared some of the quick wins that were taking place, so that everyone could see what was being achieved.

The volunteers embraced this news, and were thrilled to see that action was still being taken even in difficult circumstances. They also recognized that the organization they loved was facing some challenges, and something pretty special happened – they started looking at how they could help. Volunteers across the country began coming forward with skills or experience they had gained in their day jobs that might be useful on the inclusion journey. They offered to take on elements of the roadmap that would have originally been delivered by staff, or to support the delivery of the actions that were already underway. They shared resources of different kinds to help fill gaps. And the journey really began moving forward. Once everyone saw how committed the organization was, and how they were willing to do whatever they could to make progress, everyone rallied together to help take them even further.

Remember the (crisis) plan

In Chapter 3, we talked about the need for a crisis plan, or a 'what could go wrong' plan, to give it a slightly less intimidating title. This is where you want to try to think of every possible problem that might arise, and then set out the steps that you will take to deal with each one. Once you, and your team, know that you have a plan in place for the worst-case scenarios, they feel much less frightening and much more manageable.

A good 'what could go wrong' plan needs the following elements:

- The problem
- The potential impact
- Who needs to know?
- Who can help?
- What needs to be done?
- What needs to be communicated?

Table 12.1 shows an example of an entry on a 'what could go wrong' planning document (bear in mind that every plan will look different, depending on the nature of your organization, and this example is just to help get you thinking):

TABLE 12.1 Crisis plan

The problem	Potential impact	Who needs to know?	Who can help?	What needs to be done?	What needs to be communicated?
Social media complaint about inclusion activities	• Negative impact on business reputation • Distress to staff • Distress to wider audience • Stirring up of negative feeling towards inclusion work amongst staff	• CEO • Head of Communications • Operations Director • Board of Trustees • Relevant Employee Resource Groups	• Marketing team • Mental health partner • Employee Resource Groups • Inclusion champions	• Establish if this is a genuine complaint or a troll • Issue a public response • Follow up with complainant to establish if their complaint has been resolved • Issue a statement to staff clarifying organizational values and any relevant actions/next steps • Work with Employee Resource Groups to connect with and support impacted employees	• Outcome of the complaint • Organizational values and commitment to inclusion • Next steps • Signpost support for anyone affected

This document should be familiar to everyone involved in the inclusion journey. Your working group and your sponsor – as well as, potentially, key members of the leadership team – should be involved in creating it, and the working group should collectively revisit it regularly to make sure it's up-to-date and that everyone knows what's in it. Panic has a habit of clearing out all relevant information from people's brains, so if an issue does crop up, then, even when everyone's in the grip of all the fear and worry that is likely to ensue, they have been programmed to look to the plan for guidance.

Both your roadmap and your crisis plan need to be adaptable. Change is inevitable, and you need to build all plans with an openness to that fact. With each action on your roadmap, consider what is required to make it happen, and what you'll do if that element faces problems. Add that to your 'what could go wrong' plan. It might not seem the most cheery task to think about all the ways your roadmap might be thwarted, but it's the best way to ensure that that doesn't happen!

The cheer squad

When things go off-course, you need your cheerleaders. Those people throughout the business that you identified right at the start as being passionate and enthusiastic about this work – this is where their voices are particularly useful. Keeping them motivated and engaged along the way, and celebrating their contribution, is the best way to make sure that they'll be there when you need them.

Encourage them to have conversations with their colleagues about this work, whether informally or through elements like 'lunch and learn' presentations or team meetings. Arm them with data and information they can use to talk about the positive results of this work, and how it ties into future plans. Above all else, encourage them to be enthusiastic voices whenever they hear dissent or uncertainty, to remind everyone why this work is good for everyone. Humans are pack animals, and if negative voices are speaking unchallenged, the group is likely to assume that that's the herd mentality they should follow. If other voices rise up in support, however, people are more likely to stop and assess what they truly think of this work, and which side they want to be on. It may also cause the doubters to feel that, if the prevailing wind is blowing in that direction, they might as well flow that way too.

Managing wellbeing

One final note on dealing with challenges – they can take a toll on people's mental health. Whether it's the team working hard on this project only to see it being held back, or members of staff hearing attacks on their personal identity, or the uncovering of tensions amongst teams over how they view this work, it's vital to take care of everyone's mental wellbeing.

For the team involved in this work, setbacks and negativity can be highly demotivating. Keep everyone focused on the end goal, and celebrate how much progress you've made. Reflect regularly on the impact your work has had and why you're doing it. Whilst there will be a lot of big, long-term actions to work on, make sure these sit alongside smaller, quicker wins that you know can be completed so that everyone has a regular sense of achievement and progress.

There's also something to be said for considering how you approach challenges as an organization. Julian Roberts, an Executive Business Coach who specializes in team resilience, recommends 'flipping the script' when you face setbacks. 'Instead of seeing this as a challenge', says Julian, 'we go, "what opportunity does this represent for my business?" And the moment you do that, you start to think differently. And just the word "opportunity" in your brain is more positive, and it means, what creative ideas, what things are possible? Rather than "challenge" feels very blinkered.' Julian recommends to his clients that they work with their teams on using challenges as a springboard for creativity and expansion, and this mindset shift does a lot to support team wellbeing and resilience in the long term.[1]

You may wish to engage an external mental health partner to help you look after the wellbeing of your wider team – this is a positive thing to do anyway, not just in relation to inclusion work. You have a duty of care to your staff, and, if you look after them, they will pay you back – for every 2 per cent increase in staff happiness, revenue grows by 1 per cent.[2] Employee Resource Groups can also be valuable in supporting staff from under-represented or marginalized identities, who can then offer one another the community and shared understanding to navigate issues, as well as providing a collective voice to raise possible solutions or gaps that need to be addressed.

That sense of community is something you want to cultivate across your whole organization, too. The more that everyone feels they are all in this – both the inclusion project and the work of your business as a whole – together, the more they are likely to come through challenges together.

It can be a challenge to access a sense of community as an inclusion coordinator. Often, you're doing a lot of the heavy lifting alone, and you might not have the sense of being part of a team, of having people to turn to for help or simple camaraderie, that you find in other parts of your work. Where possible, treating the working group as you would treat any other team within the business can help – have team away days, set up communications channels for them to share ideas, challenges and general chat, and allow them to come together regularly. You can also connect with people engaged in inclusion work in other organizations, looking for forums or communities of practitioners that you can be part of. This not only allows you to share learnings with other businesses, but gives you a larger community to feel part of. You can also join The Sp_ce, which is a purpose-built community of inclusion changemakers across a wide variety of sectors, where you can access guidance and resources from the Watch This Sp_ce team, as well as sharing ideas, challenges and solutions with professionals who know what you're dealing with. You can find the details at watchthisspace.uk/the-inclusion-journey.

Notes

1 Interview with Julian Roberts, Executive Business Coach, November 2023
2 H Stewart. Happy workplaces are more profitable [blog], happy, 4 May 2017, www.happy.co.uk/blogs/happy-workplaces-are-more-profitable/ (archived at https://perma.cc/S3PH-XJR5)

13

Course correction

You'll have noticed in the previous chapter that the main way to handle any issues, challenges or disagreements on direction is to make sure you are recording and analysing relevant data. In this chapter we'll examine in more detail what you need to be tracking, and how you can use that information to guide your next move.

There are various different data and information points that you can measure, and it's important not to get overwhelmed by it all. It's vital to differentiate between what you *can* measure and what you *need to* measure, so that you're putting your valuable time and effort into tracking the right things, and the pertinent information isn't getting lost amongst the noise.

Key performance indicators

As a health check of your organization's approach to diversity and inclusion, there are a few key measures that you should be recording as standard. They are:

1 diversity across your team

2 diversity through your recruitment funnel

3 staff retention rate

4 staff engagement rate

5 pay gaps

6 external reputation

7 complaints of bullying, discrimination, harassment or exclusionary behaviour

Diversity across your team

This is a case of understanding the demographics of your organization as a whole, how they relate to the demographics of your wider community and how they are dispersed across the business.

Questions to ask here are:

- Does the demographic make-up of our staff body accurately reflect that of the geographical areas from which we recruit *and* of the customers we serve?

- Is diversity evenly spread across our organization or do we have a higher proportion of people from underrepresented identities in junior roles than senior ones?

- Are there any teams or departments that lack diversity more than others?

- Do we have different staff communities/networks to support belonging, and have we provided the support and resources to enable these networks to be created and maintained?

Diversity through your recruitment funnel

To effectively track the impact of your inclusion efforts on recruitment, you want to measure demographic data at every stage of the process – ensuring that this data is entirely anonymous and is separated from applications before they are assessed. There are a number of HR tools that will anonymize applications for you, but if you're relying on doing it manually then make sure the person that sees and files the demographic data has no influence on the assessment process, otherwise that rather defeats the point.

Figure 13.1 is what your recruitment funnel might look like.

You might have slightly different stages, and you can create a map of your own funnel that's tailored to your specific process. Then you can track the demographics at every stage: who is applying for your jobs; who makes it through the initial application assessment stage; who gets through to interview; who progresses to further stages; and what the demographics are, in general, of people who are offered jobs. You can also track who accepts jobs, and whether there are any demographic trends among those who turn you down. If you're getting a high number of female applicants dropping out of the process, for example, that could be an indication that something about the process, the personnel or the environment is putting them off as they engage further with you.

FIGURE 13.1 Recruitment funnel

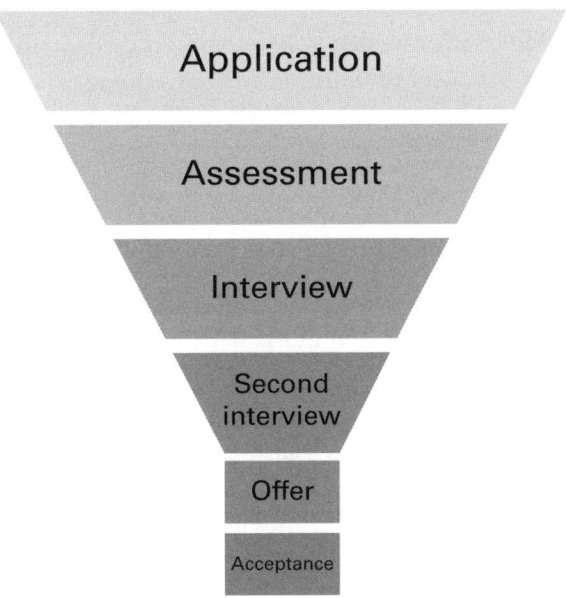

Retention rate

How included you make your staff feel, and how well you nurture a sense of belonging, will have a huge impact on how long they choose to remain in your business. When employees leave a role, 54 per cent don't feel valued, and 51 per cent don't feel they belong.[1] It isn't only their *own* sense of inclusion and belonging they're concerned with, either – staff who don't have confidence that their organization is committed to diversity and inclusion are three times more likely to quit than those who do.[2] Tracking your retention rate over time is, therefore, not only a great indicator of how your business is performing when it comes to diversity and inclusion, it's also a barometer of how much faith your staff have in you to deliver on your stated diversity and inclusion intentions.

Your retention rate will inevitably change over time, and measuring these changes, and mapping them to any new inclusion initiatives that have been introduced, will help you to understand the impact your efforts are having. It's also vital to segment your retention rate by demographics and role – it's all very well seeing that your retention rate is strong, and perhaps increasing, overall, but if you're finding that your retention rate is disproportionately low amongst staff with disabilities, for example, or that staff at a particular level or in a particular department stay with you for much less time than staff elsewhere, then there is an issue that requires further investigation. There are HR platforms that will gather all this data anonymously for you, which is the best way forward; but, failing that, you can take regular staff surveys that take demographic data and ask questions about length of service and other inclusion indicators.

Engagement rate

When staff don't feel a sense of inclusion and belonging within an organization, only around 20 per cent of them are engaged. However, amongst those who do feel a sense of belonging, engagement rises to 91 per cent.[3] That is quite the impact. When you consider that staff engagement increases profitability by 23 per cent,[4] this is clearly an area that needs attention.

Measuring engagement is tricky, as it's far less tangible than concrete elements like whether someone is actually in a job or not. There are, however, a few elements that demonstrate strong engagement:

- **Staff turnover** – as we saw above, happy and engaged staff tend to stay in their roles.

- **Absenteeism** – happy and engaged staff tend to take less time off, and also see improvements in their physical and mental wellbeing meaning that they *require* less time off.

- **Employee net promoter score** – asking a question along the lines of 'How likely would you be to recommend working here to a friend?'

- **Promotion rate** – professional growth and development are key contributors to staff engagement.

- **Employee surveys** – asking questions about how motivated, valued and engaged staff are is, of course, a good indicator, but be careful in how you put these questions together, as, even when surveys are anonymous, humans are programmed to give the answers they think you want to hear; working with someone who knows how to structure questions and dig beneath the surface can be very revealing.

One such expert is Bonamy Waddell, Data Storyteller and Founder of Bon Insight: 'I work on numerous employee surveys every year, with organizations ranging from 12 through to 3,000+ employees,' Bonamy told us. 'Each one provides valuable insight into the "temperature" of the organization at a given moment – amplifying those "water cooler" conversations into a much wider pool of evidence to show the overall "health" of your employees. Showing that, as a leadership team, you are listening to everyone – and crucially, that you are then responding to what's been said by making change – is vital. We all want to feel heard.'[5]

As with retention, it's vital to segment these results by demographics, department and seniority, and to map changes to any wider business changes or inclusion initiatives.

Pay gaps

Whether or not your staff are being paid fairly is a strong indicator of the organization's commitment to inclusion.

A note here – under UK[6] and US[7] law, it is illegal to prevent your staff from discussing salaries. Some companies still put clauses in contracts to forbid employees from disclosing their salary to one another, but, not only are these not enforceable, they don't do much to instil confidence in your staff that you're dedicated to inclusion. (And remember how much more likely they are to leave if they don't have confidence in you in that area?) Allegra once worked for a company where the MD sent round an email to all staff informing them that it was a disciplinary offence to discuss their salaries. Almost immediately, staff began to quietly gather to ask each other what they were being paid. If you tell people not to talk about salaries, they will assume they're not all being paid fairly, or why would you try to silence them? The repercussions of them then discovering that there is a glaring inequality that you've tried to cover up could be huge. Regardless of your country's legal obligation in this area, the best thing that you can do is identify and monitor any pay gaps, be transparent about these and commit to narrowing them. That way, staff don't feel that you're trying to hide anything, and they have faith in you to address the problem.

If you have HR software that anonymously collects demographic data alongside role information, then this will be easy for you to do without needing to make information requests of your staff. Otherwise, you may need to begin with staff surveys and look to implement a more efficient recording model for new joiners as time goes on.

Ideally, you would be able to measure pay gaps for a wide range of areas, such as gender identity, ethnicity, disability, sexuality, religion, parenthood (as we know there is a significant pay gap for mothers, in particular) and age. (Age is a complex one, as experience and seniority often come with age, meaning there is likely to be a natural correlation between age and salary;

but it is still worth measuring, as other factors can come into play, such as staff above a certain age being devalued.) Looking at how these factors overlap is also important, as the impact of intersectionality cannot be understated. In the US in 2022, for example, a Hispanic woman would earn $6.50 for every $10 earned by a white man, whereas the average Asian woman earned $9.30.[8]

We regularly hear organizations saying, 'We don't really have a gender pay gap, because the reason men earn more than women in our business is because the men occupy more senior roles.' That is largely the point. Yes, it's vital to know if men are being paid more than women for a role at the same level (and if that difference applies to any other demographic factor), but if a disproportionate number of senior roles are going to a particular demographic, then that, too, is a problem that needs to be addressed. Pay gaps are not only about like for like, they are also about whether one particular type of person has better financial opportunities within your organization than others.

External reputation

The public perception of your commitment to diversity and inclusion is almost as important as the reality. Doing great work is wonderful, but if your wider audience don't know, or don't believe, that it's happening, it will lead to a lack of trust amongst potential candidates and customers, and could reduce confidence amongst your staff.

This is another somewhat intangible element to measure, but there are some pointers to track:

- Ratings on review sites like Glassdoor, where current and former employees share their views on a business
- Customer reviews and feedback
- Exit interview data can tell you a lot about what former employees are likely to be saying (more on exit interviews in a moment)
- Sentiment of mentions of your business on social media platforms
- Customer surveys
- Focus groups
- Competitor analysis

You can look for feedback that relates specifically to inclusion, and at your reputation more broadly. People often have feelings towards a brand or a company without properly knowing why, so measuring how your reputation changes as your inclusion journey progresses might show you that your work is having an impact that your audience isn't even consciously aware of.

Complaints

It stands to reason that, if your business is doing well on diversity and inclusion, complaints about discriminatory or inappropriate behaviour will go down. Keeping track of incidents, and how the incident rate changes over time, is vital, as is monitoring how these incidents are dealt with and how victims feel about the resolution and the process afterwards. You can also look at the outcome of complaints, and whether these are impacted by demographic factors – are white women more likely to have complaints upheld than Black women, for example? Are complaints of racist behaviour more likely to result in action being taken than complaints of homophobic or transphobic abuse? Why might that be?

It's worth noting that, counter-intuitive though it might seem, complaints may increase when you first begin your diversity and inclusion work. If you are putting effort into making clear to your staff what behaviour is considered unacceptable and that this behaviour should be strongly dealt with, and you are working towards a more psychologically safe environment where your staff feel more able to be open and to raise concerns, then you may see more staff coming forward about problematic behaviour. It might not feel like it, but this is progress – this behaviour was happening anyway, it's just that your staff now feel able to tell you and are confident that you'll do something about it, whereas they weren't before. Now you have a better idea of the scale of the issue, and you can tackle it more effectively. Then, over time, you can expect to see complaints reducing as your journey moves forward.

There will likely still be staff who don't feel safe to raise complaints, though. It can be useful to use periodic staff surveys to ask people whether they have a) witnessed and b) experienced bullying, discrimination or harassment. If these surveys are fully anonymous – and especially when they're administered by a third-party organization who are seen as neutral – you may get a more accurate picture of the situation. You can also ask about timescales, asking whether these incidents have been witnessed/experienced in the last a) five years, b) two years or c) 12 months. This will give you a sense of whether things are improving over time. As your journey progresses, that will be even more important to know.

Deeper investigation

Whilst the above are key performance indicators that give you a sense of your impact on diversity and inclusion as a whole, there are also some more specific measures that you can look at that relate to particular issues or objectives.

For most of these areas, you will need to use staff surveys to obtain the information you need. As we've seen already, these surveys need to be completely anonymous, they need to contain demographic questions so that you can segment the data and identify any patterns, and, where possible, using a third party organization to administer the survey can encourage more honest engagement as people feel it's less likely that anyone with the power to fire them will be able to figure out what they said. You don't want to do these surveys too often, as that will be onerous for staff and will probably reduce the engagement rate. On the other hand, if you do them too infrequently then you are waiting a long time to see whether your work is having any impact. From our experience, quarterly or bi-annually tend to work well. Some organizations choose to break the surveys up into much smaller chunks, sending out 'pulse' surveys of just a few questions every week or month. This means that over the course of, say, a six-month period, all the necessary questions get answered, but they are more spread out and so take less time for staff.

Bonamy Waddell says that, in her experience:

> creating a pattern is key – employees are aware that twice yearly, for example, they will be asked a series of questions relating to particular areas of the workplace, and their role within it. But what really builds trust is action! Taking those responses, acting on what has been said, and really showing that every voice has been heard – that's the critical point. From quick wins, to longer term solutions, make sure that each survey begins with 'Thank you for sharing your views – as you might be aware, the following changes have been implemented in direct response to the last survey…' and list what you've done! This not only builds trust, it underpins their sense of belonging and feeling valued.[9]

It's not only staff that you might choose to survey, either. For some organizations, wider stakeholder surveys might be important. If you have volunteers, members, partners or other groups that are heavily involved with your work, it is worth gathering inputs from them so that you have a wider view of the situation.

Access needs

One of the most basic elements that needs to be covered before your staff can fully contribute to and engage with, and even get through the literal and metaphorical door of, your organization, is access needs for all.

Periodic anonymous staff surveys that ask staff whether their access needs are being met is the best way to monitor this, and you should also ensure that managers are regularly checking in with their reports as to whether there's any more that could be done to support them to perform at their best. In the survey, you can also ask whether staff have felt able to ask for any adjustments they need (as this will tell you a lot about the sense of psychological safety and the confidence in your commitment to inclusion amongst your team); and, if they have, whether they feel their request was fully and effectively responded to, and whether this was done in a timely fashion.

You should also keep track of all requests for adjustments, and the responses, along with dates so you can see how long it takes for adjustments to be acknowledged and provided. You can also see if any patterns emerge as to what support needs might be being neglected.

Values

We've talked a lot about the importance of clarifying your organizational mission and values, and how these are to be practically implemented on a day-to-day basis, so you need to check in with your staff that they are, in fact, clear on these matters. Ask your staff how well they understand a) the mission, b) the values and c) how these relate to their day-to-day activities. However, staff may think they understand it all very clearly, but whether their view matches the one you were trying to communicate is a different matter. So, depending on how high on your priority list this work is, you might wish to delve deeper by asking more questions about what exactly the values are and what they mean, and other more practical elements.

Another indication of your team's perspective on your values and culture is to ask them how seriously they believe that you do take, or would take, incidents of bullying, discrimination and harassment. Essentially, you're asking them whether they think you walk your talk. You can also ask questions about the culture of the organization, and how staff feel about elements like team building/social activities. As Bonamy Waddell points out, this could reveal differences in preferences and perceptions of what work culture 'should be'. 'In a post-Covid era,' says Bonamy, 'this may reveal that newer, younger and/or more junior team members place a higher value on social activities/team building than those who've been at the organization for longer, or are more senior (and often therefore more "socialized" within the organisation).' Alternatively, those who joined the business, or the workforce in general, during 'pandemic conditions' may be more comfortable with connecting remotely with colleagues than those used to more traditional approaches. Data can help you uncover and address these differences of opinion without making unhelpful assumptions.

You can also ask the staff about how valued they feel by the organization, and how important they feel their personal contribution is to the overall mission. Staff who feel truly included and engaged have a clear sense that what they do matters to the success of the business, and that that contribution is recognized and appropriately rewarded.

Communication

Effective communication and collaboration is one of the cornerstones of inclusive environments, and one of the biggest indicators of whether your efforts in this area are working. Ask your team questions such as:

- Do they feel able to communicate effectively with colleagues?
- Do they feel able to share their ideas and thoughts?
- Do they feel able to make suggestions on organizational plans?
- Do they feel able to challenge existing ways of doing things?

Remember that communication is a two-way process, so you also want to understand how well they feel they're being heard. Do they think there are enough opportunities for them to provide input and feedback to the leadership team? Do they feel that their voices are heard? On this point, you can also look at the engagement rate with the feedback mechanisms you do have in place – if people aren't using them, it's probably more likely that they're not confident they'll have an impact rather than that they have nothing to say. You can also look at how these inputs are responded to in order to assess whether they might be right.

Progression and development

As we've seen, when staff feel that there are progression and development opportunities for them within an organization, they are much more engaged.

Asking questions about whether staff feel they receive enough training and development support, and whether they receive the training and development support they need, as well as whether they believe there are career progression opportunities available to them and whether they're being supported to work towards these, will tell you a lot about whether they feel the organization is working for them as much as they are for it.

As before, segmenting these responses by demographic data will show you any patterns that need addressing. Do neurodivergent staff find it harder to access development support? Do staff who are parents feel less confident in their career opportunities? If you are using your HR software to track promotions, you will also be able to look at objective figures alongside that perception and see if they match, or if you have a reputational issue to overcome.

Exit interviews

One area that we see many organizations neglecting is their exit interviews. It's understandable that businesses feel tempted to skip this part – if the person is already on their way out the door, what's the point? Well, not only is it incredibly valuable for your reputation as an employer to do everything possible to leave that relationship on a positive note, but exit interviews are a highly valuable source of data. Bonamy Waddell agrees: 'When I'm workshopping the results of an employee engagement survey with a client, it isn't uncommon for them to say of a low mark or poor comment, "Oh, I know why they said that, but they're leaving anyway so we can ignore it." No! Whilst it might lower your scores, their comments are still valid and acting on them may be the difference between losing or retaining other members in that team – ignore these comments at your own risk!'

Outgoing staff are so much more likely to be honest with you than staff who are staying. After all, they've got less to lose – they're leaving anyway. You can ask these people some very important questions about their views on all of the elements above, as well as the reasons why they are leaving, and you'll likely receive some very interesting answers.

As well as qualitative questions, it is worth having some questions that have a numerical value attached, such as 'On a scale of 1 to 10, with 1 being not at all and 10 being very much, how seriously do you believe this organization takes inclusion?' This will give you some quantitative data that you can measure over time. You can also ask staff to voluntarily provide demographic data alongside these questions (if they are happy to do so – this data can be anonymized in the same way as data from job applicants, but in smaller organizations where staff leave in smaller numbers, it may not be possible to guarantee that people won't be identifiable from their answers by those who are monitoring the data), so that you can track any patterns.

What to do with all this data

You're now gathering a great deal of information, and it's important that it doesn't just sit on a virtual shelf. It should be regularly reviewed and used to inform the actions you take. Making sure all of your team are well versed in what the data means is an essential part of the journey.

Reporting

You will need to understand where your biggest priorities are, what data should be your main focus and what data can be looked at less often or as part of a more general health check, otherwise you will quickly find every minute of your day taken up with analysis and reporting. This will be guided by the prioritization you set when you created your roadmap, as well as the wider organizational priorities. Then you will need a plan for reviewing and taking learnings from your data. Your data monitoring schedule might look something like this:

- Monthly check-ins of top priority data with inclusion working group
- Bi-monthly review of priority data with sponsor
- Quarterly update of priority data to leadership team
- Quarterly updates of priority data to wider team
- Bi-annual health check review
- Annual full report

You want reporting to be as easy to read and understand as possible for your colleagues in the working group, for the leadership team making decisions on future resourcing, and for the wider business and your external audiences, as well as being as undemanding as possible on your time. So keep it simple, and relate everything back to those organizational priorities that everyone can connect with.

Forecasting and reforecasting

When you put together your roadmap, you identified overall goals to work towards (such as increased representation of women in senior roles or an increased level of staff engagement). So your first stage of data gathering will be identifying how you will measure each of those goals, and establishing what your baseline position is. From there, you can forecast an achievable target. For example, if your goal is to increase representation of women in senior roles, you will need to find out that, currently, 26 per cent of senior manager or leadership roles are held by women. Thinking about how many roles are actually available, how many are likely to become vacant each year and how many new roles are likely to be created, you might then determine that it's not realistic to shoot for complete gender parity within the next 12 months, but that a reasonable target might be to aim to see 35 per cent of roles at senior manager or leadership level held by women within the next three years. At the end of that three-year period, you can then look at what would be a reasonable timeframe for you to expect to reach full gender parity.

Progress is never as linear as would look nice on a graph, however. You might start out well, and at the end of year one you might have 30 per cent of senior manager or leadership roles held by women. You're 44 per cent of the way to your target and only 33 per cent of the way through your time-line. So, since such positive progress is being made, perhaps you might increase your target – could you reach 40 per cent by the end of year three? To decide that, you'll need to think about what caused this spike in progress. Have you had a recruitment drive that's not likely to be repeated? If so, increasing your target probably isn't advisable. But if new roles have been created, and you're expecting a similar rate of growth to continue in the next year, then increasing your target sounds entirely sensible.

However, at the end of year two, perhaps progress hasn't gone so well. Perhaps some of your female team members left, and, although some more were recruited, you've stayed fairly static and 31 per cent of these senior roles are held by women. Again, you'll need to look at what's likely to happen in the coming year – you might be expanding to a new region, and many more senior roles might be being created, in which case, you might still hit your target. Alternatively, you might not be anticipating much recruitment at senior level in the next year, in which case your target might have to be reduced.

Reforecasting a target to a higher level is a much more exciting prospect than reducing it down. Communicating to your core team and the wider business that you're doing so well that you've put your target up is great for morale and enthusiasm. Telling people you're behind is less encouraging. However, it's really important that you do tell everyone, otherwise it looks as though you have something to hide. You can also then involve your team in finding solutions to why you haven't made as much progress as you wanted to, and supporting you in redoubling efforts. Keeping an eye on your progress, and adjusting your targets to keep them realistic is vital for understanding what's working and what isn't, and for maintaining engagement and enthusiasm with this work. How you communicate your results and your learnings to your working group, your sponsor, your leadership team, the wider business and your external audiences is vital to the success of this project. And we'll look at how to do that in the next chapter.

Notes

1 A De Smet, B Dowling, M Mugayar-Baldocchi and J Spratt. It's not about the office, it's about belonging, People & Organization blog, McKinsey & Company, 13 January 2022, www.mckinsey.com/capabilities/people-and-organizational-performance/our-insights/the-organization-blog/its-not-about-the-office-its-about-belonging (archived at https://perma.cc/X3ZC-8F6J)

2 L Brown. Employees who don't trust their business on diversity 'three times more likely to quit', People Management, 21 January 2019, www.peoplemanagement.co.uk/article/1746697/employees-three-times-likely-quit-no-trust-business-diversity (archived at https://perma.cc/BQK2-8CDL)

3 C Herbert. Belonging at work: The top driver of employee engagement, qualtrics, 16 September 2022, www.qualtrics.com/blog/belonging-at-work/#:~:text=According%20to%20our%20research%2C%20only,and%20a%20half%20times%20more (archived at https://perma.cc/M8JU-NN8T)

4 Workplace. The benefits of employee engagement, Gallup, 20 June 2013, www.gallup.com/workplace/236927/employee-engagement-drives-growth.aspx (archived at https://perma.cc/M4NX-CAE4)

5 Interview with Bonamy Waddell, Data Storyteller, February 2024

6 Equality Act 2010, www.legislation.gov.uk/ukpga/2010/15/part/5/chapter/3 (archived at https://perma.cc/W8UD-MXJW)

7 National Labor Relations Board. National Labor Relations Act, www.nlrb.gov/
   guidance/key-reference-materials/national-labor-relations-act#:~:text=In%20
   1935%2C%20Congress%20passed%20the,workers'%20full%20freedom%20
   of%20association (archived at https://perma.cc/4V7G-Z2Z8)

8 R Kochhar. The Enduring Grip of the Gender Pay Gap, Pew Research Center,
   1 March 2023, www.pewresearch.org/social-trends/2023/03/01/the-enduring-
   grip-of-the-gender-pay-gap (archived at https://perma.cc/FYK7-APBH)

9 Interview with Bonamy Waddell, Data Storyteller, November 2023

14

Travel updates

In the previous two chapters, we've looked at how to navigate challenges, and how to keep track of, and interpret, your progress. While you're doing all of this work, it's vital that you keep everyone up to date with these learnings and changes. Part of the wider impact of inclusion work is inspiring a shift in culture within your organization, demonstrating the culture you believe in to your external audience, shaping your wider reputation and being an influence for change in the wider context of your industry, community and the world. So in this chapter, we'll go through the process of creating a long-term communications strategy that will keep everyone informed, engaged and involved, whilst also enabling and encouraging input and feedback along the way.

Establishing the need

Who needs to know?

The first thing to establish is what audiences you need to speak to. Each of them will require different information at different levels of detail, and at different frequencies.

The audiences you will have are likely to be:

- inclusion working group
- sponsor
- wider leadership team/board
- inclusion champions
- wider staff

- additional stakeholders, if applicable (members, volunteers, partners, parent company, etc)

- customers/clients

- media

- general public

Depending on your particular situation, you may identify additional audiences.

The next thing to do is to determine which audiences are your main priorities. Again, this will be unique to you, but 'Company X' separate theirs like this:

Primary audiences

- Inclusion working group

- Sponsor

- Leadership team

- Inclusion champions

- Wider staff team

Secondary audiences

- Customers

- Sister companies

- General public

- Media

For this company, the priority and the main focus is engaging with their internal team, and external audiences can have less detailed and less frequent communications on this topic. If your brand reputation is a major part of your priority objectives, then customers and the general public might be higher up the list. You might even split your audiences into three groups instead of two. There is no right or wrong way, as long as you understand the difference in attention that each audience requires – as we saw in the previous chapter, you can't do everything.

What do they need to know?

Once you know who you're speaking to, you need to consider what you want to tell them. As we now know, you have plenty of information to convey, but not everyone needs or wants everything.

The first thing to establish is, what does each audience care about and what might they be worried about? You'll have learned quite a lot about the interests and concerns of your staff and leadership team during the Discovery process, which will give you a head start on this. You can also engage the working group and inclusion champions in defining this further. For external audiences like customers, you could consider short surveys or focus groups, or you could use social listening and review customer feedback data, as well as looking at wider trends and media discussion.

Company X arrived at the conclusions shown in Table 14.1.

Once you know what they care about, and when you've done the work we covered in the previous chapter to understand what you have to say, then you can plan who to tell what to.

For Company X, their plan looks like Table 14.2.

The highlights

There are a few important elements that it is vital all audiences are aware of:

- Why diversity and inclusion matters and how it benefits the whole organization and all individuals (not just those from minority or underrepresented groups).
- You are committed to making meaningful change.
- You are grateful to everyone for their contributions so far.
- You want your work to include everyone.
- This will be a long-term project – it will take a while to see results and the work of developing and strengthening your approach will never be done.
- You are open to and eager for input and feedback.
- This is a continual process of learning – no organization or individual is perfect, and mistakes will be made, there will be differences of opinion on the best approach to take, but by working together and committing to listening and learning, you can all move forward.

How are you going to tell them?

The next part of the process to consider is the way that you will communicate all of this information. This involves the methods you'll use, the frequency of different communication elements and the way that you share your updates.

TABLE 14.1 Interests and concerns

Audience	Interests	Concerns
Primary audiences		
Inclusion working group	• How will this role benefit me? • How will I be supported in this role? • How can we make real impact? • What actions are going to have a tangible impact? • How will we know if it's working? • How can I improve my knowledge and skills in diversity and inclusion? • What are you doing to benefit people like me? • Are the leadership team committed to this work? • What changes will there be to the organizational culture? • Will this help me collaborate more effectively with my colleagues?	• How will I have time to do this work? • What if I get something wrong? • How might this impact my mental wellbeing? • Will this make me stand out (as a minority)? • What if it doesn't work? • What if there is backlash?
Sponsor	• How can we make real impact? • What actions are going to have a tangible impact? • How will we know if it's working? • How can I improve my knowledge and skills in diversity and inclusion? • How will this support the wider business objectives? • What data do we have to support this work? • What progress is being made? • What do we need to have in place to make this work?	• What if it doesn't work? • What if we make a mistake? • What if there is backlash? • Is it worth the money?

(continued)

TABLE 14.1 (Continued)

Audience	Interests	Concerns
Leadership team	• What actions are going to have a tangible impact? • How will we know if it's working? • How will this support the wider business objectives? • What data do we have to support this work? • What progress is being made? • How does this impact our reputation?	• What if it doesn't work? • What if we make a mistake? • What if there is backlash? • Is it worth the money?
Inclusion champions	• How can we make real impact? • What actions are going to have a tangible impact? • How can I make my voice heard? • Are the leadership team committed to this? • Are concerns being listened to? • What changes will there be to the organizational culture? • Will this help me collaborate more effectively with my colleagues? • What are you doing to benefit people like me? • How will I be given support to develop my career? • Will I be (better) protected from negative behaviour?	• Is this going to lead to real action? • How might this impact my mental wellbeing? • Will this make me stand out (as a minority)? • Will this make me unwanted (as a member of a majority group)? • How will leaders perceive me? • Are the people leading this work engaging with it on a deep level? Do they have the necessary knowledge and training?
Staff	• How will I be supported at work? • How will this help me do my job (better)? • How will I be given support to develop my career? • Will I be (better) protected from negative behaviour? • What changes will there be to the working environment? • What changes will there be to the organizational culture?	• Is this going to lead to real action? • Is this going to affect my role or my job security? • Are we going to have time to do this work? • Is this going to mean more work for me? • What if I get something wrong? • How might this impact my mental wellbeing?

- Will this make me stand out (as a minority)?
- Will this make me unwanted (as a member of a majority group)?
- How will leaders perceive me?
- Will this help me collaborate more effectively with my colleagues?
- How can I make my voice heard?
- How can I improve my knowledge and skills in diversity and inclusion?
- What are you doing to benefit people like me?
- Are the leadership team committed to this work?

Secondary audiences

Customers
- Is this going to lead to genuine, meaningful change?
- Why are you doing this work?
- Do you care about people like us?
- How can I make my voice heard?
- What do you believe in/stand for as an organization?
- What actions are you going to be taking?
- What impact will this work have?

Sister companies
- How will this be perceived by our customers?
- What if there are mistakes?
- What if there is a backlash?
- What impact will this have on our staff and their expectations?
- What actions are you going to be taking?
- What impact will this work have?
- How does this impact on us?
- How does this relate to wider organizational/group objectives?

General public
- Is this going to lead to genuine, meaningful change?
- Why are you doing this work?
- What do you believe in/stand for as an organization?
- What meaningful changes have you made?

Media
- How will this be perceived by our audience?
- What tangible impact is this having?
- What are you doing differently to other organizations?
- What lessons are there for others?
- What positive stories are there?

TABLE 14.2 Communications plan

Audience	Message
Primary audiences	
Inclusion working group	• What work is needed and why • Who is responsible for each action • Timelines and deadlines • Progress against objectives • Impact on wider business objectives • Any blockers or challenges • Feedback and input • Next steps
Sponsor	• What work is needed and why • Timelines and deadlines • Progress against objectives • Impact on wider business objectives • Any blockers or challenges • Feedback and input • Next steps • Any changes to roadmap • Resources/support needed
Leadership team	• What work is needed and why • Progress against objectives • Impact on wider business objectives • Feedback and input • Any changes to roadmap • Resources/support needed
Inclusion champions	• What work is needed and why • Progress against objectives • Impact on wider business objectives • Opportunities for input from them and wider team • Next steps • How they can support
Staff	• Why this work matters • How priorities have been identified • What actions will be taking place • How this work will impact you • Timescales

(continued)

TABLE 14.2 (Continued)

Audience	Message
Staff (contd.)	• Progress against objectives • Impact on wider business objectives • How you can input • What input we've received and what we're doing about it • How you can be part of taking this work forward • How we will make space for you to take part in this work • Any changes to roadmap
Secondary audiences	
Customers	• Why this work matters to us • What priorities we've identified • What actions we're taking • Progress on key priorities • How you can provide feedback • What customer feedback we've received and how we've acted on it
Sister companies	• Why this work matters to us • What priorities have been identified • What actions will be taking place • How this work will tie in with collaborative objectives and actions • Progress against objectives • Impact on wider business objectives
General public	• Why this work matters to us • What priorities we've identified • What actions we're taking • Progress on key priorities
Media	• Why we're taking action, why it matters to us and how we identified our key priorities • Key actions we're taking • Key milestone results

Methods

Given that you're communicating about plans for inclusion, it's vital that the way you communicate is inclusive. It's also important to engage, enthuse and motivate people with the project, and to make it as comfortable as possible for people who might feel uncertain or wary.

Some top tips to address both of those objectives include:

- **Keep it simple** – people don't want to trawl through loads of information, so only share what they need to know and use bullet points, visual representations (like graphs and diagrams) and pulled out stats or quotes to summarize and highlight the main takeaways, then you can also make more detail, in the form of reports or data dashboards, available for people who are interested.

- **Use a variety of methods** – people take in information in different ways, so try to vary the ways that you communicate, including writing, video, imagery, audio, presentations and meetings.

- **Make it a two-way process** – we'll talk more about feedback later in this chapter, but it's important that you're not simply broadcasting, and that you're listening as well.

- **Explain why** – keeping people aware of the reasoning behind the actions, including the organizational values and the benefits to the business, helps everyone to feel more positive about it and connect to it.

- **Make it tangible** – with inclusion work, it's easy to get lost in high ideals, but most people want to understand what, practically, is going to happen and how it's going to impact them.

- **Have a schedule** – people value knowing what information they're going to receive and when, and you also want to make sure you're not overloading people, so plan out a communications schedule (more on that shortly).

- **Never forget accessibility** – subtitles on videos, alt text on digital images, written transcripts for audio content, sign language interpreters and/or foreign language interpreters where required for meetings and presentations, being considerate of colour contrasts and font sizes, and all of the usual accessibility requirements in communications apply (see some best practice guidelines at the end of this chapter).

FREQUENCY

The frequency of your communications will depend a lot on the level of detail that your audiences need and how involved they are in the project. Company X have the communications schedule as shown in Table 14.3.

Remember that every organization is different, so your plan will be unique to your business, but this should give you a template to get you started.

TABLE 14.3   Communications schedule

Audience	Message
Weekly	
Inclusion co-ordinator	Data check-in
	Feedback review
Monthly	
Inclusion working group	Progress update
	Actions review
Sponsor	Progress update
Staff	Progress update
Quarterly	
Inclusion working group	Strategy review
	Feedback review
Leadership team	Strategy update
	Feedback review
Sponsor	Strategy update
Staff	Strategy update
	Leadership 'Ask Me Anything'
Inclusion champions	Progress update
	Feedback review
	Strategy review
Customers	Progress update
General public	Progress update
Media	Press release on key achievements
Bi-annually	
Staff	Insights survey
	Values workshop
Sister companies	Progress update
Annually	
Customers	Insights survey
Leadership team	Annual progress report
General public	Insights and progress updates

Hearts and minds

As we've already seen, people will be coming to this project from very different places. Some people will be thrilled that you're doing this work and be eager to support in whatever way they can. Some will be frustrated that this work hasn't been started sooner and have some feelings of anger about incidents from the past, or a view that you're not doing enough. Others might feel confused or fearful, others might be outright opposed to the concept of inclusion altogether. In order to communicate effectively about this project, you will need to take all of these views into consideration and speak to all these people immediately.

We've already touched on many of the ways that you can do this, so to recap:

- Regularly restate the benefits to the wider business.
- Keep everyone updated on any changes and how these will impact them.
- Ensure the leadership team frequently restate their commitment to this work and clarify that they expect everyone to support it.
- Be open and transparent about the work you're doing, why and how you're doing it, and how it's going.
- Be honest about the limitations – there are probably lots of things that need doing, but you can only do so much with the budget and resources that you have, so be clear that you would like to do more but that you have identified certain priorities to focus on (showing how you arrived at these) and that you can only deliver on these for now.

The human face

Often, people fear or mistrust inclusion work as an abstract concept. When it is made more concrete, and real human examples are given, people tend to respond more positively. If you have staff – perhaps from your Employee Resource Groups or amongst your inclusion champions – who are happy to contribute stories of challenges they've faced and ways that inclusion work has supported them to move forward, then these will be valuable to share. Allow these people to come to you though – don't ask anyone to perform that kind of emotional labour, especially as it could put a strain on their emotional health if they're not completely comfortable. If you don't have employees ready to share stories, you could use stories that are publicly available from other sources, or ask third party organizations to share theirs for the time being – once staff see these, they might come forward with their own.

You can use these real-life narratives to create videos, blogs, social media posts, podcasts, presentations, lunch and learn sessions… there are many ways to engage people with a personal narrative that helps them connect with the meaningful impact of this work.

Engagement

Whatever people's feelings towards this work, they need to know that their concerns are being taken into consideration, their voices are heard and that they will be treated respectfully by the organization. Engaging with your wider team and other key audiences, encouraging and responding to their inputs and feedback, will not only build trust and encourage involvement, but will also give you valuable insights to inform your evolving strategy.

Staff engagement mechanisms could include:

- employee resource groups
- lunch and learn sessions
- staff forums/roundtable discussions
- listening sessions where people can talk, share ideas and ask questions
- real-life and/or digital suggestion boxes
- one-to-one discussions
- surveys
- shared documents/online brainstorming tools/project boards
- regular Q&A (question and answer) sessions with the leadership team (where the option is given for questions to be submitted anonymously in advance if people wish)
- CEO AMA (ask me anything) sessions – these could be questions submitted in advance and answered in regular live streams, in-person events or pre-recorded videos
- regular updates from different teams and/or groups across the organization
- workshop/brainstorming sessions (perhaps on a quarterly or bi-annual basis) to explore opportunities for growth or organizational strategy

The good and the bad

As we've already discussed, sharing successes and celebrating achievements is very important for morale, engagement and motivation, but it's important to frame these 'wins' carefully. For staff that aren't yet convinced that this is the right thing for the business to be doing, overly excited comms might be off-putting. Good news should always be linked to business objectives and tangible outcomes for staff, so that the 'why' behind it all remains front and centre.

On the other hand, as we mentioned in the previous chapter, sometimes you will have less positive news to share. Targets that haven't been reached, or challenges that have held back planned activity, perhaps. In these situations, it's important to be honest and transparent, and to communicate the facts as soon as you're able to. Clarify the reasons behind any decisions or occurrences, and show what response you have planned or ask staff to help you come up with a solution collaboratively. Focus on what you can do rather than what you can't, and reiterate your commitment to this work. After all, it's an ongoing process of learning and you might not get everything perfect straight away, but you can show how you're growing as an organization as you try.

Listening

At some point in your childhood, a teacher probably said to you, 'You have two ears and one mouth for a reason – because you should listen twice as much as you speak.' Sanctimonious though that teacher might have been, they had a point. No communications strategy should ever focus purely on broadcasting. You'll have seen already, from the example plans we've been looking at, that you need to factor in listening mechanisms so that the audiences you wish to connect with can also speak to you.

Feedback and input

As we've discussed, feedback and input mechanisms are vital, and there are many ways that you can solicit feedback from your audiences. The key is to make sure that these inputs are responded to, so that everyone feels that you really are listening. Not every suggestion made will be possible, but just explaining why it isn't possible – or why it isn't possible *right now* – goes a long way towards demonstrating that you do care what people have to say. Of course, if you're saying no to every suggestion, people might start to feel that your interest is fairly shallow, so you need to think carefully about what and how much you're saying no to, and why.

If confidence in the leadership team's willingness to listen and respond is low, for whatever reason, at the start of the project, then you will have to make an effort to encourage input. This might mean holding workshop sessions, asking managers to speak with their teams in meetings or one-to-ones or giving staff very simple requests, such as asking them to vote on a poll related to a particular issue. Once you've started to demonstrate that you are actioning feedback and that you are making progress with the project, you'll find engagement with your feedback mechanisms will gradually begin to increase.

Collaborative design

As far as possible, this should be a collaborative process, where the whole organization is engaged. If you truly want to include everybody, then, well, do so. We began a process of collaborative design with the Discovery Workshops, where your team helped to shape your vision of the future. This approach can continue with ongoing strategy review and visioning workshops as you progress, enabling everyone to feel part of the process and invested in the outcome.

Information monitoring

As well as listening to your stakeholders, it's important to keep up-to-date with the broader inclusion landscape. You will probably wish to monitor:

- diversity and inclusion sector developments
- diversity and inclusion best practice and guidance on terminology, making sure you keep staff training on this topic regularly updated
- diversity and inclusion news from other organizations
- breaking news stories impacting marginalized or under-represented communities (such as the murder of George Floyd in the US and the murder of Sarah Everard in the UK)

Preparing to engage

Most of your communications activity will involve painstakingly collecting information and then transforming it into carefully crafted outputs. Over time, you will probably develop a range of templates for sharing certain types of update. However, some communications will have to be far more reactive and time-sensitive, such as if you need to respond to a breaking news story of the kind we mentioned above.

You can't prepare for every eventuality, but it's worth thinking about the kinds of stories or events that might occur, and putting together draft responses. Apart from anything else, getting sign-off from PR and legal teams, and quotes from relevant members of the leadership team, can take time that you don't have when an immediate response is required. Getting as much as possible ready and approved in advance can make a big difference. Your staff want to see that you're on top of a situation and that you have their best interests at heart, not that you're floundering around trying to draft a response and leaving them to face potentially distressing situations without support or acknowledgement.

A crisis communications plan might look something like Table 14.4.

Your communications strategy will need to adapt and evolve as your roadmap, your priorities and your objectives evolve, so ensure that part of your plan involves regular reviews and updates to make sure it continues to meet your needs as your inclusion journey moves onwards.

TABLE 14.4 Crisis communications plan

Event	Response required	Input prepared	Input required at the time
Tragic news story (such as the murders of George Floyd or Sarah Everard)	Offer direct support to Employee Resource Groups Issue email to all staff, expressing sorrow, letting people know who to talk to if they're experiencing distress and signposting mental health support Press release or social media posts may be required if the incident is relevant to the organization	Response plan agreed with Employee Resource Groups Draft email prepared and signed off by CEO and legal team Draft press release prepared and signed off by Head of Communications and legal team	Check with relevant Employee Resource Group on what support they feel is needed Bespoke CEO or Operations Director quote if possible (sample ones have been prepared which can be used if necessary)
Controversial news story (such as the dismissal of a university lecturer for transphobic rhetoric)	Offer direct support to Employee Resource Groups Issue email to all staff stating our organizational position and offering support to anyone who has been affected, signposting mental health services	Response plan agreed with Employee Resource Groups Draft email options prepared and signed off by CEO and legal team	Liaise with relevant Employee Resource Groups on what support they feel is needed Liaise with inclusion working group and leadership team on our organizational stance

A FEW BEST PRACTICE INCLUSIVE COMMUNICATIONS TIPS

Accessibility

General

- Separate content with clear headings to make it easy for readers to navigate and find the information they want
- Keep information concise
- Avoid jargon, technical terms, acronyms and idioms
- Aim for a reading age of 14 (most people skim read, especially digital content, so this makes it more likely that everyone will take in your message)

Digital content

- Use alt text for images wherever possible, and image captions where not
- Ensure all videos are subtitled
- Ensure a strong colour contrast between text and background
- Do not use too many hashtags, tags or otherwise hyperlinked text close together in social media posts as this makes posts difficult to read
- Make calls to action clear – explain where any links will go to and state clearly what you want people to do next

Emails

- Emails should be written in a font size of 14 or above, *or* with a clear and easy-to-use option to increase or decrease font sizes
- The most accessible fonts are Tahoma, Calibri, Helvetica, Verdana and Times New Roman
- Avoid unusual fonts as these might not be recognizable by certain accessibility devices
- Avoid fonts that have letter shapes that might be easily confused (e.g. lowercase ls, number 1s and uppercase Is which all look very similar)
- Provide a bullet point list summary at the beginning of the email so that readers know what is within the email, then supply the detail below

Inclusion

- Provide a variety of ways that information can be consumed (e.g. written, audio, video) to support different processing styles

- Include imagery, charts and diagrams amongst written or presented content to support visual learners

- Enable people to contribute in different ways (e.g. some people will prefer to discuss ideas openly in a meeting, others might prefer to provide thoughts in writing – meetings and brainstorming sessions could make space for both discussion and for thoughts shared on Post-it Notes or digital whiteboards)

- Before a meeting, provide relevant information for people to review beforehand to give those who want time to consider their views or inputs, and then provide opportunities for those who want to contribute their thoughts later when they have had time to reflect

- Streamline communications – avoid sharing too many updates, for example, and keep content simple and to the point

- Use gender-neutral terms

- Avoid making assumptions about your audience, their experiences, lifestyle and background

15

Sharing the driving

Inclusion isn't the responsibility of just one person. You need a strong ecosystem of people who can collectively drive inclusion progress to drive changes in behaviour and see meaningful impact. Cultivating that ecosystem is vital.

NATALIE RATHNER, HEAD OF SOCIAL IMPACT AT SIMPLY BUSINESS[1]

One person will not be able to design, steer and drive the whole inclusion journey as a solo driver. There are people all around an organization who need to join the journey and see how it connects to the goals and objectives they are responsible for delivering on. In this chapter, we will look at the importance of sharing the work with people as you progress on your journey, ensuring that this includes diverse voices. Given the nature of this work, it's critical that those who have faced under-representation or marginalization are involved in the steering, and that all different perspectives are taken into consideration. Otherwise, the inclusion journey will not be addressing the core areas of focus.

People across the organization will need to learn about being an ally, and passing the microphone to those who may not have had a voice to speak up until now. How can you listen to and involve different types of people and elevate their voices so that different people are in the spotlight and centred in this work?

Shared visions

Simply Business is an insurance provider for small businesses and landlords, with 1 million customers in the UK. It has 1,200 employees, with teams in the UK and the USA covering a range of functions from customer support to technology. It is a B-Corp certified company,[2] with goals around sustainability and social impact. It focuses on inclusion both as an employer and in its customer community of small business owners. Natalie Rathner is Head of Social Impact. Her role is focused on working with colleagues across Simply Business to create connections which drive social impact. Key pillars of work focus on sustainability, diversity, equity and inclusion. Simply Business continues to progress in its inclusion journey, consistently collecting data and putting goals in place to help the company develop. It now has five Employee Resource Groups set up, with networks for neurodivergent, LGBT and Black staff, as well as networks dedicated to gender diversity and mental health.

Each employee network has an Executive Sponsor to ensure there is budget and support, and that priorities are addressed effectively. They see this work as an evolving ecosystem where the work is never 'done', it just progresses to different priority areas. Rathner works with people across all levels and communicates with a variety of people to reach all around the company. They strive to create a culture where people can have open discussions and feel that it's OK to make mistakes and learn as you go along.

Rathner stresses the importance of taking time to listen and speak the language of the people she is talking to. She believes this is important so that people can understand what the areas of focus are and not feel bombarded by jargon. People need to know that what they are saying will be heard and understood. When talking with the employee networks, Rathner focuses on community, belonging and culture. When she talks with Executives, she focuses on the link to business goals, evidence and performance. They see the next stage as developing their work to include a link to inclusion performance objectives for people across the company. They already have a Social Impact Committee of the Board, chaired by the Chair of the company. So as well as engaging with people, they have a shared responsibility for this work at board level, and they have an external Board Advisor on diversity and inclusion.

Sharing the work across teams has led to momentum developing in different areas of the company. A great example is in their US teams, where they are engaging with education, specifically with historically Black colleges and universities[3] to help people develop their careers. In the UK, they work with Codebar[4] to help encourage people into technology careers through support and training. The next focus area is on inclusive entrepreneurship, so that they build a business community of founders from different backgrounds, supporting diverse founders to start and scale their businesses. Their Business Boost award has been running since 2020 and has won industry awards itself.[5] This is an annual competition in which small businesses can win a cash grant to help boost their growth. The award has been granted on four separate occasions to female founders (including us at Watch This Sp_ce in 2021![6]). They now want to go even further in creating communities to help entrepreneurs from different backgrounds to grow and scale their businesses with training and other support. They will look at how to provide information people need, as well as support to access funding and mentoring, and they have already started a Women In Business community group.

This example of Simply Business and the progress it continues to make shows the importance of sharing the work and responsibilities across the organization, not leaving the accountability to sit with one person or one team, as well as the value in listening to under-represented voices. There has to be shared ownership of the work in different teams. Staff need to be involved in employee groups to share information and feel listened to, as much as leaders need to be involved and have conversations at board level to ensure there is focus and progress. Having a Head of Social Impact helps them with coordinating this, but having someone in that type of role does not mean that people do not need to get involved in the journey themselves. That ecosystem has to be created with different people taking responsibility for delivering on actions.

If we look at how you can apply this to your organization, we can break it down into key areas of focus. This will help you consider how to ensure that the work is shared across the people who need to be involved and heard.

Allyship – pass the mic

Centring the voices of those who may not have been listened to before is at the heart of the concept of allyship. Instead of taking centre stage yourself, how can you pass the mic to people who have previously been sidelined, and make their stories the centre of your work? This will require people who may be used to doing most of the talking to learn to step aside to make room for someone else, and stopping to listen to others who have a different perspective. For leaders, this involves thinking carefully about who gets airtime to speak and how this can be done differently to centre different people. Those people may well need support if this is the first time they are being asked to speak up and say what they think.

FIGURE 15.1 Allyship definition

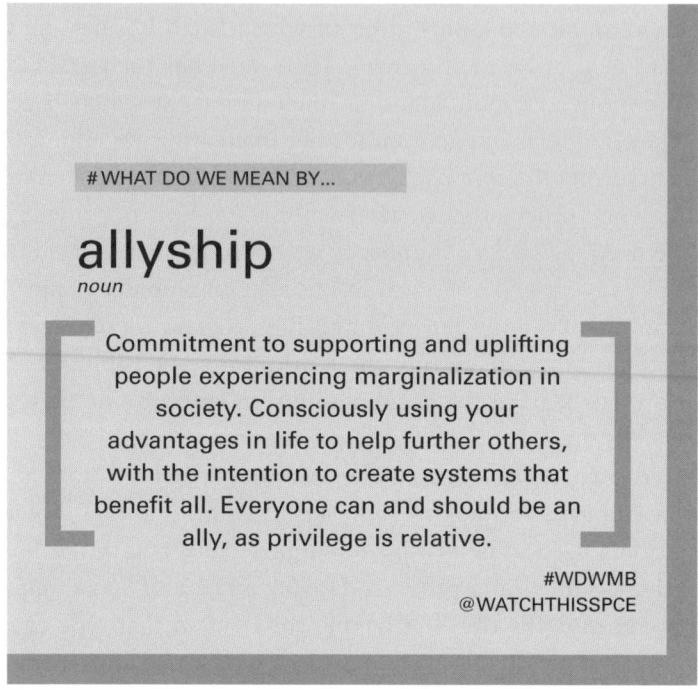

Allyship terminology

First of all, what do we mean by allyship? This is the definition (Figure 15.1) that features in our free 'What Do We Mean By...?'[7] guide, which you can download at watchthisspace.uk/resources.

PERFORMATIVE AND PROACTIVE ALLYSHIP

When it comes to allyship, many people see themselves as allies, when the reality is often different. For example, 80 per cent of white employees see themselves as allies to people of colour at work,[8] but only 45 per cent of women of colour say that they have strong allies in the workplace.[9] The difference in those statistics shows that true allyship is about the actions you take. Those people who think they are allies may be strong in their intent, but perhaps not in their implementation. Allyship is not about silence, or the performative action of sharing a social media post, but about changing your behaviour. We often use the example of the companies who shared black squares on Instagram in the summer of 2020 following the murder of

George Floyd in the USA.[10] Those companies wanted to show their support, but what has happened since then? Have those companies taken any actions to create more inclusive teams and address discrimination? Without the follow-up to drive change, the short moment of solidarity shown in sharing a social media post is lost, and it begins to look like it was more about making the business look good than any genuine support. This is what is called *performative allyship*.

Being a proactive ally means taking actions and doing things differently. When you are working on your inclusion journey, take the time to think about who has not been heard, and who can offer a different perspective. You can sponsor those people and support them to speak up, instead of speaking yourself. They could be the people to lead on some of this work instead of the people who usually lead projects in your organization. Consider how to address any injustices, and centre people who have previously been marginalized. This may mean making some difficult decisions for those who are usually centre stage. Perhaps it means stepping down from chairing a prestigious meeting yourself. Or it could be that you lead on speaking out on behalf of others. How can those in positions of privilege use their advantages to help other people to be seen and heard?

There are two other useful definitions here, of privilege and intersectionality.

For people who want to become allies, understanding their own privileges helps to see how they have a position that they could use for the advantage of others. Having a privilege in one aspect of life does not mean someone is privileged in every way. And the concept of privilege is not necessarily linked to wealth. So a person can be privileged through their skin colour, but also have experienced a tough life with economic disadvantages. Or they could be disadvantaged owing to their gender, but come from a background of wealth which changes their opportunities in life. That brings us to the second definition in Figure 15.2 – intersectionality – where different identities and factors combine to give someone a different and unique experience of life.

For the work on your inclusion journey to have depth and impact, consider how to reach and engage with people who have these unique experiences. You are very likely to need to reach beyond the obvious teams and people you usually work with, to seek out those who need to be heard. Make space for what might be difficult conversations and difficult things to hear. Give people different ways to communicate and tell their stories. And make sure there are options for these communications to be anonymous so that people feel safe to share their thoughts and feelings.

FIGURE 15.2 Privilege and intersectionality definitions

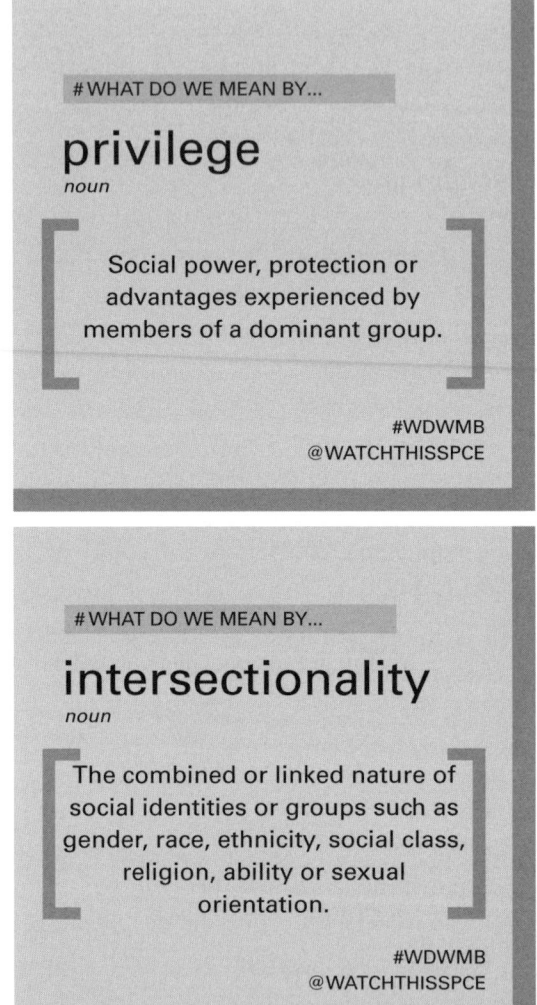

ORGANIZATIONAL ALLYSHIP

An organization can lead on taking strong actions, too, to show allyship; this is not only about individuals. We spoke to Karen Dobres, Ambassador and former Board Director at Lewes FC Football Club.[11] This organization made a bold move in 2017 when it became the first football club in the world to pay the men and women's teams equally.[12] It describes itself as the 'mouse that roared'[13]: a small football club in Sussex that took a strong stance and showed bigger clubs how to drive change. And it continues to do that in other ways:

- Defender Mitch Nelson stopped playing during a match when an away fan shouted homophobic abuse at another Lewes player.[14]

- The men's team led a campaign, 'Call Him Out', to encourage men to call out sexism and challenge sexist language and behaviours when they see it.[15]

- It set up a Sisterships Network for organizations who empower women to become owners.[16]

- It set up the Rooker Prize for under-represented writers, which is now sponsored by Hachette.[17]

All of these actions have created a reputation and a following for fighting for equality. Their brand is about taking actions and showing they are strong allies to under-represented communities. At Lewes Football Club, engagement with this comes from the board right through to the players, trainers and fans. And they encourage people in their community to become owners of the club and help them in their mission.

For organizational allyship to be a success, everyone involved also needs to consider how you hold people accountable and challenge discrimination. What happens when things are said? Do people have the courage and support to challenge it and speak up? Some people might have tried to speak up before and not been heard. How will you win back trust? This requires the creation of safe spaces for people to come forward, and where different people know their voices are all valued.

Inclusive leadership

To create a culture where people understand allyship and the importance of listening to under-represented voices, change needs to be led from the top. At Lewes Football Club, it was the board who took a lot of the decisions on the actions they have taken. They had the initial idea back in 2017 to pay the teams equally. They then support players and staff to keep calling out discrimination and to drive change.

There are other organizations who do this successfully too. In Chapter 11 we looked at the example of teal leadership, where the overall vision and goals are shared with everyone, and then individuals and teams share responsibilities to work in the way they feel is best to achieve the outcomes they want. This method is used by Here – Care Unbound, the healthcare social enterprise we looked at in Chapter 4.

Here – Care Unbound uses this model to enable people to work without hierarchies in how decisions are made. People are encouraged to bring their whole selves to work and speak up about the things that are important to them. The leaders guide and support decision-makers, but they do not command people to do things in the way they have decided they should be done. The work on communicating about the purpose of the organization is a priority so that people can make their decisions with an understanding of how it relates to that purpose. This is about fostering an environment of listening to people, empowering people and, as leaders, focusing on how to include people and help them feel they can belong.

Here – Care Unbound is also trialling a method of 'reverse mentoring', which we have seen successfully used by other organizations too. This is where, instead of someone in a senior role mentoring an employee, an employee mentors someone in the senior leadership team. So someone in a functional role might reverse mentor the CEO, for example. This helps leaders to understand more about the everyday experiences of employees, and for those employees to see how leaders work. If leaders are open to this, it's a powerful way to understand the experience of others and think about how to become an even more inclusive leader.

To create a culture of inclusive leadership, leaders may need to learn new skills, and perhaps 'unlearn' behaviours of the past.

Leaders who can focus on developing these behaviours will show employees that they are leaders they can trust. A key behaviour in this is listening, which is listed in Table 15.1. Many of the people we interviewed talked about the importance of listening, and creating spaces for active listening so that people can share their stories. Danielle Alsey at Plus X Innovation,[18] the company we looked at in Chapter 10, talked to us about how, as they scale and grow their business, they want to keep in mind how to continue listening to employees. They hold 'listening circles' to hear from different people about what changes they want to see and what their experiences are. Alsey does not feel the goals around inclusion are just for her to hold in the leadership team. She wants everyone to feel accountable and responsible so that there is a culture of inclusive leadership.

For your work on your inclusion journey, consider the skills that your leaders may need to work on and develop to become inclusive leaders. Are there behaviours listed in Table 15.1 that you could work on with those who are leading people? And could your leaders benefit from some focused training on this to help them become leaders who show that they are ready to listen, learn and collaborate in order to help everyone feel involved in the inclusion journey?

TABLE 15.1 Inclusive leadership behaviours

Behaviour	Action	Impact
Listening	Giving time and space to listen	People feel heard
Empathy	Understanding other people and their situation	People feel understood
Centring others	Giving different people the opportunity to lead	Different voices are heard
Relationship building	Taking time to get to know people	Different leadership methods for each person
Connecting people	Building connections with other people	Teams network and reach grows
Recognition	Celebrating successes and sharing them	People feel valued
Encouraging participation	Encouraging people to do things and get involved in things they may need support with	Builds people's skills and confidence
Curiosity	Always learning about themselves, their biases and new skills	Team is empowered to learn new things
Collaboration	Seeking to connect and collaborate with others to achieve goals	Different voices are centred and connections are made
Making mistakes	Not being afraid of getting things wrong and talking about mistakes	Empowers team to try new things and not worry about mistakes
Seeking feedback	Asking people how things are going and for their feedback	People feel they can say how things are going and ask for feedback themselves

Shared goals and destinations

It is not only the leadership team who need to share responsibility and accountability. For an inclusion journey to make meaningful progress, everyone must feel a shared responsibility for the destination and be travelling in the same direction. How can you create a culture where people want to help carry each other's bags and support with navigation when someone gets lost?

We have looked at setting the vision and communicating this to your teams in Chapter 6. Keeping a focus on your communications around this will help people feel connected to the journey all the way along. What drives real progress on this is thinking about how you connect the inclusion journey goals to people's work performance objectives. Dina Knight, Chief People Officer at Datatec and Logicalis,[19] talked to us about the challenges of doing this in a decentralized company with big teams. They are a technology company operating in more than 30 territories, with over 100 offices and 7,000 employees. That's a lot of people to share information with. They have to work hard on sharing the mission, goals and vision, and see this as a key skill for leaders. They offer ongoing development to build the skills they want to embed, and to create a culture where leaders are viewed as inclusive. Knight believes this is crucial for both attracting new employees and engaging and retaining the employees they have.

They bring their leaders together to embed collaboration, so that leaders talk to each other and share challenges and ideas. And the People team works hard on aligning with the commercial business divisions so they are not operating separately. They have more than 100 people in HR and People and Culture roles, and Knight believes in the people in these roles understanding the business divisions well. By understanding their business goals and challenges, inclusion can be embedded in how they work so that they drive the behaviours they want to see. Knight coaches people to understand the business objectives and then makes the links to the People objectives, so that there are shared goals and responsibilities. They bring a similar focus to their sustainability objectives and are working towards net zero, where they ask people to align with the overall business goals and see where their sustainability goals fit with what they are already working on.

In terms of tangible outputs, this varies across the business divisions and geographies. For example, in South Africa, there are processes in place to score companies on inclusion. So in their South African divisions, Datatec works closely with schools and universities to encourage more girls to learn about technology, and for those of different ethnicities to consider careers in technology. They then build on those links to help build their recruitment pipeline and share opportunities with people. This type of work on inclusion takes time, and results are slow. So the leaders in the business need to understand this and be bought into it to make sure the work is prioritized and supported on an ongoing basis. The longer-term objectives of working with communities takes a shared understanding, and also a willingness to share in driving these things forwards.

Who is missing from your journey?

This chapter has looked at the different ways to make sure you include different people in your journey and share responsibilities for driving without leaving anyone behind. There will be key stakeholders with insights, experiences and perspectives to share, if they are given the opportunity and space to contribute. Think about how you centre conversations with different people. And work on the different ways in which you can help people feel psychologically safe enough to contribute their thoughts and ideas and get on board with the journey.

Giving people different options to contribute will enable people to feel they can share with you as you progress on your journey (we looked at different employee engagement mechanisms in Chapter 14). For those steering the work, different people can get involved in different areas and use different methods to engage people. Leaders can use these techniques to work with their teams, and employee groups can have sponsors from the leadership team to help support the discussions, work and outputs. This kind of collaboration across teams, departments and levels of seniority is so valuable in bringing together different perspectives, increasing shared understanding and moving work forward.

Hopefully by now you are starting to feel that you are all travelling together towards those outcomes and goals you worked on at the beginning. In the next section, we will look at how to appreciate the view from the destinations you have reached. How do you celebrate the successes of all the work you have done to get there? And how do you keep your eye on the road and consider the directions you need to take next to shape your future?

Notes

1 Interview with Natalie Rathner, Head of Social Impact at Simply Business, November 2023

2 The UK B Corporation movement, https://bcorporation.uk (archived at https://perma.cc/G2EV-L2AW)

3 US News & World Report. Historically Black Colleges and Universities, www.usnews.com/best-colleges/rankings/hbcu (archived at https://perma.cc/U9H3-PRRE)

4 Codebar, https://codebar.io (archived at https://perma.cc/R2YP-5EKQ)

5 Simply Business. Awards & recognition, www.simplybusiness.co.uk/about-us/awards (archived at https://perma.cc/D887-8NWX)

6 C Smith. Diversity and inclusion consultancy wins our £25K Business Boost grant, Simply Business, 22 October 2021, www.simplybusiness.co.uk/knowledge/articles/2021/10/inclusion-consultancy-wins-business-boost-grant/ (archived at https://perma.cc/QRT6-W9CM)

7 Watch This Sp_ce. What Do We Mean By…, www.watchthisspace.uk/what-do-we-mean-by/ (archived at https://perma.cc/4GX9-L47F)

8 C Connley. Over 80% of White employees see themselves as allies at work, but Black women and Latinas disagree, CNBC make it, 24 August 2020, www.cnbc.com/2020/08/21/over-80percent-of-white-employees-see-themselves-as-allies-but-black-women-and-latinas-disagree.html (archived at https://perma.cc/K9L8-HFNQ)

9 C Connley. Over 80% of White employees see themselves as allies at work, but Black women and Latinas disagree, CNBC make it, 24 August 2020, www.cnbc.com/2020/08/21/over-80percent-of-white-employees-see-themselves-as-allies-but-black-women-and-latinas-disagree.html (archived at https://perma.cc/6PHM-UZAF)

10 P Monckton. This is why millions of people are posting black squares on Instagram, Forbes, 2 June 2020, www.forbes.com/sites/paulmonckton/2020/06/02/blackout-tuesday-instagram-black-squares-blackouttuesday-theshowmustbepaused/ (archived at https://perma.cc/U9WT-4349)

11 Interview with Karen Dobres, Ambassador, Lewes Football Club, December 2023

12 M Christenson. Lewes FC become first professional club to pay women and men equally, *Guardian*, 12 July 2017, www.theguardian.com/football/2017/jul/12/lewes-fc-first-club-equal-pay-men-women (archived at https://perma.cc/KB5E-A84E)

13 Interview with Karen Dobres, Ambassador, Lewes Football Club, December 2023

14 K Dobres. How Lewes Football Club runs on community values, Global Values Alliance, https://valuesalliance.net/fans-of-change/ (archived at https://perma.cc/M7QQ-NXWE)

15 Jack. #Call Him Out, Lewes FC, 8 February 2023, https://lewesfc.com/news/call-him-out/ (archived at https://perma.cc/96FA-L4F3)

16 SisterShips Ownership offer, Lewes FC, https://lewesfc.com/sisterships-discount/ (archived at https://perma.cc/Z6YD-8PV9)

17 Jack. The Rooker Prize 2023, Lewes FC, https://lewesfc.com/news/the-rooker-prize-2023/ (archived at https://perma.cc/Y4UY-GZWB)

18 Interview with Danielle Alsey, Director of People & Culture at PlusX Innovation, December 2023

19 Interview with Dina Knight, Chief People Officer at Datatec and Logicalis Group, December 2023

PART FOUR

Look how far you've come

16

Has it been worth the effort?

We have looked, in previous chapters, at the importance of gaining buy-in from key stakeholders, and how you can keep them updated and engaged. However, simply keeping people updated on progress is not enough. At some point, the people who have put their trust, energy and investment into this project will want to know if it's all been worth it. You will also need to be clear on what you've achieved and what tangible impact that has made, and evaluate whether you've made progress in the right places. Therefore, in this chapter, we'll look at how you can calculate the return on investment and broader impact of your work, as well as how to approach your progress reviews so that you can maintain buy-in and secure ongoing commitment.

Playing the long game

As we saw in Chapter 14, large-scale reviews of progress won't be taking place straight away. It's critical to stress to key stakeholders – particularly members of the leadership team and the board who hold the purse strings – that results won't be seen overnight. This is a lengthy process, the impact of which will take a long time to be visible in any tangible way.

Setting goals for work that you want to achieve, rather than results that you expect, will be crucial in the early stages, and it's important that everyone understands that progress is measured in this way to begin with. For much of the first year, it's likely that you will be working on developing, implementing and improving different policies, processes and approaches, so it would be unrealistic to expect to see these changes driving quantifiable results until they've had some time to become embedded within the organization. That review of tangible, quantifiable results is more likely to be beneficial from your second year.

In the example communications schedule we shared in Chapter 14, there were monthly check-ins, just for the working group to monitor progress and identify any necessary changes to the strategy; quarterly strategic reviews, to assess whether everything is on track and moving in the right direction; and an annual progress report, which offers a chance to give a wider view of overall progress. You don't have to adopt this exact schedule – your approach will depend on the particular needs and reporting practices of your individual business – but we recommend using some variant on this model, where there are regular opportunities for those *doing* the work to check that it's all moving in the right direction, less frequent but still regular opportunities for all key stakeholders to review progress and then a much more spaced-out point to look at results in comparison to previous data points to look at the impact of the work.

Your annual review – or whatever takes its place in the model you choose to adopt – is your chance to look at results in detail. Whilst you can keep an eye on data from month to month and quarter to quarter, big changes to the fabric of your organization are not likely to be as visible at this granular level. It is only by taking the long view that you'll understand how far you've truly come.

It's likely that your first annual review, then, will be a look back at the action plan you started with, an assessment of how much of it you've completed and where you identified changes that were needed to your approach, or blockers holding you back, and how these were dealt with. By the time you get to your second annual review, you'll be more likely to be in a position to look at tangible return on investment.

Calculating return on investment

Financial returns

At its most basic level, return on investment is a comparison of the costs of the work that you've undertaken with the financial benefit that it has produced, showing you what you've got back in return for the money you put in. The formula for calculating this is shown in Figure 16.1.

FIGURE 16.1 ROI calculation

$$\frac{(\text{gains} - \text{costs})}{\text{costs}} \times 100$$

If you calculated that you had spent £10,000 on your diversity and inclusion work and that the benefits to the business had generated gains of £100,000, then your ROI is 900 per cent, and your benefits to costs ratio is 10:1 (meaning that you've generated £10 for every £1 spent).

That's the simple part. However, when it comes to diversity and inclusion work, calculating those financial gains isn't quite so straightforward. As with much of what we've talked about in this book, exactly what you calculate will depend on your specific goals and actions, and will relate to the wider business objectives to which you have mapped these actions. Some of the potential financial measures you might take into account are:

- recruitment savings as a result of an increased retention rate
- increased profits resulting from increased productivity
- increased sales from a broadened and/or more engaged customer base
- market expansion from diversifying teams
- increased profits resulting from an improved reputation or increased visibility
- increased profits arising from new innovations
- decreased spending on legal and HR fees owing to a reduction in diversity and inclusion related complaints
- decreased costs arising from a reduction in sickness absence, stress and other relevant wellbeing issues

It's unlikely that, for any such measures, you will be able to attribute 100 per cent of the financial gain to your diversity and inclusion work – other factors are also likely to contribute. How much did your diversity and inclusion work contribute to your increased customer engagement, for example, and how much was it driven by that new marketing campaign you launched in Q3? So, you will be looking to calculate an estimated percentage split between the different factors, taking into account the weighting likely to be given to each one by the amount of work undertaken, the timing of different actions and the level of influence of each factor. If there was a big spike in sales straight after that Q3 marketing campaign, and a dip in sales when the campaign had ended, then it's likely that the majority of the weighting lies there. But if customer engagement and sales began creeping up in Q2, before the campaign even launched but after you began introducing more inclusive communications practices, and has continued to grow from the baseline point (excluding that big spike around campaign time) ever since, then you have to give considerable credit to your diversity and inclusion work. Data from staff and customer surveys will help you here, as you can gain insight into how important each factor is to the people concerned.

Types of return

Financial gains aren't the only returns you will be looking at, though. There are a number of different ways that your organization can gain a return from diversity and inclusion work, which go beyond monetary income and savings. These fall into the following categories.

OUTPUTS
This is the quantifiable measure of the actions that you have taken, tracking elements that have been delivered or numbers of people who have been engaged. Here you will be reporting on the number of training sessions delivered, the number of employees/customers who responded to surveys, the number of attendees for Discovery or Strategy workshops, the number of people who have been reached by your diversity and inclusion messaging, and other similar metrics. Whilst these don't represent growth or change in and of themselves, they are gains in terms of skills, knowledge and experiences accessed.

PERCEPTION
Here you are measuring your staff's, customers' and other stakeholders' view of your organization's approach to inclusion. This will be captured through internal and external surveys, measurement of your external reputation (of the kind we discussed in Chapter 13), reviewing exit interview data and input from focus groups and/or staff networks. You can also measure complaints about discriminatory or exclusionary activity, and queries related to your organizational plans and priorities regarding diversity and inclusion – if complaints and queries of this kind are reducing, then your work is paying off in terms of your reputation, staff and customer satisfaction, and time-saving from staff having to handle these inputs.

SKILLS
Your action plan will almost certainly involve the delivery of training, learning and development for your staff. As part of this, you should measure the extent to which staff feel they have improved their knowledge and skills, and how able they feel to put this learning to use in their day-to-day jobs. This is then a valuable return on your investment, when your workforce has increased their knowledge, gained new skills, and improved their

understanding – not only of diversity and inclusion, but of how to work well and communicate effectively with one another. (It will likely also be possible to map these increased skills to tangible financial gains in terms of productivity and profitability.)

APPLICATION

This is where you can track how effectively your action plan has led to changes in the way things are done within your organization. What changes in process or approach have been implemented, and how have these improved ways of working and staff/customer satisfaction? What efficiencies or initiatives have been introduced (e.g. streamlining meetings or introducing new communications mechanisms), and what impact have they had? Are staff finding it easier to do their jobs, or to work with other teams? Has the quality of staff output increased as a result of more effective collaboration mechanisms and/or better provision for staff needs? What impact has your diversity and inclusion activity had on the way your business works?

WELLBEING

As we've discussed in previous chapters, diversity and inclusion increases staff engagement, job satisfaction, collaboration and staff happiness, whilst reducing stress, anxiety, conflict and sickness absence. It is often possible to attribute financial benefits to these elements, but they also hold intrinsic value in themselves.

Types of cost

Just as there are a variety of types of gain from this work, there are also a variety of types of cost. Financial costs will include elements such as:

- salary of an internal diversity and inclusion lead
- costs of external diversity and inclusion experts
- admin costs (survey software, communication tools, etc)
- time staff spend on diversity and inclusion work
- costs of delivering training and workshops
- production of communications materials

When you're considering a question like 'Has this all been worth it?', you also have to take into account the emotional impact on the staff working on this project, and what their time has been taken away from to make space for this work.

What if it wasn't worth it?

At the end of these calculations, what if you conclude that the returns haven't repaid the investment? Should you just give up on the whole thing? Absolutely not. The benefits of diversity and inclusion are too great to abandon, and we've seen how much it can cost you to leave these elements neglected. But if the activity you're investing in isn't giving you value, it's time to go back to the drawing board. Go back to the data you're collecting and look at where challenges are arising and why things aren't working. Talk to your staff and key stakeholders and identify the issues. Then recalibrate and find a new direction. Perhaps start out with a smaller investment that you can test to be sure that this path is the right one.

Success stories

At Watch This Sp_ce, ensuring that our clients gain real value from their inclusion journeys is of the utmost importance to us. Let us give you a few examples of the benefits this work has generated in different sectors.

Hospitality

We introduced you to Richmond Hill, a luxury hotel just outside London, in Chapter 4. Their Discovery Workshops and staff survey had a huge impact in engaging staff and improving internal perception of diversity and inclusion. Their programme of training and learning had a quantifiable impact on knowledge and skills, and improved staff collaboration. At the end of the first year of their inclusion journey, their retention rate had increased from 46 per cent to 72 per cent, which, having reviewed the other potential contributing factors, they attribute predominantly to the diversity and inclusion work. All of this will have generated financial gains and cost savings, as well as non-financial improvements.

Technology

The company we talked about in Chapter 6 is a clear example of how non-financial gains can be a higher priority to a business than monetary ones. The main measure of success for the leadership team is the fact that their team no longer raise questions about diversity and inclusion, or worry that the business isn't doing enough. This has increased staff engagement and motivation, and improved the working environment. The knock-on effect for productivity, retention and cohesion can be linked to financial returns, but the key priority for them in the initial stages was for their team to know that inclusion was something highly valued in the business and to feel that they, as a leadership team, were meeting their staff's needs.

Local authority

The Diverse Talent Programme that Watch This Sp_ce delivered for a Local Authority saw 20 per cent of participants receive a promotion within six months of completing the programme, with a further 47 per cent putting themselves forward for promotion opportunities. Confidence in current roles and future career development increased amongst participants by 50 per cent, and 85 per cent said they would recommend the programme to others. These are tangible financial benefits – in terms of staff retention and development – and also non-financial gains in terms of engagement, personal growth and job satisfaction.

The big picture

Whilst looking at individual metrics is valuable to demonstrate what areas are providing the greatest impact and where growth is both needed and felt, you will also want to step back and take a wider view. Ultimately, if everything you are doing is working, you'll see an overall impact on the success of your business as a whole. The bottom line is, if profits have increased for the business, it's likely that your diversity and inclusion efforts have contributed towards this.

What are the metrics by which you measure the success of your business? Whether it's profits, revenue, market share or a combination of factors, we've seen that diversity and inclusion impacts all of these. Other factors will contribute, certainly, but by tracking the data and mapping the actions you have taken to changes in your results, you will be able to estimate the value that your inclusion journey has contributed.

Once you've demonstrated return on investment and wider business gains from this work, future buy-in and investment becomes easier. Not only that, but you can start to make projections concerning what might be achievable with increased investment. If you achieved a benefits to costs ratio of 10:1 with an investment of £10,000, what might be possible with an investment of £20,000? As a business, you can begin to envisage where this journey might be able to take you next.

17

Celebrating progress

When you reach these important milestones and demonstrate return on investment, how do you celebrate your achievements? If you're honest about your usual organizational approach to success, do you pause to celebrate reaching goals with your team? A common theme we have seen with most organizations we have worked with, and with people we have interviewed, is that successes are not always acknowledged. We all have a tendency to be tough on ourselves and minimize our own achievements, and we get caught up in a sense of needing to push on to the next destination. We're so busy looking forwards to where we're heading next that we forget to look back at how far we've come. This can often mean that fabulous achievements and successes can be missed by those who were not closely involved in the work, leaving people in the dark about progress the business is making, and that the people who have been working so hard to produce these results feel unappreciated and disengaged. In this chapter we will look at why the celebration stage of the journey is not one to miss out, and how you can make the most of it.

Why the celebrations?

We are as keen as you to keep progressing to the next destination. But pausing can be as important as moving forward sometimes. People have put in a lot of effort, produced big results and learnt a lot, so showing appreciation encourages them to keep going and validates the work they have done. It reminds people why they were on the journey in the first place and shows everyone how far they have travelled together. In a survey of US employees, 46 per cent said they had left a job because they felt unappreciated,[1] so this is not an area you want to neglect.

As we saw in Chapter 11, change management methodologies all have a stage in the process to evaluate the work that has been done. This stage is about reflecting on and appreciating the progress that has been made. As you check back on goals achieved and targets hit, this is a time to thank everyone for their hard work and show them the tangible impact so that they can see why what they're doing matters. After all, employees who are recognized for their work are 3.7 times as likely to be engaged in their roles, and almost half as likely to experience burnout as those who are not recognized and thanked for work they have done.[2] This is also a chance to evaluate how things have been working and see if changes need to be made for the journey ahead. This is a time, too, for re-energizing everyone to plan new stages to the journey and to generate new ideas for future work.

We spoke to Alex Farbon, Talent Acquisition Lead at GFT UK,[3] a financial technology business offering bespoke solutions to companies in the financial services and manufacturing industries globally. As part of their inclusion journey, they have done a lot of work to address gender representation, as this is an industry that is very male dominated. Only 10 per cent of their engineering team were female in 2021 when Farbon joined, and by 2023 they were at 20 per cent. So in just under two and a half years, they really moved the bar forward. The average tech company has around 23 per cent women,[4] and GFT UK had progressed to 26 per cent across the whole business by the end of 2023. They have done this by looking carefully at recruitment, retention and career progression. And they have purposefully supported and sponsored Women In Tech events and conferences. When women join their teams, they encourage them to get involved in events to help people to see that they are doing positive things to address gender representation.

Despite all of these successes, when asked how they celebrate them, Farbon is more hesitant. He works closely with the Internal Communications team, who are now linked to the People team, to embed internal communications more widely. Their challenge is that many of their staff work on client sites, often spending more time on those sites than at a GFT UK office location. All-staff meetings are held regularly, but not all employees will necessarily dial in, so this means communicating about successes can be challenging. What does work well is that they hold four employee events throughout the year. They have two 'Connect' events, to which all employees are invited, where they talk about successes and future strategy. They also run awards, which celebrate their values and the employees who embrace those values, and these are showcased at a summer event and a winter event, which celebrate successes linked to their values and strategy.

GFT UK is proud of its successes, and the progress it has made in two years, achieving what has taken many of the big tech corporations far longer.

In its 'Great Place To Work' survey[5] 85 per cent of its employees said they would recommend working for them to others. This is seen as a strong success indicator and something it needs to communicate well, both internally and externally, to celebrate their success.

GFT UK is not the only company that thinks it could do more to celebrate successes. When we talked with Dina Knight from Datatec and Logicalis, another technology company, she told us that a common theme in all of her roles is that there is so much to do to continue progression. People are constantly thinking 'what's next?', so stepping back and celebrating the successes can get missed in the rush to progress on to the next set of tasks. Yet actually taking the time to celebrate and recognize the work people have done is a key way to keep people focused and energized on the next thing they are going to work on.

Knight talks about the launch of their Employer Value Proposition (EVP), which went really well, and completing three talent programmes to develop future leaders. All great things to celebrate. They do talk about these successes in her regular calls with their People Leaders, but they could do more to recognize all of the teams involved, and to publicly share with other teams that this work is taking place. In our conversation with Nathalie Rathner, Head of Social Impact at insurance company Simply Business[6], she said a similar thing: that one of the hardest parts of her role, and similar roles, is that there is always more work to be done. So, pausing to celebrate can be easily missed as you move on to the next thing.

A key part of planning your roadmap, then, should be factoring in pauses to stop and celebrate your milestones. Not only does this keep people motivated and enthused for the next stage of the journey ahead, but it keeps the wider team aware of what is being done so that they see the value and believe in keeping moving. It's also a way of enhancing your external reputation as an employer and to potential customers. Your celebration planning might look something like Table 17.1.

Now let's look at some of the different ways you can celebrate your progress.

Celebration styles

Everyone will have different preferences and ideas about how to celebrate. Each organization will also have its own approach to marking successes. You will need to be mindful that any celebrations are inclusive, too. Not everyone enjoys a noisy celebration with hordes of people, and some people prefer private thanks to public ones. Here are some ideas to think about.

TABLE 17.1 Celebration planning

Goals	Year One				Year Two			
	Q1	Q2	Q3	Q4	Q1	Q2	Q3	Q4
	Diversity and Inclusion targets in place	Data collection framework introduced	Staff participation in inclusion survey to reach 75%	Inclusive recruitment policy to be in place	Website to be fully accessible	Future leaders programme launched	75% of staff feel they are being supported to progress their career	100% of staff who require adjustments to say these have been fully provided
Celebration	Communication to all of roadmap and goals	Online event to explain what it is, why it matters and how it works	Thank you to all staff and to inclusion team	Lunch and learn to explain policy Thank you to team responsible End of year inclusion review celebration	External and internal communications Team celebration budgeted for	Launch event	Share staff stories Thank you to inclusion team	Rewards for teams responsible End of year inclusion review celebration

What are you celebrating?

Is it a project milestone hit? Is it some fabulous external feedback? Or perhaps you have hit a target you had set early in the journey? Or sometimes it's great to celebrate the fact that more people are getting involved and have joined the journey team. Schedule pauses along your route to take the time to take a look at what has been achieved and look at what can be celebrated. If you are a large organization with lots of people spread across teams and different locations, consider how the things you are celebrating impact different people. Do they know about the inclusion journey? What changes that have been made will make things better for them? And how can they talk about what you are celebrating? You will also want to allow for more spontaneous celebrations, perhaps if something is achieved ahead of schedule or you get some amazing feedback that you want to recognize. Think about what you can do to be reactive if these events occur.

How are you celebrating?

You will need to involve everyone, so your celebrations need to be inclusive and wide-reaching. Do you have teams working across different locations? How will you involve all of them? If you are considering an event, think about times of day, and, if the event is in-person, accessible venues and ease of travelling to the venue. If food is involved, consider different dietary requirements. Will you include alcohol, and if so, how will you then allow for people who don't drink or might be uncomfortable around situations involving alcohol? In one survey, 45 per cent of people said that alcohol should not play a part in work social activities.[7] In another, more than one in three workers see drinking alcohol with colleagues as outdated.[8] Evenings also mean that some people will need to make childcare arrangements, so that needs to be considered. Some work events now offer crèche facilities.

We see lots of great ideas for celebrating successes with employees when we work with different organizations. And we see that offering people choices has a positive impact too, so that the celebrations show the organization is inclusive. Here are some other ways you might want to celebrate:

- Create communications to be shared with all teams
- Prizes or awards (making sure prizes are inclusive and judging is fair)
- Events to bring people together to celebrate
- Individual communications to thank people who have been involved

- Rewards – perhaps financial or in the form of gifts or other benefits – which can be shared with teams or individuals
- Recognition for the people who have been involved in the journey
- Celebration fund for employees to choose how they want to celebrate

People really value recognition, and often the simple act of thanking people individually or publicly, or both, can help people to feel appreciated and valued for the work they have done. More and more large employers are now putting in place rewards schemes to celebrate different types of work achievements. With rewards schemes and any gifts or prizes, remember to consider different preferences and ideas people have about what is a great reward.

If you progress to the point where you want to look at putting in place a regular way to reward employees, there are companies who offer exactly that. There are software platforms that allow employees to give each other 'kudos' or thanks for particular things they have done, which can be viewed by all employees.[9] These systems are an effective way to build employee engagement as they introduce an element of competition as well as the public recognition people often crave which motivates them. There are also platforms such as Perkbox[10] or huggg,[11] where you can reward employees with gifts and discounts that they can choose themselves from an allocated budget. Thanking people in some way is proven to be a strong motivator. A survey by Great Place To Work[12] found that there was a 69 per cent increase in the likelihood of employees bringing extra effort to their work if they have received a genuine 'thank you'. Thanking people and celebrating their efforts in some way creates a culture of recognition and appreciation for employees, which motivates people to do more.

Who is celebrating?

Whilst you want to include everyone, you should also give people options in how they can be involved. If the celebration is an event of some type, do give people the option not to attend, particularly if it is during their free time. There are many who choose not to attend work social events; in fact, 34 per cent of people avoid them.[13] Check in with people to make sure that everyone who has been involved in the work is given the option to be included in the celebrations and ask people for ideas about how they would like to celebrate.

When you are celebrating work that has been achieved, leaders need to be cautious of taking all the credit for themselves. Who has actually delivered the work? Make sure they are centre stage. This is a nice way to shine a light on people who have stepped out of their comfort zone to get involved. And do you want to share the celebrations with everyone in the organization in some way? This is a nice way to help everyone feel involved in the journey, and also to enable them to find out more about it if they are not directly involved themselves. What you do not want is anyone feeling like they have been excluded from celebrations, so plan for this carefully. We have seen that, for the best impact from celebrations, make sure there is good communication, options for different ways to celebrate and that there is always a thank you to the people who have achieved goals so that they receive recognition for their work.

Sharing celebrations

As well as the celebration itself, sharing the fact that you are celebrating spreads the word to people externally. This could be through sharing on social media platforms such as LinkedIn or on your company careers page to show people what it is like to work for you. Celebrating your successes along the way is a great thing to share in external communications to your wider audience, as well as internal communications to employees. Telling people about the journey you have been on will help people see that you are one of the organizations actually working on change and not just talking about it. There are different things you can communicate externally to celebrate your successes, and these methods will all help you to reach and engage with more people.

- **Share examples** – Use examples of the work you have done and the results you have achieved from it; this will show people that you are not just talking about inclusion, you are doing something about it and achieving results. Sharing key statistics and stories shows people evidence that the work is creating impact.

- **Tell people how** – Share how you progressed with your journey, with examples of how you achieved these results, and be open about any hurdles you had to overcome. That will mean your communications are authentic, and people will relate to that and see that they can embark on similar work themselves. You will also be establishing yourself as an authority and a thought leader in this space – this will be discussed more in the next chapter.

- **Share objectives** – There are now many organizations who link inclusion objectives to their organization's objectives, and many share these publicly in annual reports or impact reports. This can be a very effective way of sharing the results of your work. If you are including objectives on inclusion for leaders or for all employees, then sharing that is a very effective way to celebrate your achievements.

- **Link to financial rewards** – Some organizations are starting to link objectives to financial rewards too, so this could be team bonuses shared if particular goals are reached. There are also some organizations who link to individual bonuses. This might be something that is shared in an annual report or impact report.

- **Get involved in volunteering days** – There are organizations who celebrate by continuing their work and contributing to their communities. This is a way of sharing celebrations externally by engaging with charities and community organizations. Many employers now give staff time to volunteer out of their standard working hours. We have seen examples of teams joining together to do beach cleans, serve lunches, clean an area or make things for community groups and charities.

- **Enter awards** – There are many different types of industry awards you can enter, with many specific ones for diversity and inclusion. Most industry awards now include a category for diversity and inclusion. With any awards, consider which ones really celebrate progress with inclusion and which ones are relevant to your organization. Some awards may require you to pay to enter; talk to your team about whether they are happy with this, and get their buy-in to enter awards. If you do decide to enter, write your entry using lots of examples to evidence your progress. If you are shortlisted, or, indeed, if you win, this is another great piece of news to share.

Celebration unhappiness

On the flip side, as we've discussed before, not everyone in your organization may be on board with or comfortable with your direction. Therefore, when you come to celebrate, there is always a risk that some people will see any sharing of successes as an opportunity to voice their displeasure or negative views. There are those who might feel that their particular cause or idea has not been considered or worked on yet, so they see a celebration of other work achieved as frustrating. Keeping everyone informed throughout the journey about what you are working on and why will help to minimize these reactions. We have to remember, though, that even regular communications might pass some people by. A survey by Gallup[14] found that only 13 per cent of employees believe that their leaders communicate effectively with the organization. We have worked with many employers who think they are communicating effectively, but they are relying on methods that are not necessarily reaching everyone. For example, we worked with one employer who shared all important employee communications in an email at 3pm every Friday afternoon. When they looked into why people were not aware of things that were happening, they found that most people were not reading that Friday email. They had other priorities at that time of the week. You need to use a variety of methods of communication to engage different people, so they know about the work as well as the great things that are achieved. When you are telling people about successes, remind people what the work is about and who they can talk to with any concerns.

When you communicate about achievements, show people where this sits in the journey roadmap. A visual diagram helps with this to show people the context of the work. An example can be seen in Figure 17.1.

It's worth acknowledging how much there is still to do and clarifying that you are going to continue with the next destination on your journey. Link the celebrations with the next goal or milestone, and you might find that this means you pick up more people along the way with new ideas for the next stage of the journey. In fact, being open about this and saying that you are looking for more people to join the next stage is an effective way to bring more people into the work you are doing next.

As well as those who are still looking for more things to be worked on, be aware of detractors and disgruntled employees. There will be those who might have experienced issues which you are addressing as part of the inclusion journey. So if they see communications about successes, it might bring back memories of bad experiences they had and make them feel uncomfortable or unhappy. If you share celebrations either through internal or external communication and you get feedback from unhappy employees, or ex-employees, then do take the time to engage with them. Show them you are listening, ask for their ideas and share with them the actions you still have to progress so they can see you want to address their concerns. Sometimes these types of communications can come through on social media, so talk to the people who look after your accounts so that they are equipped and know how to respond. Often people who are unhappy want to know that someone is listening and that will help with your communications with them.

FIGURE 17.1   Inclusion targets

	Year One				Year Two				Year Three			
	Q1	Q2	Q3	Q4	Q1	Q2	Q3	Q4	Q1	Q2	Q3	Q4
	Diversity and inclusion targets in place	Data collection framework introduced	Inclusive communications processes in place	100% of staff to know where to find policies and processes	Formal appraisal process for staff in place	Future leaders programme launched	75% of staff feel they are being supported to progress their career	100% of staff who require adjustments to say these have been fully provided	Increased representation of ethnic minority groups across organization	Fewer than 10% of staff to have experienced bullying, discrimination or harassment in last five years	90% of staff feel they are being supported to progress their career	Increased representation of women in leadership roles
		Diversity and inclusion training programme launched	Staff participation in inclusion survey to reach 75%	Inclusive recruitment policy to be in place	Website to be fully accessible		Staff participation in inclusion survey to reach 85%	100% of staff to say they understand the procedures for reporting bullying, discrimination or harassment and would feel comfortable reporting an incident			Staff participation in inclusion survey to reach 90%	

Key
Target met
Behind target
Ahead of target

We will be talking more about how you shape your communications, and build your wider reputation, in the next chapter.

Notes

1   V Kahn. Survey says: Appreciation matters more than you think, bonusly, 2 March 2022, https://bonusly.com/post/employee-appreciation-survey (archived at https://perma.cc/Y939-PNKQ)

2   P Davis. The power of employee appreciation, Psychology Today, 19 October 2023, www.psychologytoday.com/gb/blog/pressure-proof/202310/the-power-of-employee-appreciation (archived at https://perma.cc/2M55-DR7W)

3   Interview with Alex Farbon, Talent Acquisition Lead at GFT UK, December 2023

4   Women in Tech. 8 facts about women in the tech industry, www.womenintech.co.uk/8-facts-women-tech-industry (archived at https://perma.cc/M7JQ-CR69)

5   Great Place To Work. GFT Technologies, July 2023, www.greatplacetowork.com/certified-company/7002227 (archived at https://perma.cc/AK7U-V5T3)

6   Interview with Natalie Rathner, Head of Social Impact at Simply Business, November 2023

7   M Carnegie. Why workplace drinking culture is fading fast, BBC, 27 March 2023, www.bbc.com/worklife/article/20230320-why-workplace-drinking-culture-is-fading-fast (archived at https://perma.cc/BZ3W-E55D)

8   M Carnegie. Why workplace drinking culture is fading fast, BBC, 27 March 2023, www.bbc.com/worklife/article/20230320-why-workplace-drinking-culture-is-fading-fast (archived at https://perma.cc/H4CU-KMA6)

9   S Benstead. 5 simple ways to sky-rocket employee engagement, breathe, 10 April 2023, www.breathehr.com/en-gb/blog/topic/employee-engagement/want-to-drive-employee-engagement (archived at https://perma.cc/NQB8-5VYJ)

10 Perkbox, www.perkbox.com/ (archived at https://perma.cc/32DU-YBZ2)

11 huggg, www.huggg.me/ (archived at https://perma.cc/4V8K-AN77)

12 C Hastwell. Creating a culture of recognition, Great Place To Work, 2 March 2023, www.greatplacetowork.com/resources/blog/creating-a-culture-of-recognition (archived at https://perma.cc/RK7D-5454)

13 S Haththotuwa. Sober October: 34% of employees avoid work socials because of alcohol – is there an alternative?, HR Grapevine, 16 October 2023, www.hrgrapevine.com/content/article/2023-10-13-34-of-employees-avoid-work-socials-because-of-alcohol-but-is-there-an-alternative (archived at https://perma.cc/WJW7-6SD8)

14 S Mullen O'Keefe and J Buono. Crisis communication: How great leaders stop rumors before they start, Gallup, 3 April 2020, www.gallup.com/workplace/297545/crisis-communication-great-leaders-stop-rumors-start.aspx (archived at https://perma.cc/NU7E-EDJG)

18

Look at this view

You've come so far and achieved so much. In the previous chapter, we looked at how you can celebrate that success and appreciate the impact that your work has had; and in Chapter 14, we talked about the practicalities of creating a communications plan and the different ways you can share updates about your work. Here we're going to take a wider view of the story that you want to tell about this project – and how you can shape the story that you want to tell about your organization.

What makes a good story?

Storytelling is fundamental to how humans understand the world. Ever since we started walking upright, we've been interpreting and sharing our experiences by creating narratives to explain them. The oldest cave painting in the world was created around 64,000 years ago,[1] and some researchers have suggested that art was made inside caves because the flickering lights of our ancestors' flame torches made the pictures move – making them the first forms of cinema.[2] Our brains are still hard-wired to respond to stories more powerfully than to simple facts – and we remember stories more effectively too.

This is why storytelling has become such a powerful tool for organizations. When Bill Gates said, in 1996, that 'content is king',[3] he was predicting that most of the money made online would come from content – and he was right. Digital content is a richly lucrative industry, and there are few large businesses on the planet that don't use content marketing in some form to attract and convert customers. We know, then, that shaping a good story can have a powerful impact on reputation, sales, retention of both customers and staff, and long-term behaviour change. As a diversity and inclusion leader, you don't just want to talk about how brilliant your work is – you want people inside and outside your organization to make real changes, to come together to build a better world and to be part of the movement you are creating.

Storytelling has been shown to be extremely influential in changing behaviour, and it enhances positive behaviours like altruism and kindness.[4] Stories help us relate to a situation, make it more tangible in our minds and enable us to see issues from different perspectives. Our brains also react to stories as if we were experiencing the events in real life. All of this is why we are 22 times more likely to remember a story than simple facts.[5]

You can use stories to:

- encourage your team to buy into the overall vision for this project
- show the benefits of diversity and inclusion work
- celebrate the impact your diversity and inclusion project is having in your business
- lessen tensions between people with differing views, and encourage engagement and allyship
- enhance your reputation as an inclusive organization

In order to equip you with the skills to inspire your external audiences and motivate your internal team, so as to enhance your reputation and drive ongoing engagement, we're going to give you a quick crash course in how to tell a great story.

The story arc

You might have heard of the Hero's Journey[6] (a concept attributed to Joseph Campbell and since developed and debated by numerous theorists), which summarizes the essence of the most common narrative arc. Firstly, as the name suggests, there is a hero. Readers (especially Western readers, who are used to individual protagonists) connect more easily with one person who is at the centre of the story. Too many viewpoints can dilute the impact or distract your audience from the point you're trying to make. So you need your hero. Then, something will happen to throw a challenge or an opportunity in their way. The hero will try to resist dealing with it, because the challenge or opportunity is scary, but in the end, they will be put in a position where they have no choice. They will face many obstacles, but also encounter some helpers and guides. Then a point will come where everything

FIGURE 18.1 The hero's journey

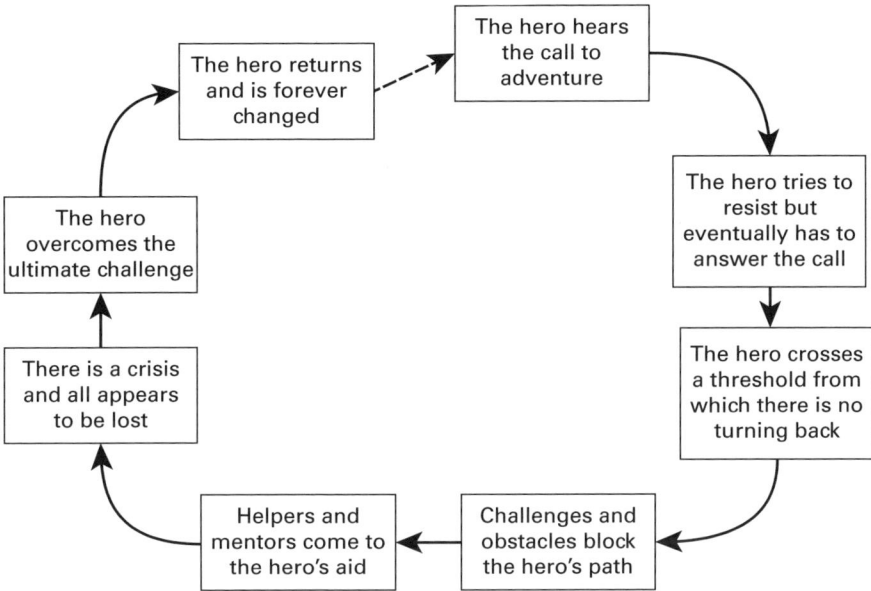

appears hopeless, but they will battle through to overcome it, and return back from their journey forever changed in some way (see Figure 18.1).

You're not writing a great novel, so the stories you create will use the essence of this story arc in its simplest form – you need a character that the audience can connect with, you need to show the struggles and challenges they face, and then you need to show how they have overcome those obstacles to triumph, and what that outcome means for them.

Making it land

For this story to have impact, it needs to resonate with your audience. This means that it has to feel relevant to them, they have to connect with the characters and they need to become emotionally invested in the outcome.

RELEVANCE

Your story should reflect the world of your listeners (or at least have enough recognizable elements that relate to their world that they can identify with it and feel at home within it). The challenges and opportunities the story offers also need to connect to the values of your audience – you need to understand what they feel is important and meaningful so that you can tap into that.

CONNECTION

You need to be able to foster empathy in your audience – that means that they can see things from your hero's perspective and put themselves in their shoes. They need to feel the emotional impact of the events unfolding, and that needs to feel real and relatable.

INVESTMENT

There need to be some stakes involved, and your audience needs to feel that they matter. You need to set up a sense of potential peril if the hero doesn't succeed, and, if the story has felt relevant to them and they have connected with your hero, then they will feel a strong desire to see the hero triumph.

Narrative elements

In addition, there are a few other key elements for you to consider in crafting your story:

- **Novelty** – human brains crave newness, so a story that feels different and original will pique interest much more than one your audience feels they've heard a million times before.

- **Show, don't tell** – this is an old writing adage, and one that's popular for a reason; audiences don't want to be told what conclusions to draw, they want to draw their own. As Anton Chekhov said, 'Don't tell me the moon is shining; show me the glint of light on broken glass.'[7] Or, in the case of stories about diversity and inclusion, don't tell people that certain behaviour is upsetting, show them the distress it causes and help them experience it for themselves.

- **Repeat yourself** – people won't necessarily pay attention the first time; don't be afraid to tell several similar stories, or tell the same story in different formats using different media (such as blogs, videos and newsletters). As we've discussed previously, there are a variety of ways that people take in different information, so sharing your story using a variety of methods is more likely to broaden its impact.

- **Engage the senses** – the more real a story feels for us, the more active a role our brain plays in taking it in, and therefore the more we remember and internalize it. Your goal is to fully transport your audience into the world of the story, and engaging the senses through vivid description, sensory details and relatable experiences is one of the best ways to do that.

- **Streamline** – we have short attention spans as a species, especially in our modern world of constant conflicting demands. Keep your story succinct, to-the-point and fast-paced to keep your audience engaged. If you need it to be long, consider breaking it into segments or instalments to allow people to digest it in manageable chunks.

- **Prime your audience** – research shows we are staggeringly suggestible. Stories can prime us to take certain actions just by dropping in hints or examples. In one study, people who had read a story about someone behaving in a foolish and mindless manner subsequently performed significantly worse in a general knowledge test.[8] If you want your audience to take a particular action after they've been told your story, consider how you can prime them for that.

- **Call to action** – depending on the situation, you may want to directly tell them what action to take next. If you're recruiting for people to join your inclusion working group or you want staff to take your next survey, then say so. People are much more likely to take an action if it's clearly pointed out to them, and if it's a simple action they can take straight away.

Telling the world

Now that you know how to tell a great story, let's look at how you can get that story out to the world.

Press releases

One simple way you might want to go about this is to send press releases to relevant media. This might include national, local, business or industry press. Before you do this, though, you'll need to consider whether you really have a story. Many a business has sent out press releases about their new logo or change of premises and wondered why they haven't received any coverage – now that you're an expert storyteller, you know the answer. There isn't relevance for the reader, there's no hero they can connect with, and there are no stakes or revelations for them to become invested in.

To have a story that will capture the imagination of the media, you will need at least one, preferably several, of the following:

- **Something new and innovative** – for example, an initiative or approach that you have introduced that no one else is doing (or at least not many people), or that you are doing in a brand new way.

- **Stats or data** – if you can show tangible impact, through original findings or results that you've produced, journalists will be much more interested.

- **A big picture view** – media outlets don't want to just promote your business, unless you pay them for advertising space; if you're going to generate a news story, you need a message that's bigger than yourself. You can share your particular perspective, but you also need to be able to look at the wider landscape and how your experience can provide learnings or insights for others.

- **A topical element** – a connection to a big news story or a calendar date is very attractive to journalists (a huge success story on helping female staff return to work after having babies could be a good news story around Mother's Day, for example).

- **Clear targeting** – you need to understand exactly which audience will be interested in this, and which publications/platforms, and which journalists within each of those, write for that specific audience (e.g. is this a story about overcoming discrimination that might be of interest to the general public or is this about specific innovations in the finance sector that would be of interest to people in particular roles within that industry?).

Thought leadership

You don't have to rely on other people to tell your story for you. There are plenty of ways you can share your insights with your audience, and potentially build a wider audience in the process. Similar rules apply to sharing stories with the media, though. Whilst you can publish whatever you like on your own platforms, if the content you're producing isn't resonating with and engaging your audience, they won't respond to it, and they may even be actively turned away from your brand. In this age of the algorithm, a lack of engagement also means a lack of visibility – the fewer people that interact with a post, the fewer people the platform will show your future posts to. Ensuring that you have a story that will feel relevant, emotionally resonant and important to your audience remains vital, even when you're the publisher.

Thought leadership means sharing insights and learnings that can inspire and educate others. By doing this, you establish a reputation as an organization that is committed to this work as well as being at the forefront of understanding and grappling with the challenges it presents. This cements you in the minds of your audience as a business that is walking the talk – even if you're not perfect yet. As we've said before, no one expects you to have nailed it, and being honest about challenges and shortcomings actually builds trust. When your audience sees that you're doing the real work – and they recognize that this involves facing real struggles – they come to see you as an inclusive business, and an inclusive employer, and one that shares their values. They see you as a business they want to support.

Here are some ways you could share thought leadership on diversity and inclusion with your audience:

- **Blogs** – for example, a regular (maybe quarterly) update from your CEO on the progress of your diversity and inclusion work, and what results have been produced, as well as what challenges you've faced and how you dealt with them.

- **Social media** – short and concise messages work best here, so celebrating milestones that you've reached, sharing a solution you found to a problem, announcing new projects that you're embarking on to address specific issues or sharing individual people's stories work well on social media.

- **LinkedIn articles** – although social media posts need to be concise, LinkedIn offers the option to write long-form articles, where you can take a deeper dive into an issue, and encourage discussion from readers.

- **Email newsletters** – if you send out a regular email newsletter, incorporating a diversity and inclusion update to share progress and challenges would be valuable. You could even create a specific newsletter for your diversity and inclusion lead to provide updates on your progress and share your learnings.

- **Podcast** – if you already have a podcast for your business, you could introduce a segment on diversity and inclusion and the impact it's having, as well as the learnings and challenges you've encountered. Or, if you think you have the time and resources, your diversity and inclusion lead could create a new podcast to share this journey. You will need to find your niche – the unique angle that will attract and engage your audience – so perhaps this is understanding how to implement diversity and inclusion work within your specific industry. You can then interview other people in your space – or in other industries to gain their insights – and discuss the challenges and solutions you've discovered.

In the worksheet at the end of this chapter, you'll be able to take a look at your existing channels and see how you could utilize them effectively for storytelling. Regular updates work well, so that your audience can see this is an ongoing project for you, not something you're mentioning briefly for the sake of appearances. So consider the schedule you came up with in Chapter 14, and how your storytelling can integrate with that.

As you begin to build a reputation as thought leaders in this space, you may find yourself being invited to share your message on other platforms – and you don't need to wait for an invitation; you can research platforms that you think would be a good fit for your business (in terms of crossover with target audience and core values) and offer yourself as one of the following:

- **Guest blogger** – other platforms that cater to a similar target audience to yours may well be interested in a guest blog from you about particular learnings or insights you've gained.

- **Podcast guest** – there are a wide range of business podcasts, some of which are specifically interested in diversity and inclusion or related HR/ People topics, and some of which will look at all facets of your specific industry, that may well be interested in having you as a guest to discuss your journey.

- **Interview subject** – a wide variety of different platforms, from traditional media to blogs and vlogs to networking groups and a whole host of others often create content using interviews. Keep an eye on the platforms that your target audience are engaging with and look for opportunities to offer yourself as an interviewee to any of these.

- **Content collaborator** – collaboration is becoming a popular way to create new forms of content and reach wider audiences by teaming up with someone else; when you work with a collaborator, you can access their audience and they can access yours. There are so many different ways to create collaborative content, from interview series to co-created events and projects – it's worth watching how other people do it for a while to gain inspiration. If you identify people who you think would be good collaborators (these are usually people with a large audience of the kind that you want to tap into and who complement but don't compete with you), then you might suggest getting together to brainstorm some ideas.

- **Speaker or panellist** – from industry conferences to business events to TEDx and other general interest speaking slots, there are so many places that you can talk about your journey if you craft a good story around it.

Professional networks

We mentioned in Chapters 8 and 12 that being part of professional networks to discuss diversity and inclusion can be a valuable way to learn from others. You can also contribute to these networks by sharing your story and the learnings you've taken. Often people are hesitant to admit that they've faced challenges, particularly if they think competitors are watching. They don't want to show weakness. But hopefully throughout the course of this book we've convinced you that honesty is not a weakness. Every business is facing challenges in this area, and attempting to cover over them or pretend they're not happening is what causes the biggest reputational issues. Openly admitting to difficulties is a great show of strength – you are demonstrating that you're truly working and growing, and that you're not afraid of feedback.

The more that you show your willingness to work with, learn from and share with others, the more you establish yourself as a leader in this space, and in your sector. You will also gain so much from others – being open in your sharing encourages others to share with you. That means that you'll be given insights into other businesses' struggles and the solutions they've found, so that you can avoid some of the pitfalls they've encountered and get a head start on some areas of your work.

The internal work

It isn't just about what the wider world thinks of you, though. It's important not to lose sight of the value of internal perception. For this project to succeed in the long term, you need your team to be behind it, driving it forward. This means they need to be fully bought in, engaged and convinced of its worth. They need to feel heard, supported and valued as part of the process, and that their contribution not only matters but is recognized. They need to see progress, but they also want to know that you're aware of gaps and blockers. How you shape the story of this project will be vital to its ongoing success.

Shaping your narrative

We have already vigorously underlined the need for honesty and transparency, but it is particularly crucial when it comes to your internal storytelling. The people on the ground know the reality – if you try to tell them everything is rosy when they're fully aware that it isn't, all that's going to happen is that they will lose faith in you as an employer and lose complete trust in this project. They won't want to engage on a meaningful level if they don't believe that you're looking deeply and openly at the issues. Talking about your challenges and blockers, whilst being willing to be vulnerable about how hard the journey really is, is actually a very effective way to encourage people to get behind it. Tell them a story about the problems that exist (which they already know about), whilst inspiring them to believe that overcoming those problems is possible with their help, and you'll have a team raring to take action.

We all see ourselves as protagonists in our own lives, and in telling this story you have a chance to make everyone the hero. You can show how the actions your team have taken, the feedback and insights they've shared and the culture they've built together, have made tangible differences. You can share stories of individual successes and collective triumphs. You also give your audience a chance to get inside the story and write the next part with you. As this story is continuously unfolding, it can be fully interactive, and you can invite contributions from across your organization.

Telling a story effectively invites empathy, by enabling the audience to place themselves in the protagonist's shoes. If your team is divided on the value of diversity and inclusion work, some well-told stories can help people see the societal and institutional barriers that impact people's lives, and start to feel more willing to address these. You need to be subtle here, though – if sections of your audience are already sceptical about inclusion work, going in hard with a story clearly designed to show the evils of injustice is only going to make them roll their eyes. Your story will need to reflect the complexities that this audience perceive within this situation, and speak to them in language that resonates with them, so that they are willing to engage and open themselves up to being won over.

Sharing the stage

As a leader, you don't want to make yourself too much of a hero in this story. If your team feel like you're trying to centre the people at the top in all this, they will quickly suspect you of being disingenuous and you will lose their attention. In the majority of organizations, the leadership team are not the heroes of the story. The heroes are the people who face systemic inequalities and personal challenges, and who are finding ways to overcome them. The leaders in your organization might be part of the team of helpers that support the hero on their journey, but they shouldn't be the centre of the story. A relatable, engaging protagonist that we all want to root for is one that we feel is just like us. Your team want a story about a colleague whose experience feels relevant to their own.

This is a chance to centre the voices of people who are often marginalized and unheard – both in your organization and in wider society. Whether it's through blog content, videos, podcasts, interviews, newsletters, internal talks or any other kind of content you care to create for your staff, you can use these platforms to share stories from a variety of different people, and give your staff insight into a wide variety of different experiences. Through hearing first-hand from diverse individuals, your team gains a greater understanding of their colleagues' experiences, challenges and strengths, and can better recognize how to work effectively together.

In addition to creating content, we have seen a number of organizations hosting innovative events that celebrate and explore diversity and inclusion. For example, one client that we worked with hosted a one-day conference to share their progress on their inclusion journey so far, and invited their team to discuss how the work was going and what more should be done. This organization invited a range of people to speak who they knew would challenge them – they identified people who they knew had been frustrated or unhappy about inclusion-related issues in the past, and asked them to give a talk as part of the conference that would ask tough questions and provoke deep thought. They put individual members of staff and other key stakeholder groups at the centre of the day – the leadership team's only contribution was to underline how important this work was and that it was a key part of the values of the organization.

Remember that you don't always need to be the one creating the stories – you can create a platform for other people to create content, speak and share. You can collate a library of individual voices, and connect to Employee Resource Groups, staff networks and other relevant groups to provide them with a mouthpiece for their community. Often stories are most powerful when they're not scripted by a third party but come organically and naturally from an individual with no agenda but their truth.

FIGURE 18.2 Inclusion journey storytelling worksheet

Core messaging matrix
This section will identify the main elements that underpin your stories.

Organizational values	Inclusion journey goals
Desired actions (what do you want your audience to do next)	**Points of interest** (key data, big successes, major challenges, individual stories)

Audiences
This section will help you understand your different audiences and what stories are right for them.

Audience (Who are they?)	Interests (What matters to them?)	Points of interest (What will resonate with them?)	Actions (What do you want them to do?)

Platforms
This section will help you identify the different platforms you have available to you and how best to use each one.

Platform	Audience (Who do you reach on this platform?)	Content (What type of content works best here?)	Key messaging (What stories will you tell here?)

Timeline

This section will help you to plan your storytelling for the next 12 months (you can adapt this timeline to suit a longer timeframe if you prefer). Plot on the line key targets, milestones, internal or external events, and then map any key stories / messages you expect to share at different times.

Month	1	2	3	4	5	6
Targets/milestones						
Events						
Messaging						

Month	7	8	9	10	11	12
Targets/milestones						
Events						
Messaging						

Always learning

As we've discussed previously, this is an ongoing journey of learning and growth, that will necessitate a willingness to stay open to feedback. You will never be able to recognize the actions that need to be taken or deliver work that makes a meaningful impact if you are not willing to listen to inputs that are sometimes uncomfortable. In order to build trust, credibility and authenticity, a huge part of your internal and external narrative will need to be an active solicitation of these inputs, and ongoing demonstrations that you are hearing and responding to feedback. If you can tell people what you've learned and show how you've grown as a result, then that is a story they will want to hear.

What's your story?

The inclusion journey storytelling worksheet (Figure 18.2) will help you craft the story that you want to tell, and develop creative ideas for sharing that story with the world. Use that worksheet to explore the unique story that you have to tell.

Notes

1 H Barnard Gerber. Ten oldest known cave paintings in the world, The Archaeologist, 18 December 2022, www.thearchaeologist.org/blog/ten-oldest-known-cave-paintings-in-the-world (archived at https://perma.cc/L2NZ-VKU7)

2 S Cascone. Was cave art actually a form of cinema? How prehistoric lamps suggest a surprising new way of looking at ancient paintings, artnet, 2 August 2021, https://news.artnet.com/art-world/prehistoric-cave-art-proto-cinema-1994505 (archived at https://perma.cc/G27E-NLEZ)

3 H Evans. 'Content is King' — Essay by Bill Gates 1996, Medium, 30 January 2017, https://medium.com/@HeathEvans/content-is-king-essay-by-bill-gates-1996-df74552f80d9 (archived at https://perma.cc/DB3T-J3TU)

4 B Passon. The power of storytelling for behavior change and business, *American Journal of Health Promotion*, 2019, 33 (3), 475–76, https://journals.sagepub.com/doi/full/10.1177/0890117119825525d (archived at https://perma.cc/7QYG-H4T7)

5 B Passon. The power of storytelling for behavior change and business, *American Journal of Health Promotion*, 2019, 33 (3), 475–76, https://journals.sagepub.com/doi/full/10.1177/0890117119825525d (archived at https://perma.cc/7QYG-H4T7)

6 reedsy blog. The hero's journey: 12 steps to a classic story structure, https://blog.reedsy.com/guide/story-structure/heros-journey/ (archived at https://perma.cc/2FH7-5XT7)

7 A Chekhov (trans. A Yarmolinsky) (1954) *The Unknown Chekhov: Stories and other writings hitherto untranslated by Anton Chekhov*, Noonday Press, New York, Introduction p 14

8 M Appel. A story about a stupid person can make you act stupid (or smart): behavioral assimilation (and contrast) as narrative impact, University of Linz, Austria, www.appel-lab.com/wp-content/uploads/2014/08/Appel2011_Media-Psychology_Narratives-and-Performance_PREPRINT.pdf (archived at https://perma.cc/TBE6-ZULB)

19

Where to next?

You got there! You have now checked everything off the roadmap, celebrated your progress and told people about all the fantastic work you have done. Most importantly, you have seen the impact of changes you have made on the organization and people. You are getting great feedback about all the progress made from people, and it feels like a wonderful sense of achievement for everyone who has worked so hard on the inclusion journey. This isn't the end though. Inclusion work is never actually done, and never something you can forget about. The work to create an even more inclusive organization continues as you all grow and learn more. The world keeps turning and changing. If you imagine that you have travelled to the top of a mountain, what can you see? From your vantage point you can see the next mountain you want to reach or perhaps the next valley you need to explore. The work continues and evolves as everyone in the organization learns more and mindsets change. This final chapter looks at where you might want to travel to next, and the things to consider as you continue along your way.

Review the map

When you get to the point that you have achieved all the goals and milestones you set out in that original roadmap, appreciate how far you have come. We have looked at how you might mark the successes along the way in Chapter 17, but this calls for a special celebration, and a chance to bask in that feeling of accomplishment. Getting to the final milestone on your roadmap is also a time to review everything. Have a look at what you set out to achieve, and what the original vision and mission were.

At this point, it's great to look at all your data again to assess where you are now. What metrics have changed? What are people saying in your latest employee survey? And what external feedback have you had? When we work with organizations, at this stage, we suggest looking at all the data points again to reassess your current situation, just like we did at the very beginning. Then you can see and understand what needs to be looked at in your next stage of work as the organization evolves. You will not need to complete all of the initial analysis again; this is about checking back on the key data points and metrics to see what has changed. If you do not already run a regular employee survey or perhaps pulse surveys throughout, then it's a good idea to re-run your original staff survey and see the results now. This is also a useful time to review other metrics you may have set up. An example schedule for reviewing your data is shown in Table 19.1.

Looking at the data again at this point and reviewing your roadmap actions will show you a lot about where you have progressed to. You might find at this point that the review shows you even more things to celebrate, as some key things have changed which you might not have paused to notice. Or you might find that there are areas still left to explore in some more detail. Useful metrics here will show you what your current situation is so that you can plan ahead. Consider at this point what you want to focus on next. It might be that you are now getting great employee feedback about

TABLE 19.1 Example re-run of inclusion journey data

Item	Frequency	Additional note
Employee survey	At least annually, preferably more frequently	Could be adapted to regular pulse surveys
Demographic data	At least annually	Can be reviewed more regularly in reporting
External feedback	At least annually	Should be ongoing reviews
Exit interviews	When anyone leaves	Check regularly for any themes
Recruitment date	At least quarterly depending on size of organization	Should be ongoing review of these metrics
Retention and progression	At least annually	Depending on size of organization, this should be checked regularly
Buildings and technology review	At least annually	Keep track of system and technology changes regularly with a process for anything new
Supplier reviews	At least annually	Process should be in place to check new suppliers have their own checks and metrics in place
Training analysis	At least annually	Check that all employees are participating in ongoing learning

inclusion; how can you ensure that continues? What are some key things to continue to check in on?

For employee surveys, there are many great software platforms you can use to help engage your employees. As well as annual or quarterly surveys, a lot of employee survey tools use 'pulse' data, which ask employees questions in short form throughout the year. This can be an effective way to continue to measure how employees are feeling and any feedback from them. Each software provider will give different examples of good questions to ask employees and you can usually customize them for your team.

Examples of good questions to ask for continuing engagement are:

- Would you recommend our organization as a great place to work?
- Do you feel a sense of belonging at this organization?
- Are you excited about our organization's future?
- Does our organization have a great culture?
- Are you satisfied with how decisions are made at this organization?

As part of your review, it's also so inspiring to collect feedback in the form of conversations and quotes. Ask people for their thoughts. Ask them how they feel now to have been part of this journey. Collect feedback from people who were recruited along the way, as well as those who were involved from the start. These stories are a powerful way to show people how far everyone has come. We have seen some great examples of people sharing stories in the form of videos and anecdotes from employees to bring everyone together and show why this was a priority.

Learning journey

Learning about diversity and inclusion and the different concepts is a journey as well. We suggest to our clients that their teams learn about different subject areas as they progress through the journey. As we have already seen, people learn and process information in different ways, so learning programmes need to consider this. It's useful for everyone in the organization to do a certain level of training so that there is shared understanding, although some roles might require additional specialist or more in-depth learning.

As we said before, there is some truth in the media stories claiming that diversity and inclusion training does not work. A one-off, one-hour training course will not embed deep learning and drive change. There has to be a programme of ongoing education and development, which includes support for people to embed new ways of working and communicating on an ongoing basis. When we look at where you travel to next, learning and development should be a key part of this. If you have not already got an ongoing learning programme in place, here are some things to consider:

- Learning budget allocated for each employee
- How training is selected and offered to people
- Whether any of the training is mandatory
- How different roles have time allocated for learning
- Equipping leaders to understand their team's learning needs

Then there are different ways you can offer learning to people. To help your teams engage with learning, offer them different opportunities which are researched. We have seen some great examples where teams are given a learning budget to then select some different options, and we have also seen examples where training is mandatory for everyone. There are some suggestions in Table 19.2.

TABLE 19.2 Types of learning

Type of learning	Advantage	Disadvantage
In-house training	Cost effective Tailored to your team	Takes up time May require research Time to develop training
External supplier	External expertise Brings experience	Needs budget Time to research suppliers
E-learning	Self-led Uniform training Assessed	Lack of engagement Lack of shared learning Not tailored No opportunity for questions Can be disengaging
Open training courses	Meet other people Share learning Share ideas	Not tailored Can be tricky to share information Time constraints
Conferences	Industry learning Network with others	Time and expense to travel Time to research conferences Does not suit all personalities Not tailored
Membership groups	Network with others Share ideas and learning	Not always specific on learning People at different stages Requires individual effort to engage

FIGURE 19.1 Typical diversity and inclusion training subjects

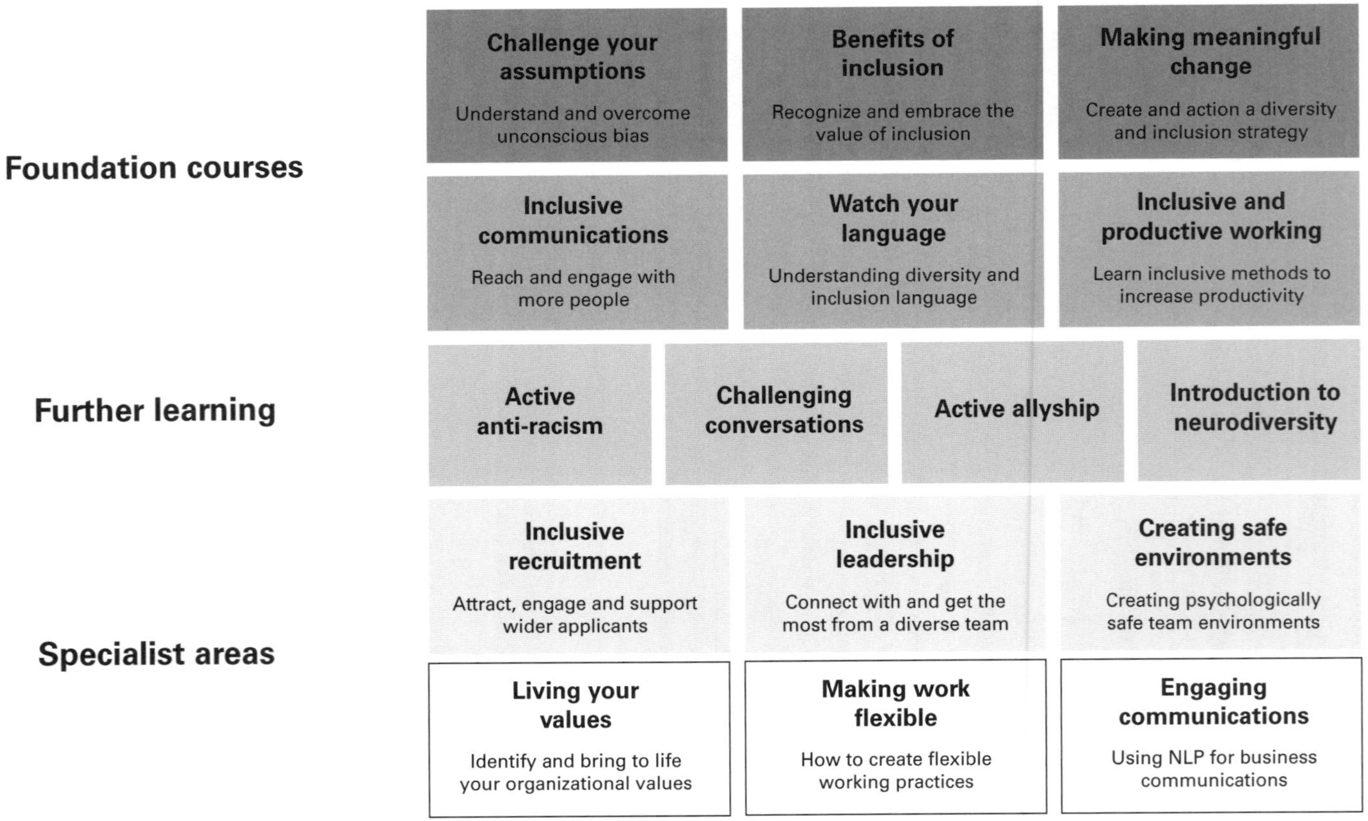

Foundation courses

Challenge your assumptions
Understand and overcome unconscious bias

Benefits of inclusion
Recognize and embrace the value of inclusion

Making meaningful change
Create and action a diversity and inclusion strategy

Inclusive communications
Reach and engage with more people

Watch your language
Understanding diversity and inclusion language

Inclusive and productive working
Learn inclusive methods to increase productivity

Introduction to neurodiversity

Further learning

Active anti-racism

Challenging conversations

Active allyship

Inclusive recruitment
Attract, engage and support wider applicants

Inclusive leadership
Connect with and get the most from a diverse team

Creating safe environments
Creating psychologically safe team environments

Specialist areas

Living your values
Identify and bring to life your organizational values

Making work flexible
How to create flexible working practices

Engaging communications
Using NLP for business communications

The main thing to consider is how interactive the training is and how easy it is for people to engage with it, ask questions and take actions back to their roles. Consider how you offer training to any new starters to bring them up to speed on where the organization is. How is learning introduced in your onboarding process? And how will you ensure that any new starters are given opportunities to learn? As you develop your learning programme, this is a great thing to talk about in recruitment processes too, and factor in questions around different areas of inclusion so you can see where people are on their personal inclusion journey. It is incredibly valuable to ask people about learning during recruitment processes and when they start working with you. Your new recruits may bring brilliant ideas which they have learnt about in other organizations, which you can introduce as part of your learning programme.

For the subjects that people learn about in training sessions and workshops, there are many providers who can help with subjects to learn about. Some organizations work with suppliers to design specific training programmes. Good examples are training around biases, language and inclusive ways of working. There will be other subject areas relevant to your organization which you discover in the initial stages and as you progress. A typical approach to structuring learning is shown in Figure 19.1.

As well as training, do also consider other ways you can offer learning and development to people in the organization. Coaching will help people to develop their skills and mindset; mentoring programmes can help people to network, learn and progress their careers; and we have seen great examples of reverse mentoring, where leaders can learn from people in more junior roles. This is all about embedding a culture of ongoing learning so that everyone is thinking about how they can grow as they move forward.

Future leaders

Linked to learning and development is retention and progression for people in the organization. A key part of continuing your inclusion journey involves considering who will be the next people to move into leadership roles. Who has shown that they are ready to step up? Who has shown they are capable of leading in a way that embodies the values and culture that you are building? Who can bring a fresh perspective and approach to senior-level decision-making? This thinking is part of the ongoing work to continue to drive change. Without continuing focus on this, you risk going back to square one in the make-up of your leadership teams.

In Chapter 10 we looked briefly at Future Leaders programmes. These types of programmes are a brilliant way to embed ongoing development and create a pipeline of diverse future leaders. Research by the CIPD (Chartered Institute of People Development) in the UK found that more than 6.5 million people intended to quit their jobs in the next 12 months,[1] with a third of those people looking for better pay and benefits. A survey by CareerAddict found that 82 per cent of people would leave their job owing to a lack of career progression.[2] In the USA, a survey by Guild showed that 41 per cent of workers quit their roles owing to a lack of career progression.[3] Delving into some of the reasons why shows us that people do try to progress their careers with their employer, but they are sometimes held back. A US survey showed that, although women receive higher ratings than men for performance, they were 14 per cent less likely to be promoted.[4] Now, these are factors you will have already looked at as part of your inclusion journey; you need to be mindful that the focus remains on these areas, and on driving meaningful change in the places it's needed most.

Often what people are looking for is learning and development opportunities that will enable them to progress to their next role. And people will usually look in their current organization for those opportunities first. It is when they are not given those opportunities that they look elsewhere. The MIT survey of US workers shows that staff who are passed over for a promotion are up to 50 per cent more likely to leave.[5] Continuing focus on future leaders is a way to retain and develop talent, by showing them a roadmap to a more senior role and showing that you care about their growth. Programmes can be tailored to suit the organization, and a typical programme might provide some of the benefits shown in Table 19.3.

TABLE 19.3 Future leaders programme design elements

Who?	Element	Learning objective
Participant	Application and selection process	Career planning
Participant	Welcome event	Networking
Participant	In-person workshops	Learning
Participant	Online workshops	Learning
Participant	Sponsor 1:1 sessions	Relationship building, career development
Participant	Change project	Networking, team working, strategy
Participant	Celebration event	Networking, celebrating success

(continued)

TABLE 19.3 (Continued)

Who?	Element	Learning objective
Sponsor	Sponsors volunteer and are selected	Networking
Sponsor	Sponsor workshops	Learning
Sponsor	Celebration event	Networking, celebrating success
Line Manager	Support with applications	Career planning for team
Line Manager	Ongoing reviews	Career planning
Line Manager	Celebration event	Networking, celebrating success

Including a change project as part of these programmes is another effective way to build networks and drive ongoing change. Typically, participants are encouraged to think of ways in which they think the organization can be changed or improved. Then they form small teams of perhaps three or four people to work on their change project alongside their work on the programme. They are supported by their Sponsors, and then introduced by their Sponsors to relevant people who can help them progress the project, which also enables them to grow their network. We often see that these small groups then join Employee Resource Groups at the end of the programme to continue the ongoing work on the inclusion journey.

With these programmes, as people progress their careers, cohorts of alumni form strong networks. For ongoing career development for people who typically face systemic barriers, these types of networks can be incredibly valuable, and they can offer a great deal to the future development of your inclusion journey. This is how you develop the culture of the organization and your leaders of the future, by empowering diverse people with different perspectives and lived experiences who have learnt about collaborating with, and working with others so you create teams of leaders who embrace your new ways of working.

Case study – a local authority

Many organizations use Future Leaders programmes to address specific areas of under-representation, guided by data they have about their employees. We worked with a local authority on a programme similar in content to our programmes for future leaders. This programme was to address diverse talent.

The Local Authority represents a population of more than 200,000 people and was already working on equalities and anti-racism. Through this work they looked at their data on their employees. They wanted to not only retain but also develop their staff from under-represented groups. Their data showed that BAME and White Other staff were not proportionately represented in senior roles. Their staff survey also showed them that these employees were less likely to believe they had opportunities to develop their careers.

We developed a bespoke Diverse Talent Programme specifically for them, which followed another programme of this kind that they had run the year before. All employees who worked in the relevant grades were encouraged to apply for the programme, and those who applied were supported by their Line Manager, with expectations made clear about the time commitment required to participate in the programme. Fifteen people were selected to join, and the programme ran for six months.

The programme included:

- Matching each Participant with a Sponsor in a senior role, who would develop their relationship with the Participant, and meet with them regularly to mentor them
- Monthly workshop training sessions with Watch This Sp_ce
- Access for all Participants to the Council's 'Learning Zone' for training
- Two individual coaching sessions with Watch This Sp_ce for all Participants
- Work on career development plans throughout the programme

The Sponsors also had training sessions with the Watch This Sp_ce team on subjects such as Allyship, Unconscious Bias and Inclusive Leadership. This encouraged Sponsors to learn about the experiences of the people they were working with, gain skills that would help them effectively provide support and to network with other Sponsors.

We collected feedback from both Sponsors and Participants throughout the programme, to enable us to develop the sessions and adapt as we moved along. People were open about frustrations in progressing to next level roles, which meant that everyone could have open conversations about how to address areas of frustration.

The training workshops we ran were a mixture of online and in-person sessions, taking place once a month. Coaching sessions and Sponsor sessions were on-line. The Participants networked during their sessions and formed strong relationships which have continued beyond the programme.

What were the results?

The Local Authority saw some significant results after the implementation of the Watch This Sp_ce Diverse Talent Programme.

Of the 15 Participants, three were promoted within six months of the programme's completion, with a further seven applying for new, more senior roles.

We received positive feedback from Sponsors individually, and from the Sponsor/Participant partnerships, expressing that the partnerships had worked really well to help people, introduce them to and develop new relationships and provide them with advice and work shadowing opportunities.

Many of the Sponsors have continued to support Participants after the programme ended. For the metrics that were set as indicators of success for the programme, 40 per cent said they felt more confident to progress to their next role, 50 per cent said they were more confident in their communication skills for work and 85 per cent would recommend the programme to others.

And the feedback from individual people involved in the programme was positive too. The programme Participants were able to learn and make progress in their careers. What was fascinating was the insight that the Sponsors gained from working with people in different roles. This led to developing longer-term relationships where they continued to meet.

The programme has shown the leadership that this is an effective way to progress people's careers. They plan to run more programmes like this for future leaders to address areas of under-representation and create more representative leadership teams.

New people, new direction

Employees in the organization will progress their careers into more senior roles, but you will also recruit new people for roles where you need to bring in new skills. The work on your inclusion journey should form part of the recruitment process so that you are recruiting people who want to work in the inclusive ways you have developed. They are very likely to have taken learnings on inclusion from previous employers, too, so they will bring new ideas, perhaps question how things are done and re-energize the direction you might take next. New people joining provides a great opportunity to listen, learn and consider new opportunities. This should form part of the onboarding process for new employees.

This approach can also be applied with existing employees who progress to a new role or team. They might have seen great ways of working in their previous role, which they then introduce to their new team. When someone starts a new role, take the chance to find out what their thoughts and ideas are, and also give them opportunities to get involved in any potential new areas of work.

New directions will also come from those who are learning about different areas and developing new skills and ideas. Encouraging an environment where new ideas are welcomed will create an ongoing learning culture. People will continue to share new thinking and new ideas as you progress, which keeps the journey refreshed. This will also encourage everyone to keep thinking about where the inclusion journey should take you next, as you move into the future.

Mindset

As you have progressed on your inclusion journey, there will have been a fundamental mindset change in the organization. This takes place gradually, as people progress through different stages of the journey. All of that initial work to get buy-in across the organization will have changed how people think about inclusion, and their understanding will have deepened as they take part in training and see the results the work creates. People are now likely to be working in different ways, and using language differently. The way things are done in your business is likely to have undergone a significant change.

For your ongoing work, it is important to remind people about that mindset shift and consider how you embed that in all the ways of working as a continuous process. Particularly when people are under pressure, as that is often when things can go backwards. In the moments of stress, people might find themselves slipping back into ways of working that make people feel excluded. Put in place support mechanisms and learning to support your new approach. And it should form a key part of the competencies for leaders to check in with their teams about how they are working. As well as ongoing learning programmes for everyone, we recommend embedding coaching and mentoring so that people can talk things through and build sustainable ways of working inclusively.

We have also seen effective ways in which inclusion journey objectives become embedded in performance reviews. Instead of one annual appraisal, ongoing reviews work well to check in on progress and challenges, keep key

TABLE 19.4 Typical diversity and inclusion training subjects

Question	Competency
How are you making your team decision-making inclusive?	Decision-making
Which perspectives are you including as part of your team recruitment?	Recruitment
How are your team learning from other teams?	Collaboration
How have you expanded your learning over the last year?	Learning
What methods are you using to empower people who work with you?	Delegation
Have you adapted any processes in the last year to make them more inclusive?	Adaptability
How do you ensure all meetings and events include people?	Planning
Have you adapted any working practices in the last year to account for your biases?	Adaptability
How have you acted on feedback in the last year around inclusion?	Response to feedback

objectives front of mind and give people space and time to work on goals throughout the year. To support the mindset change, it's useful to include 360-degree reviews, where people ask others who they work with for feedback. This, along with objectives around inclusion, can help to embed that inclusive mindset for the future.

Table 19.4 shows examples of the types of questions people can be asked in regular review discussions. Each organization can also include specific questions which relate to their unique inclusion journey. Asking people to review their learning around inclusion will help embed inclusive ways of working and encourage an ongoing learning environment.

The mindset shift in your working culture links to ongoing wellbeing and mental health work which you can embed with your teams as ways of working. We have looked at why it is important to consider support for mental health throughout the journey, and this should continue. Alongside this, your teams will benefit from wellbeing training and coaching. This could be around subjects such as resilience, so that you create the mindset, behaviours and cultures for resilient teams.

Collaboration

Working effectively with colleagues and across teams will have already been part of the work on the inclusion journey, and you will want to ensure this continues so that you embed a culture of collaboration. The next stage on your journey will be about collaboration with other organizations. Connecting with organizations that have also been working on an inclusion journey, as we have seen, helps you to learn, make progress and build your reputation. As well as connecting with organizations that are both ahead of you and at earlier stages, you can connect with community groups and campaign groups connected with relevant areas.

We encourage organizations we work with to connect with each other so that they collaborate and learn from one another. There are always opportunities to refine what you are doing and consider new opportunities. There can be ways to collaborate on ideas, but also potentially on career opportunities for people, resources shared, events to go to, and more.

Looking outwards and working with other people helps keep a check on the direction too. It's often the case that a partner organization can see something you cannot, or they might have new ideas to re-energize the work you are doing.

Future direction

What we have seen all the way through this book is that the inclusion journey does not stand on its own in terms of direction and strategy. If we think back to the reasons why you decided to embark on this journey, it was all linked to your business goals and priorities. Creating inclusive teams and ways of working helps with innovation, productivity, problem-solving, happiness, recruitment, retention, team development and more. So why would you want to stop? This is about the future direction of your entire business. The more you work on this, the more it all becomes linked to your organizational strategy and direction.

Linking objectives, perhaps financial rewards and your strategy to your inclusion goals will ensure that your future direction both informs, and is informed by, your inclusion strategy. From the companies we have worked with and talked to who are further along in their inclusion journey, this is the approach they are taking to their next stages. For example, insurance company Simply Business and tech companies GFT, and Datatec and Logicalis have all made strong progress in their inclusion journeys, and they told us about continuing focus through objectives. Natalie Rathner at Simply Business talked to us about changing political and business landscapes, which will drive agendas. To ensure they continue on their journey, they are working on embedding diversity and inclusion metrics into performance reviews.

Dina Knight at Datatec and Logicalis talked to us about developing strong leadership attributes which have inclusion competencies built in. She wants to see resilience, positive mindset and acting with integrity as core leadership skills, with work done to look at how leaders address any inequalities into the future. She says 'resilience is absolutely critical'[6] so that there is a focus on inclusion going forwards and the culture created is inclusive by design.

The future is about inclusion work becoming embedded in corporate strategy and it being measured as part of corporate reporting. At GFT UK, Alex Farbon sees the work on inclusion becoming a core part of their corporate social responsibility goals. They already have measures in place for sustainability to work on their carbon footprint.[7] He says the ongoing work is to constantly review the inclusion metrics and measure them alongside those goals. And a common theme from all organizations who have progressed on inclusion is that the responsibility for this work and focus has to be across teams, including leadership teams, so that it does not get forgotten.

Instead of seeing the inclusion journey as a one-off exercise, it becomes something people plan for and work on as an ongoing process. After all, everyone wants to have an exciting destination to travel towards.

Notes

1 CIPD. 6.5 million workers plan to quit in search of better jobs in the next year, but it's not all about pay, shows new CIPD research, Press Release, 27 June 2022, www.cipd.org/uk/about/press-releases/220622-cipd-workers-plan-to-quit/ (archived at https://perma.cc/XN69-6A85)

2 M Theodorou. 9 reasons why employees quit their jobs (infographic), CareerAddict, 13 January 2020, www.careeraddict.com/why-employees-quit (archived at https://perma.cc/H9RP-VETD)

3 Guild. Guild's American Worker Survey Report: The new 'Up or Out', www.guild.com/report/guilds-american-worker-survey-report/ (archived at https://perma.cc/L2NJ-6RNU)

4 M Somers. Women are less likely than men to be promoted. Here's one reason why, MIT Management Sloan School, 12 April 2022, https://mitsloan.mit.edu/ideas-made-to-matter/women-are-less-likely-men-to-be-promoted-heres-one-reason-why (archived at https://perma.cc/FFU6-TNZQ)

5 M Somers. Women are less likely than men to be promoted. Here's one reason why, MIT Management Sloan School, 12 April 2022, https://mitsloan.mit.edu/ideas-made-to-matter/women-are-less-likely-men-to-be-promoted-heres-one-reason-why (archived at https://perma.cc/4LFQ-X5HT)

6 Interview with Dina Knight, Chief People Officer at Datatec and Logicalis Group, December 2023

7 Interview with Alex Farbon, Talent at Acquisition Lead at GFT UK, December 2023

Conclusion

We began this book by reflecting on the huge amounts of disruption that businesses have faced in recent years. We have all survived a pandemic, a global financial crisis and the impact of wars around the world just in the first half of this decade. So it's not surprising that we're feeling hesitant about embarking on further disruptive activities. Can't everything just be straightforward and steady for a while? Who else yearns for *precedented* times?! There's no doubt that inclusion work can be disruptive and uncomfortable. But the fact is, we don't know what future challenges might be on the horizon, for individual organizations or for our planet. We need to be prepared to face what the future has to throw at us, and the best way to do that is to bring together the varied perspectives and skills that a diverse workforce can offer us so that we can be stronger as a group. By creating spaces where everyone can be heard and contribute their best, we build businesses, and, indeed, a world that is not only happier, healthier and more resilient, but that benefits from a much wider range of insights and strengths. We truly can go so much further together.

As we've seen throughout this book, diversity is not limited to particular demographics, or to particular areas of legislation. There might be elements of your team's diversity that you are never aware of, because they don't want to talk openly about it or maybe because they don't even know about it themselves. By applying inclusive principles to everything you do in your organization, you can create an environment where people don't need to tell you everything, but where everyone can find a way of working that works for them – and, therefore, means they can work best for you.

This *will* all be worth it

Hopefully we've convinced you that the benefits of diversity and inclusion are well worth the challenges and the costs. The improvements to your innovation and creativity, communication and collaboration, reach and engagement, recruitment and retention, problem-solving, productivity, resilience and so much more can open up so many opportunities for your business and its future growth. Ultimately, the data is clear – inclusive organizations make more money. The bottom line is, this work is only going to benefit your bottom line.

There's no doubt that this is a long road, a big investment, and something that might shake up your whole organization. But this is about future-proofing your business; setting you up for long-term success and giving you the skills to navigate the ever-changing landscape of the future.

There is a reason why we called this book *The Inclusion Journey* – it really is a journey. An ongoing, ever-evolving one. There is no final destination where your organization will have achieved perfection, although you will make incremental improvements along the way. This is a commitment to continual learning, listening and growth. This is a commitment to being constantly willing to ask what you could do better, to look for new ideas and perspectives, to make mistakes and then try again. This is a commitment to opening yourself up to curiosity and opportunity, to letting go of your preconceptions and certainties and being more eager to improve than to be right. Are you ready to make that commitment?

If so, this commitment will require time, energy, resources and budget. You can't reshape the fabric of your organization on good wishes alone. It's time to put your money where your mouth is, and put in the work that will drive genuine change. But, as we've seen, the cost:benefits ratio is well worth it.

It's not always an easy journey, and we're grateful to you for being willing to embark on it. The world needs leaders like you to stand up and show what's possible so that we can all learn and improve as a global community. Leaders who are willing to face the resistance they encounter, and work to bring everyone on board. Leaders who will ride out the bumps in the road, and be prepared for and adaptable to changes and challenges as they come.

You can do this together

Remember that most resistance and negativity comes from a place of fear – fear of change, fear of how individual people will be impacted and fear that more opportunities and acknowledgement for some people will lead to less for others. Carefully managing that experience of change is critical, as is making sure that everyone understands what's happening and why. Hopefully the models and tools we've shared in this book will help you to smooth the path ahead and help your whole team to recognize the benefits of this work. We need to keep talking to our colleagues, and showing them that the world is not a pie – we have capacity and capabilities to create space for everyone. A rising tide lifts all boats, even if some boats are being lifted from a lower starting point than others.

As the work moves forward, you will find momentum building. Small successes early on encourage and motivate your team, and inspire people who might have seemed disinterested to begin with. As this work becomes more familiar, and it is apparent that it isn't actually going to lead to some of the catastrophes envisioned, much of the initial fear and discomfort will subside. A large number of people will simply get on board because they see this is the way the wind is blowing anyway. Some people, it's true, will never be comfortable with this work. Maybe that means they won't want to be part of your organization anymore, and that's OK. You don't have to be a perfect match for everyone, and it's OK to thank people for their contribution and wish them well in a future elsewhere. If you're staying true to what you believe is right for your business, you'll attract the people who want to be a part of that, and the ones who don't will fade away.

The discomfort and disagreement is not something to shy away from or to fear, though. Often our greatest learning and growth comes from experiences of discomfort. Growing pains are real. Equally, some of the best ideas and plans come from disagreement and in-depth discussion. Your job is to facilitate an environment in which all of this can take place in a constructive and healthy way. As Jennifer Wright says, 'People talk about caterpillars becoming butterflies as though they just go into a cocoon, slap on wings, and are good to go. Caterpillars have to dissolve into a disgusting pile of goo to become butterflies.'[1]

So if you feel as though you are in the messy goo stage right now, know that this is all part of the process of powerful transformation.

Mistakes will be made on this journey. That's OK. We are human, we make errors, we mess up, but we recover, and that's how we learn. As babies, learning to walk, we fell down a hundred times before we got the hang of it. We spelled our own names wrong before we could write them reliably, we made multiple mistakes before we nailed our five times table. Somewhere along the line, we forgot that getting things wrong is part of learning how to get them right. We need to remember. No one judges us harshly for trying and failing, but they might judge us for not bothering to try at all. The risks of not doing this work – to your reputation, your ability to recruit and retain talented staff, your productivity and quality, and the future survival of your business – far outweigh the risks of a few missteps.

You might be the one reading this book and driving this work forward, but this work isn't all on you. Inclusion is everyone's responsibility. It takes a whole team to make it a success, and it's imperative that everyone is heard and engaged throughout the process. You will need to bring people together from all across your organization to do the work itself, and you will need to hear the voices of absolutely everyone connected to your business for this to yield the results you want to see.

You will need leaders ready to throw their weight behind this project, and to model the change you want to see. But, as a leadership team, you will also need to be willing to share the stage and centre other people's stories. You need to be a genuine ally to the people across your business. The fact that the work isn't all on you also means that the success isn't all yours, and you need to celebrate and value every person who contributes along the way.

Whilst the glory isn't all yours, the struggle isn't, either. This journey will be tough going sometimes, and you need to make sure that you take care of everyone's mental and physical wellbeing along the way – including your own.

Opening up the conversation

Communication is key to the progress of this journey, and how you engage your internal team and your external audiences is crucial. Consider what people need and want to know, how you can keep them updated, and how you will listen and respond to them. Communication is a two-way street, after all. You need to be open, honest and transparent in your communications at all times – this is never going to work if anyone thinks that you're trying to pull the wool over their eyes, cover over the cracks or overstate your achievements.

It would also be damaging and detrimental to your efforts, not to mention deeply ironic, if your communications surrounding your inclusion work were not, themselves, inclusive. You need to be able to talk to everyone in a way that they can fully understand and engage with, as well as providing different mechanisms that allow all perspectives to be heard and all contributions to be valued. You also need to make sure that different skills can be effectively utilised, and different stories can be told. And telling stories here is vital. The way you shape the story of this work will go a long way to shaping the story of your whole organization – and stories, ultimately, are how humans understand and relate to the world.

This all comes down to the question of what kind of organization you want to be. What impact do you want to have on the world? What do you stand for? How do you want to move forward? What future do you want to create? If this work is grounded in your mission and values, and if those are truly meaningful and unique to the work you do, then you can't go far wrong.

Information is power

If you take nothing else away from this book, we hope that you recognize the importance of getting a clear picture of where you are now before you set out. You need to gather the data and inputs to help you understand your current situation, and set SMAART goals and timelines that you can measure your progress against. Linking your inclusion goals to your business objectives not only enables you to better understand the bigger picture impact of this work, but helps you to get buy-in and support for future development of your journey. It's important, though, that everyone is realistic about what it is possible to achieve and when – setting overly ambitious targets only leads to a demoralized workforce, and a leadership belief that this isn't working. Setting your bar too low, on the other hand, will just make everyone think it's not worth bothering in the first place. Understanding what's possible, breaking your goals down into manageable steps, and tracking what you achieve effectively, are vital to your success.

All of this information is pointless without action. So the most important thing is to identify your priorities and get moving. You will learn as you go. You should be constantly reviewing and reflecting, and redrawing your map. You will also be keeping a constant eye on the horizon. What's next for your team? Who are your future leaders? What challenges are up ahead? Where will this journey take you next? As is so often the case, you need to look backwards to look forwards, and learn to do both at once.

Where will you start?

This work requires a fundamental mindset shift. It will challenge you to rethink everything about your business and how it works. It will ask you to redefine success, to reimagine the nature of strength and performance, to reconsider why your business and other businesses – and the very world around us – is set up the way it is. But that can be so exciting – if nothing is fixed, then anything is possible.

Hopefully this book has provoked a great deal of thought and analysis, and helped you to open up some important conversations. Talk is the first step. But it can't be the last. We have seen time and again that organizations get stuck in discussions and consideration, afraid to move forward. This is not an area that you can afford to be non-committal, or where you can bury your head in the sand. Your team and your external audience won't stand for lip-service or empty rhetoric. The time has come to move from talk to action. We know you can do it, and that you'll achieve great things.

We'd love to hear how you get on. If this book has inspired you to move your journey forward, or if you have any questions about how to progress, please do contact us at hello@watchthisspace.uk. Sharing stories and learning from and supporting one another is the most powerful way to help everyone move forward.

After all, that's what this work is all about. When we listen to different ideas and perspectives, when we take time to fully understand other people, when we collaborate with others and allow other people's work to build on our own, then we can achieve far more than we could by ourselves. At the end of the day, we all work better together.

Note

1 Jennifer Wright @JenAshleyWright. X (formerly Twitter), 21 June 2019, https://x.com/JenAshleyWright/status/1141896207666688000?lang=en (archived at https://perma.cc/683S-FRED)

GLOSSARY

There are many different terms used for diversity and inclusion work. This is a selection of our definitions of key terminology and concepts to help you navigate your inclusion journey. Please note, alternative definitions from other sources may be found elsewhere.

You can find a version of our definitions in our 'What Do We Mean By' dictionary available at watchthisspace.uk/what-do-we-mean-by.

Ableism: Attitudes in society that limit the potential of people with disabilities.

Accessibility: The act of making spaces, technology or products usable by everyone, especially those who may typically be excluded.

Accountability: To accept responsibility for what is within one's control, and to share goals and progress openly.

Adjustments: Sometimes called 'reasonable adjustments', a workplace adjustment is a modification to a work process, practice, procedure or setting that enables a person with a particular need to perform their job in a way that minimizes the impact of barriers they face at work.

Affinity bias: Natural unconscious tendency to be inclined towards people who resemble ourselves in appearance, background and behaviours.

Ageism: Discrimination or bias on the grounds of a person's age.

Allyship: Commitment to supporting and uplifting people experiencing marginalization in society. Consciously using your advantages in life to help further others, with the intention to create systems that benefit all. Everyone can and should be an ally, as privilege is relative.

Anti-racism: Deliberate efforts and intentional actions to challenge systemic inequality and provide equitable opportunities.

Belonging: An affinity with and connection to a certain place or a group. A sense of comfort, safety and acceptance in a particular environment. In a workplace, a sense of belonging enhances psychological safety and increases engagement and motivation.

Bias: An inclination or prejudice towards or against a particular person or group, usually without any basis in logical reasoning.

BIPOC: Black, Indigenous and people of colour.

Bullying: Behaviour that seeks to intimidate, coerce or harm (physically, emotionally or psychologically) another person, particularly someone who may be vulnerable or who holds less power than the perpetrator.

Burnout: A reaction to prolonged or chronic stress that can show up as extreme exhaustion, cynicism, defeat, detachment, loss of motivation and decreased satisfaction.

Bystander effect: Phenomenon whereby a person is less likely to help someone in distress if other people are present. Everyone assumes someone else will step in and feels embarrassed or unqualified to do so themselves, and so no one goes to the aid of the person in need.

Cisgender: Describes a person whose gender identity is the same as the sex assigned to them at birth.

Code switching: When a person alters the way they culturally, linguistically or even physically express themselves to fit a certain environment or situation, like the workplace.

Complicity: Choosing neutrality or silence in the face of social inequality or violence, which in effect upholds the oppressive nature of said inequality and/or violence.

Confirmation bias: Interpreting evidence to confirm existing beliefs, opinions or theories.

Critical race theory: A cross-disciplinary approach to exploring how race and racism have shaped society.

Cultural appropriation: Unacknowledged or inappropriate adoption of the customs, practices or ideas of a particular group (ethnic, religious, etc), usually by people from a group that is typically more dominant in society.

Culture add: In recruitment this is a method of considering who you do not have in your team and who would add something different.

Culture fit: In recruitment, a candidate considered likely to conform to the common behaviours, attitudes and perspectives of the existing group. Hiring for culture fit is likely to lead to a team that lacks diversity of thought.

Deadnaming: Referring to a person by the name they were given at birth after they have changed their name. Usually associated with trans people.

DEI: Diversity, Equity and Inclusion. An acronym commonly used as the umbrella term for programmes, policies, strategies and working practices to create inclusive environments.

Dignity: Recognizing the right of all people to be valued and respected for their own sake, and to be treated ethically and fairly.

Disability: Defined by law as an impairment that has an impact on a person's ability to access places, take part in activities or have equitable access to elements of society. Disabilities can be cognitive, developmental, intellectual, mental, physical, sensory or a combination of multiple factors.

Discrimination: Treating a person differently and more negatively because of certain attributes, characteristics or elements of their identity.

Diversity: The condition of being varied; inclusion of many different things or people; representation of these things or people.

Diversity of thought: A group that contains a variety of perspectives and ways of thinking. This requires an understanding that our ways of thinking are shaped by our culture, background, identity, nature, experiences and personalities.

Dominant group: The most common demographic group in a particular environment; a group of people with power, privilege and social status in society.

EDI: Equality, Diversity, and Inclusion. A commonly used acronym used as an umbrella term (similar to DEI) to ensure that environments are created that are inclusive, incorporating equality for all with teams created from different types of people who feel included.

Emotional labour: The work required to suppress emotions in formal settings, such as at work, particularly in the face of offensive behaviour. Also used to describe the effort people from marginalized groups are forced to expend to educate others about bias and protect themselves.

Employee Resource Group (ERG): An employee-led group, usually voluntary, that leads and advises on organizational objectives and actions to contribute towards a more inclusive workplace.

Equality: A state in which everyone is treated in the same way.

Equity: The acknowledgement that we don't all start from the same place and must therefore be committed to addressing these imbalances, meaning that treating people fairly might not mean treating them equally.

Ethnicity: A state of belonging to a social group that has a common national or cultural tradition.

Ethnocentrism: A tendency to believe one's own ethnic group is of primary importance or focus, and to judge other groups by the standards and customs of your own.

Fascism: A far-right political ideology that promotes extreme nationalism and homogeneous culture.

Feminism: A socio-political movement aiming to establish equal rights and opportunities for people of all genders.

Fight or flight response: Also known as 'acute stress response' or 'fight, flight or freeze response'. A psychological state, brought on by anxiety or fear, in which the body prepares itself to either forcibly resist or run away. This causes changes to the nervous and endocrine systems, including the release of the stress hormone cortisol.

Flexible working: A system whereby people are able to work outside the standard 9–5, Monday–Friday pattern and/or unrestricted to a standard office environment. This might include, but is not limited to, condensed hours, flexitime around core hours, annual hours, remote working and hybrid working.

Fragility: Often used in the context of 'white fragility' or 'male fragility'. Discomfort or defensiveness of someone from a dominant group around discussions of inequality and systemic injustice. Based on the concept that not having to deal with these issues on a regular basis makes people from dominant groups less robust when facing them.

Gaslighting: A form of psychological manipulation that forces a victim to question their own memory, perception, judgement and understanding of the world around them.

Gender dysphoria: Discomfort experienced by those whose sense of their own gender does not align with the sex they were assigned at birth.

Gender equality: Refers to a state in which access to rights and opportunities is unaffected by gender. In a business context, this means ensuring that elements such as recruitment, pay, promotions, performance management and support are not influenced by gender.

Gender non-conforming: A person who does not identify with or follow traditional societal conventions in relation to sex and gender.

Generational trauma: The psychological impact that the collective trauma experienced by a group has on subsequent generations.

Gentrification: The process by which a dominant group from a wealthy socioeconomic background changes the demographics of an area, excluding and/or displacing the people living in that area.

Groupthink: A psychological phenomenon whereby a group of people will unconsciously strive for harmony and conformity, leading to poor quality decision-making.

Harassment: Threatening, intimidating or pressuring behaviour, either physical or verbal, towards an individual.

Hepeating: Where a man repeats a woman's comments or ideas as if they were his own, often followed by him taking the ensuing credit or praise.

Heteronormativity: The belief or implication that heterosexuality is natural, ideal or superior to other sexual preferences.

Homogeneity: The state of all being the same or of the same kind.

Human rights: The basic rights and freedoms to which all human beings are entitled.

Hypersensitivity: A strong or intense response to an external stimulus (e.g. sounds, textures, sensations, colours, lights, smells), characteristic of certain neurodivergences. Contrasted with hyposensitivity, which is a low response to external stimuli.

Imposter syndrome: An internalized fear of legitimate work or expertise being exposed as fraudulent, often present in members of under-represented groups.

Inclusion: The act of creating environments in which any individual or group will feel welcomed, respected and able to fully participate.

Institutional racism: The impact created when the policies and practices of an institution create different outcomes for different racial groups. This may not be explicit or intentional, but nevertheless has the effect of advantaging one group and/or disadvantaging another.

Internalized racism/sexism: When members of a racial group or gender have absorbed negative messages about their group from society and participate in attitudes and behaviours that support or maintain existing power structures.

Intersectionality: The ways in which multiple social identities (race, gender, sexuality, etc) intertwine to create unique advantages and disadvantages.

Intersex: A person born with reproductive or sexual anatomy that does not align with binary concepts of male or female.

Invisible disabilities: Disabilities that are not immediately apparent.

LGBTQIA+: An acronym standing for Lesbian, Gay, Bisexual, Trans, Queer (and/or Questioning), Intersex, Asexual (or Ace) and others.

Mansplaining: Typically describes a situation in which a man explains to a woman, in a condescending or patronizing manner, a subject that the woman is already highly familiar with.

Marginalization: The process by which society excludes, ignores or devalues certain groups, limiting their economic and social power.

Meritocracy: A system in which the leaders are selected purely according to merit.

Microaggression: Everyday behaviour, often seen as minor or unnoticed entirely by those from dominant groups, and perpetrated casually and/or without awareness, that communicates hostile, derogatory or negative messages to people from certain under-represented groups.

Microassault: An explicit racial derogation characterized primarily by a verbal or nonverbal attack meant to hurt the intended victim through name-calling, behaviour or purposeful discriminatory action.

Misgender: To refer to someone using a gendered word, pronoun or form of address that does not reflect the gender with which they identify.

Multiculturalism: Coexistence of a range of cultures, religions, races and ethnicities in a way that acknowledges and respects their differences and practices.

Neo-colonization: Contemporary policies adopted by Western nations and organizations that exert power and control over less economically advantaged nations in the name of humanitarian assistance or aid.

Neurodivergent: An individual whose cognitive function operates outside the standard range expected by society.

Neurodiversity: The variation in human cognitive function regarding sociability, learning, attention, mood and other brain processes.

Neurotypical: An individual whose cognitive function operates within the standard range expected by society.

NLP (Neuro Linguistic Programming): An approach to communication and personal development that focuses on how individuals organize their thinking, feelings and language, and on how to change that programming for desired outcomes.

Non-binary: An adjective describing a person who does not identify exclusively as male or female. A non-binary person may identify as both, neither or somewhere in between.

Oppositional sexism: The belief that femininity and masculinity are rigid and exclusive categories.

Oppression: Systemic and institutional inequality whereby certain groups are disadvantaged, treated unjustly and/or exploited.

Othering: Treating or creating a perception of a person as different, alien or an outsider because they are from a non-dominant group.

Outing: The act of revealing someone's sexual orientation or gender identity to an individual or group without the person's consent or approval.

Patriarchy: A social system where power and authority are held by men.

Pay gap: The discrepancy in average salary between people from dominant and non-dominant groups.

Performative allyship: Professing support and solidarity with a marginalized group in a manner designed to attract praise or positive attention, but that is not supported by meaningful action or acceptance of personal responsibility.

Positive action: Measures that enable or encourage members of under-represented groups to overcome disadvantage. (Contrasted with 'positive discrimination', which is an illegal practice of discriminating in favour of under-represented groups.)

Privilege: Social power, protection or advantages experienced by members of a dominant group.

Proximity bias: An unconscious tendency to favour or give preferential treatment to those in our immediate vicinity.

Psychological safety: Confidence in individuals that they are free to share ideas, questions, concerns or mistakes without fear of punishment or humiliation from the group or its leaders.

QPOC/QTIPOC: An acronym standing for Queer People of Colour, sometimes extended to Queer, Trans and Intersex People of Colour.

Queer: A term of identification used by some people who do not identify as heterosexual or whose gender identity is outside traditional binary concepts. This was previously used as a derogatory term, and is still viewed as such by some. However, many members of the LGBTQIA+ community have reclaimed the term and find it empowering.

Questioning: A term referring to anyone who is exploring or considering their sexual orientation or gender identity.

Race: A social construct that artificially divides people into distinct groups based on characteristics such as physical appearance, ancestral heritage, cultural affiliation, cultural history and ethnic classification.

Racial profiling: The act of suspecting, targeting or having negative expectations of someone on the basis of their race, ethnicity, religion or national origin. Most often used in the context of law enforcement.

Reasonable adjustments: See **Adjustments** above.

Reclaimed language: Word or phrases that have traditionally been used to degrade certain groups, but which that group has taken control of in order to use them in an empowering way.

Representation: Visibility of individuals from particular groups, backgrounds or identities in spaces where these groups have traditionally been excluded.

Respect: Having, and showing, due regard for the feelings, wishes or rights of other individuals or groups of people.

Safe space: An environment in which all people, particularly those from marginalized groups, feel able and comfortable to fully express themselves and participate without fear of attack, blame, ridicule or denial of their experience.

Scarcity mentality: A mindset that focuses on lack; seeing the world as a finite pie, so that if one person takes a big piece it automatically leaves less for everyone else. This often causes people to be resistant to increasing opportunities for others as they believe it will reduce those available to them.

Silencing: Exerting social dominance over a space or discussion so as to overpower or block voices of those from under-represented groups.

Social justice: A vision of society in which the distribution of resources is equitable and all members are physically and psychologically safe and secure.

Stereotype: A widely held but fixed and oversimplified image or idea of a particular type of person or thing.

Stereotype threat: Fear caused by a person believing themselves to be at risk of conforming to a negative stereotype about their social group.

Sustainability: The practice of using natural resources responsibly, promoting a holistic lifestyle of working with (rather than against) our environments through conscious, ecological actions.

TERF: An acronym for Trans Exclusionary Radical Feminist. A self-professed feminist who denies the legitimacy of a trans woman's gender identity and does not believe that trans women should be given sex-based rights. Sometimes the term gender-critical feminist may also be used.

Tokenism: The practice of including only one or a few members of an under-represented group as a performative gesture.

Tone policing: A tactic used in debate or conversation to dismiss, invalidate or distract from the substance of what the other person is saying by focusing on the way they have said it and claiming this was too hostile or emotional. Normally used against people from under-represented groups.

Trans: A person whose gender identity does not align with the sex they were assigned at birth.

Transitioning: The process that a trans person goes through to align their gender expression with their gender identity.

Two-Spirit: A Native American term for someone who identifies as having both a male and female essence or spirit.

Unconscious bias: Deep-seated assumptions and preferences that we all hold without being consciously aware of them.

Under-represented group: A group that is less represented in one subset (e.g. employees in a particular sector or organization) than in the general population.

Unity: The state of being united or joined as a whole. The term 'unity in diversity' refers to harmony between varied individuals or groups.

Universal design: The process of designing products and environments to be usable by all people (inclusive of abilities, different characteristics and different needs) to the greatest extent possible.

Upstander: A person who speaks or acts in support of an individual or cause, particularly someone who intervenes on behalf of a person being attacked or bullied.

White centring: Placing the needs, experiences, feelings and norms of white people above those of people from other racial groups.

White privilege: The preferential treatment in society, freedom from discrimination and subtle advantages given by institutions and societal systems to white people and not to those from other racial groups.

White tears: Offence and distress, often to a seemingly excessive and perhaps performative degree, taken by white people to suggestions of racial injustice or criticisms of their own behaviour.

Whiteness: The social, political and cultural ideology that benefits, prefers and privileges white people over people from other racial groups in societal hierarchy.

Work/life interface: The intersection of people's work and personal lives, and how these two things impact and affect one another.

INDEX

NB: page numbers in *italic* indicate figures or tables

Looking for another book?

Explore our award-winning
books from global business
experts in Human Resources,
Learning and Development

Scan the code to browse

www.koganpage.com/hr-learning-
development